INTERNATIONAL TOURISM

INTERNATIONAL TOURISM
An Economic Perspective

François Vellas
and
Lionel Bécherel

Foreword by
Eduardo Fayos-Solá
Director of Education and Training
World Tourism Organisation
Madrid

First published 1995 by
PALGRAVE
Houndmills, Basingstoke, Hampshire RG21 6XS and
175 Fifth Avenue, New York, N. Y. 10010
Companies and representatives throughout the world

PALGRAVE is the new global academic imprint of
St. Martin's Press LLC Scholarly and Reference Division and
Palgrave Publishers Ltd (formerly Macmillan Press Ltd).

ISBN 0–333–61522–0 hardback
ISBN 0–333–61523–9 paperback

This book is printed on paper suitable for recycling and
made from fully managed and sustained forest sources.

A catalogue record for this book is available
from the British Library.

10   9   8   7   6
04   03   02   01   00

Copy-edited and typeset by Povey-Edmondson
Okehampton and Rochdale, England

Printed and bound in Great Britain by
Antony Rowe Ltd, Chippenham, Wiltshire

Contents

List of Tables

List of Figures

List of Boxes

Acknowledgements

We are very grateful to the World Tourism Organisation for its support and for providing information and statistics. We would particularly like to thank Mr Antonio Enríquez Savignac, its Secretary-General, Mr Francesco Frangialli, the Deputy Secretary General, Mr Enzo Pacci, responsible for statistics, and Dr Eduardo Fayos, Director of Education and Training.

We are also indebted to Mr Simon Wilde for his guidance on language and style and Mr Alex Noble, Lecturer in Financial Management at the University of Surrey, for his direction and advice on the section dealing with finance and investment in the tourism industry.

FRANÇOIS VELLAS
LIONEL BÉCHEREL

List of Abbreviations

ACP   Africa, Caribbean and Pacific
ADB   African Development Bank
ANTO   Austrian National Tourist Office
BTA   British Tourist Association
CRS   Computer reservation system
EDF   European Development Fund
EFRD   European Fund for Regional Development
EIB   European Investment Bank
ETB   English Tourist Board
EU   European Union
GATS   General Agreement on Trade and Services
GATT   General Agreement on Tariffs and Trade
GDS   Global development system
GEI   Grouping of economic interests
IATA   International Air Transport Association
IATM   International Association of Tour Managers
IBRD   International Bank for Reconstruction and Development
IBST   International Bureau for Social Tourism
ICAO   International Civil Aviation Organisation
IDA   International Development Association
IFC   International Finance Corporation
ILO   International Labour Office
IMF   International Monetary Fund
IUOTO   International Union of Official Tourism Organisations
NITB   Northern Ireland Tourist Board
NTO   National Tourist Office
OECD   Organisation for Economic Co-operation and Development
PATA   Pacific Asian Travel Association
STB   Scottish Tourist Board
UNCTAD   United Nations Conference on Trade and Development
UNDP   United Nations Development Programme
UNEP   United Nations Environmental Programme
UNESCO   United Nations Educational, Scientiic and Cultural
         Organisation
USTTA   United States Travel and Tourism Administration
WATA   World Association for Travel Agencies
WHO   World Health Organisation
WTB   Welsh Tourist Board
WTO   World Tourism Organisation

Foreword

After several decades of rapid growth, the tourism industry has reached a critical point in its development. We find ourselves in the midst of a business paradigm shift, where the old rules for profitability and long-term success are losing validity.

The new paradigm is primarily characterised by the supersegmentation of demand, flexibility of supply and distribution, and achieving profitability through system economies instead of economies of scale.

In a mass production system of tourism such as the one which has predominated in the last few decades, the only choice the client had was to consume totally standardised and, hence, very rigidly structured products. However, the new conditions in the market require a far more sophisticated approach.

Certainly, the scenario of the tourism industry for the coming years includes a new map of competitiveness in which enterprises must compete globally, not only within the tourism sector, but often with companies in the larger leisure industry at world level.

In order to do so, businesses and professionals must adapt their skills and strategies (i.e. their *culture*) to the new market environment by: (i) improving their tourism information systems, to better understand demand requirements and the strategy of the competition, and to communicate the products offered; (ii) improving knowhow acquisition through increased efforts in R & D, enabling the most competitive product to be offered at any time; (iii) investing in human capital, streamlining the entrepreneurial culture, which often constitutes the key element for success; and (iv) instilling a philosophy and methodology of total quality in service, in which products and processes are selected by their capability to give satisfaction to consumers.

In this context, *International Tourism* represents a productive new approach to the knowledge of contemporary tourism in its global perspective. Its authors, Professor François Vellas and Mr Lionel Bécherel, are well known for their significant contributions to tourism research and education. François Vellas has wide experience in teaching tourism in his capacity as Professor of International Economics at the University of Toulouse. He has acted as consultant and adviser on tourism policy matters for the World Tourism Organisation, the Commission of the European Union and many other public and private institutions. He is also the author of numerous publications on tourism and aviation and an active member of prestigious academic associations in tourism. In addition,

Lionel Bécherel has been very actively involved with the educational undertakings of the Surrey Research Group at the University of Surrey and with tourism departments in the United Kingdom on the local and national level. He has also acted as consultant in several international projects and lectured extensively in tourism, economics and business studies, both in Guildford and at the University of Toulouse.

International Tourism is an ambitious book. With a direct, pragmatic approach, Vellas and Bécherel cover very extensive ground. From basic definitions to predicted trends through demand and supply conditions, marketing, finance, sociocultural and ecological impacts, development issues, and tourism policy. All is here – in clear, concise language; very effective in its descriptive capabilities, and notably able in summarising state-of-the-art tourism knowledge.

I particularly like the treatment of topics not usually analysed in textbooks – for example, the theories of international specialisation (comparative advantage, demand theory, etc.) in their application to tourism, the consideration of the economic and environmental impacts of tourism; the analysis of aviation policies (specifically deregulation in the USA and Europe); and, last but not least, tourism policies in industrialised and developing countries.

The authors are well aware of the ongoing paradigm shift in the tourism industry and the need for a broad, comprehensive view of the main issues at stake – together with a subtle, astute insight of the causes underlying the changes. Hence, the book responds well to the needs of students and professionals in the four above-mentioned areas: information, knowhow, education and total quality management.

While it is true that we cannot always have the future we would like – and this is especially certain for our increasingly complex and environment-dependent tourism industry – *we can adapt and prepare for the real future*. Vellas and Bécherel's book does an excellent job in helping those of us who think and work in one of the most dynamic industries of contemporary society

Director of Education and Training,   EDUARDO FAYOS-SOLÁ
World Tourism Organisation, Madrid

Introduction

There are few economic sectors which generate as much added value, employment and currency for such a low cost as international tourism. All tourism products and services consumed by foreign visitors are exports which avoid the costs of distribution and transport to other markets. International tourism both provides foreign currency and distributes purchasing power throughout the visited country.

Tourism has become the world's most important economic activity.

- According to the World Tourism Organisation (WTO), *annual expenditure worldwide on tourism* is more than 2,000 billion US dollars (of which US$324 billion is attributed to international tourism). In 1994, tourism accounts for 12 per cent of the world's Gross National Product (GNP).
- The travel and tourism industry has become the principal source of *job creation* in many countries and employs more than 100 million people worldwide.
- The economic impact of the industry has been considerable. It is responsible for approximately 7 per cent of *global capital expenditure*.

International tourism not only influences economics, it also affects social, environmental and land development policies.

Although vast tourism movements are a recent phenomenon, they actually reflect a long tradition of migrations and mixing of populations. Nowadays, these population movements are not just confined to certain regions. They affect virtually every country in the world, either as tourist receptors or tourist generators or both. Even today, international tourism is transforming previously closed societies of insular inward-looking states into an open universal society where contact between peoples becomes a daily reality. It satisfies a deep need for encounters and exchanges with other cultures, for escape, health and social progress. It is undeniably one of the most influential phenomena (possibly even the most influential) in the economic and social development of our society.

However, the growth of international tourism also creates a number of difficulties which can cause severe crises. These have led to questions from certain quarters about its social, cultural and even economic consequences. In contrast to the positive effects on employment and the production of revenue are some strong negative effects: inflation, the destruction of the environment and of the traditions of local populations. These are particularly sensitive issues in developing countries, where tourists from industrialised countries impose, by their very presence, a way of life and a level of consumption which can often offend local sensibilities. Similarly, in certain regions, particularly the European Mediterranean, high tourist concentrations, resulting from uncontrolled development, contribute to the destruction of the economic and social fabric as well as the cultural heritage of the local population.

It is therefore imperative to assess not only the contribution of international tourism but also its consequences, in order to increase the advantages that it brings and avoid its damaging effects. This is the objective of economic and international tourism policies.

The economic approach to international tourism is based on a methodology which uses the knowledge and techniques of economic analysis to design and implement policies adapted to its needs. First, the methodology requires an in-depth understanding of tourism activity, followed by the economic analysis of this activity and, finally, the communication of the results to decision-makers in both the public and private sectors, so that tourism policies can be developed and implemented at local, national and international levels.

The *in-depth understanding of tourism activity* concerns both the international tourism flows of populations and the financial flows of currency in and out of countries, as well as the impacts of these flows on national economies. Additionally, it involves an understanding of sectors of economic activity which depend partially or totally on tourism, such as transport (in particular, air transport), accommodation (the hotel and catering industries), the commercial sector (travel agencies and tour operators), administrative services and international tourism organisations.

The *economic analysis of tourism activity* focuses on the determinants of international tourism and on its economic mechanisms. The methodology uses techniques of international economics based on the theory of international exchange in conjunction with empirical studies and the analysis of case studies. This approach analyses the causes of international tourism by evaluating the role of the determinants of exchange (factor endowments, comparative costs, absolute advantages, representative demand). The economic analysis is also applied to the mechanism which spreads the receipts generated by international tourism throughout the economy, using the tourism foreign account system and the multiplier techniques.

Tourism policy is a result of actions planned at local, regional, national and international levels, and its analysis determines the necessary *level of intervention by the public authorities*. In industrialised countries, decentralisation has resulted in a development of tourism better adapted to the needs of the population of each region. In developing countries, tourism development programmes set up with the financial and technical help of international organisations have resulted in regional planning. This has reduced the financial burden on developing countries and increased the profitability of tourism infrastructures that have been created.

Tourism policy must take into account a number of external variables such as demographic and social change; the economic and financial situation of generating countries; currency exchange-rate fluctuations; political, legal and statutory change; technological progress; shifts in trading patterns; transport infrastructure; the security of travellers; and the protection of sites and the environment.

Three determinants affecting tourism play a particularly significant role in the evolution of international demand in industrialised countries:

1. Demographic changes and social evolution;
2. Increased leisure and holiday time;
3. Fragmentation of holidays and market segmentation.

1. Demographic changes

By the year 2000 there will be more than 144 million Europeans aged between 35 and 45 years. This is 16 per cent more than in 1985. The over-65-year-old age group will have increased by more than 14 million people (from 61 million to 75 million) in the same period.

The 35- to 54-year-olds generally enjoy the highest disposable income and this group is increasing at a faster rate than any other age group – a very favourable situation for the future expansion of the industry.

Nowadays, over 65s also have higher incomes and more free time. Furthermore, older travellers are more flexible with their time and can travel during offpeak periods, thus contributing to a longer tourism season.

2. Increased leisure and holiday time

The working population of industrialised countries is enjoying increased leisure time and more holidays. Although this is common to all industrialised countries, there are significant differences between nations. For example, the length of the annual paid holiday in the United States and Japan is generally less than a month and sometimes just a fortnight. Western European workers are entitled to longer paid holidays. France, in particular, allows its workforce five weeks of statutory annual paid leave. If national holidays are included, the French enjoy up to eight weeks of paid vacation a year.

3. The fragmentation of holiday time

This is a direct consequence of the increase in available holiday time. Now that total annual holiday periods are longer, the traditional 'four-week holiday' is disappearing. Tourists are abandoning the concept of the one-month vacation and replacing it with several shorter breaks of one to three weeks spread over the year.

The international market has been transformed by this fragmentation and increase in the number of holidays. New products are being created for each market segment to satisfy the demand for shorter breaks. The family holiday and the traditional rest and relaxation holiday, based solely on bed and board, no longer meets the requirements of today's tourist.

As a result, industrial and commercial strategies, adapted to the new conditions of the market, need to be developed and implemented.

The aim of this book is to contribute to the understanding of the economic factors and agents which create international tourism and to relate the reasoning, techniques and processes adopted by professionals, administrators and politicians who have particular responsibility for developing and evaluating tourism programmes and policies.

■ *Chapter 1* ■

Definitions and Trends in International Tourism

Definitions: the domestic visitor; the international visitor; the international tourist; the excursionist

Accounting and economic indicators in international tourism: statistical sources; OECD tourism accounts system; economic indicators for international tourism

International tourism trends: world and regional tourism trends; international tourism flows and the level of economic development; the main destinations

International tourism flows produce some of the most dynamic economic exchanges that occur between countries. Between 1970 and 1993, international arrivals more than trebled from 165 million to 500 million. Over the same period, international tourism receipts experienced an 18-fold increase, passing from US$17.9 billion to US$324 billion annually.

International tourism is especially important for European countries (particularly those in the south such as France, Italy, Portugal and Greece) as it can represent the largest export contribution to their balance of payments. These countries are therefore very sensitive to fluctuations in tourism volume and value. However, trends are changing and the 'new industrial countries' – principally those of Asia (Thailand, Malaysia, Singapore and Hong Kong) – are experiencing the fastest growth in international tourism.

To monitor the impact of such an important economic sector, it is imperative that reliable and accurate statistics based on definitions recognised by all countries should be internationally available. This is one of the main tasks of the World Tourism Organisation (WTO) which is the principal source of statistics on international tourism.

■ Definitions

The economic analysis of international tourism is based on accurate and universally accepted definitions which describe the characteristics of

1

international tourism, classify the different types of tourism flows and explain their economic impact and the economic activities they generate.

The World Tourism Organisation distinguishes between three basic forms of tourism:

- *domestic tourism*, involving residents of the given country travelling only within the country;
- *inbound tourism*, involving non-residents travelling in another country;
- *outbound tourism*, involving residents travelling in another country.[1]

International tourism consists of *inbound tourism* and *outbound tourism*.

Tourism expenditure can be defined as 'the total consumption expenditure made by a visitor or on behalf of a visitor for and during his/her trip and stay at destination'. The WTO offers definitions of international tourism payments for both inbound and outbound tourism:

- *International tourism receipts* are defined as expenditure of international inbound visitors including their payments to national carriers for international transport. They should also include any other prepayments made for goods/services received in the destination country. They should in practice also include receipts from same-day visitors, except in cases where these are so important as to justify a separate classification. It is also recommended that, for the sake of consistency with the balance of payments recommendations of the International Monetary Fund, international fare receipts be classified separately.

  International fare receipts are defined as any payment made to carriers registered in the compiling country of sums owed by non-resident visitors, whether or not travelling to that country. This category corresponds to transportation, passenger services, credits in the standard reporting form of the International Monetary Fund.[2]

- *International tourism expenditure* is defined as expenditure of outbound visitors in other countries including their payments to foreign carriers for international transport. It should in practice also include expenditure of residents travelling abroad as same-day visitors, except in cases when this is so important as to justify a separate classification. It is also recommended that, for the sake of consistency with the balance of payments recommendations of the International Monetary Fund, international fare expenditure be classified separately.

  International fare expenditure is defined as any payment made to carriers registered abroad by any person resident in the compiling country. This category corresponds to transportation, passenger services, debits in the standard reporting form of the International Monetary Fund.[3]

Basic definitions of tourism were established at the United Nations (Conference on Tourism and International Travel, Rome 1963) and by the United Nations Commission on Statistics (April 1968). These definitions were revised and updated at the World Tourism Organisation (WTO) conference in Ottawa in June 1991 and certain recommendations were formulated. These have been adopted by most countries. The WTO has published these recommendations in its report *Recommendations on Tourism Statistics*. The WTO's definition of the traveller moves away from the concept of the 'visitor' and distinguishes between the 'tourist' and the 'excursionist'. In fact, travellers can be categorised in four ways:

- Domestic visitors
- International visitors
- International tourists
- Excursionists

☐ *The domestic visitor*

For statistical purposes, the term 'domestic visitor' describes any person residing in a country, who travels to a place within the country, outside his/her usual environment for a period not exceeding 12 months and whose main purpose of visit is other than the exercise of an activity remunerated from within the place visited.[4]

Domestic tourism is very significant in world tourism as it represents, on average, over 80 per cent of all tourism movements. However, it should be noted that if domestic tourism is particularly important in the industrialised countries of Europe and North America, it is still limited in many developing countries, generally because their population does not have sufficient funds to travel within their own country and because few governments in the developing world have introduced social legislation concerning paid holidays to encourage domestic tourism.

☐ *The international visitor*

For statistical purposes, the term international visitor describes any person visiting a country other than that in which s/he has his/her usual place of residence but outside his/her usual environment for a period not exceeding 12 months and whose main purpose of visit is other than the exercise of an activity remunerated from within the country visited.[5]

Two factors differentiate visitors from other international travellers: their country of residence and their motivation for travel.

☐ The country of residence

Visitors are travellers who do not reside in the country they are visiting. These include nationals of the visited country living permanently abroad. Thus, a national from country A, resident of country B and visiting country C, spends money he has earned in country B. This person is influenced by country C's promotional efforts in country B. In order to understand accurately the different tourism markets and the transfers of currencies, the visitor in our example is recorded according to his country of residence rather than his nationality.

A resident has lasting economic links with the country he is living and working in and would normally have lived in his adopted country for a minimum of one year. It is therefore the country of economic ties rather than the country of nationality which determines a person's residency.

Certain types of travellers are excluded from the category of *tourist* for reasons other than that of residency. These are:

- people travelling for political reasons: refugees;
- people travelling for political/professional reasons: migrants, members of the armed forces, diplomats, embassy staff;
- people travelling for professional reasons: nomads, border workers, seasonal workers, couriers;
- people sent abroad by their companies or government. These are considered residents of the country where they normally live (temporary immigrants);
- transit passengers and permanent immigrants.

☐ The motivation for travel

People who travel to work in a foreign country and are paid by this country have different motives for travelling than other visitors to the country. The WTO has devised a system of classifying international travellers which separates visitors that should be included in international tourism statistics from those that should not. There are, however, still a number of practical difficulties in compiling these statistics: for instance, differentiating between visitors and immigrants, visitors and people who live or work near an international border, transit passengers and foreign airline crews. It is often difficult to identify and classify accurately each traveller in the global movement of people crossing borders. Are they in transit? Are they in transit for more or less than 24 hours? Are they remaining in the airport or staying at an airport hotel? Will they visit the town? And so on.

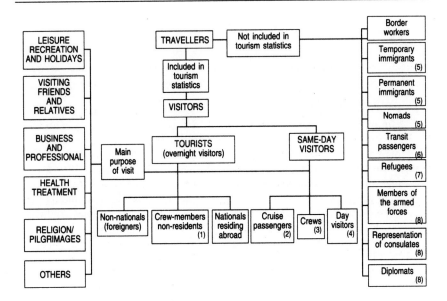

Notes: 1. Foreign air or ship crews docked or in layover and who use the accommodation establishments of the country visited.

2. Persons who arrive in a country aboard cruise ships (as defined by the International Maritime Organisation (IMO, 1965) and who spend the night aboard ship even when disembarking for one or more day visits.

3. Crews who are not residents of the country visited and who stay in the country for the day.

4. Visitors who arrive and leave the same day for: leisure, recreation and holidays; visiting friends and relatives; business and professional purposes; health treatment; religion/pilgrimages; and other tourism purposes, including transit day visitors en route to or from their destination countries.

5. As defined by the United Nations in the Recommendations on Statistics of International Migration, 1980.

6. Who do not leave the transit area of the airport or the port, including transfer between airports and ports.

7. As defined by the United Nations High Commissioner for Refugees, 1967.

8. When they travel from their country of origin to the duty station and vice versa (including household servants and dependants accompanying or joining them).

Source: WTO.

Figure 1.1 *Classification of international visitors*

☐ *The international tourist*

A visitor whose length of stay in a country reaches or exceeds 24 hours, thus spending at least one night in the visited country, is classified as a *tourist*. If his length of stay in the country is less than 24 hours he is categorised as a *same-day visitor*.

Box 1.1   *Visitors included and excluded in tourism statistics*

<table>
<tr><th>Visitors included
in tourism statistics</th><th>Visitors excluded
in tourism statistics</th></tr>
<tr><td>

(a) People travelling for pleasure, for family reasons, for health etc. (including nationals who live permanently abroad;

(b) people travelling to attend meetings or for assignments (sports, scientific, management). Employees of large organisations on assignment abroad for less than one year are also included;

(c) people travelling for business (employees of commercial or industrial firms who are travelling to install machinery or equipment abroad etc.);

(d) students and young people at boarding schools or colleges and those who travel or work temporarily during their holidays;

(e) visitors from cruise ships even if their stay is less than 24 hours. They can be registered in a separate group which does not take into account their place of residence;

(f) transit passengers who cross the country in more or less than 24 hours;

(g) foreign airline and ship crews on stopover in a country;

(h) musicians or artists on tour.

</td><td>

(a) People arriving in a country for work with or without a contract (including service personnel and people accompanying them);

(b) people who emigrate;

(c) people who live or work on an international border including those who live in one country and work in another;

(d) diplomats, embassy staff, members of armed forces stationed abroad (including their service personnel and people accompanying them);

(e) refugees;

(f) nomads;

(g) transit passengers who do not leave the transit area in the airport or at the port.

Source: WTO.

</td></tr>
</table>

International tourists are defined as:

Temporary visitors staying at least 24 hours in a country whose motive for travel can be described as being either for:
– leisure (pleasure, holidays, health, study, religion or sport);
or for:
– business, family or work assignments.[6]

This definition clearly encompasses both business travellers and holiday-makers in the tourist category. Business travellers include tour guides, commercial travellers and representatives, and artists.

☐ *The excursionist or same-day visitor*

The excursionist is a foreign visitor whose stay does not exceed 24 hours. The economic impact of the international excursionist is very important to small isolated countries which receive cruise-ship passengers. In fact, visitors spending the night on board ship are classified as same-day visitors and not tourists. The excursionist therefore does not spend the night in the country he is visiting.

It is difficult, however, to determine the tourism definition of a short trip. Generally, a journey is considered to be a trip when a minimum distance has been covered or when there has been a change of administrative district. Commuting (daily journeys between home and work) and shopping trips are excluded from the excursionist category. Apart from these exceptions, excursionists tend to be registered in domestic tourism statistics.

The business excursionist is generally an official representative or an agent travelling for his company. If his journey is not considered to be commuting to work he is registered in international tourism statistics. However, some countries now apply special restrictions when it comes to classifying the business excursionist. They are either excluded from the international tourist classification or recorded in a category apart, even if they stay overnight in the country.

Excursionist tourism is particularly important for small insular countries like the Caribbean islands. A large proportion of their market is tourists arriving on cruise ships, who visit during the day but are actually accommodated on board.

▌ Accounting and economic indicators in international tourism

The objective of accounting in tourism is to collect financial information which describes tourism as a economic phenomenon. The information is necessary to analyse tourism within the context of the National Accounts System and for international statistical comparisons. To this end, important studies have been conducted by the WTO and the Organisation for Economic Cooperation and Development (OECD)[7] to establish a common conceptual base. The resulting database offers a body of information which can be used for economic modelling and for the international analysis of tourism. In particular, tourism accounting should cover all tourism activities within the borders of a given country and detail the conditions of supply and demand.

☐ *Statistical sources*

Statistical information used in tourism accounting is drawn directly from sources supplied by the National Accounts System and the Balance of Payments System and from statistics compiled by the WTO. The Tourism Accounts System should be compatible with the National Accounts System while reflecting and emphasising the characteristics of tourism specific to the country.

Statistics are available from three main sources: statistics collected at borders, accommodation statistics and transport statistics.

- *Statistics obtained at borders* record international tourism flows. They are collected by immigration controls and by survey interviews. Random samples of visitors are surveyed at borders to gather precise tourism information on the country of origin and the country of residence of tourists, length of stay, reasons for travel, modes of transport and expenditure during the visit. The information collected by these surveys is also useful for associated areas. For instance, the additional data they supply contributes to estimating the share of tourism in the balance of payments and provides extra information on the different types of accommodation used by international tourists.
- *Accommodation statistics* are particularly valuable in the analysis of tourism supply. They also provide information on tourism demand. They measure both accommodation capacity and occupancy. It is, however, difficult to collect reliable data from some types of accommodation, such as private homes or accommodation rented directly from private sources.
- *Transport statistics* are usually obtained directly from tourism transport firms and provide information on modes of transport used by tourists, on volume and, by studying the firms' receipts, on the economic impact of tourism.

There are several other statistical sources which are also used in estimating the tourism account of the country. *Household surveys* are conducted either at the home of past and potential tourists or at tourist destinations (at points of sale, in trains or coaches, at stations, at accommodation sites, etc.). Additionally, further resources are provided by governments who regularly compile vast amounts of data on economic activity.

☐ OECD *tourism accounts system*

Although there are several different tourism accounts systems, the OECD has developed a model which is a particularly useful reference for international comparisons. This system has the following characteristics:

- it is descriptive and lends itself to practical implementation;
- it consists mainly of economic (particularly of a monetary and financial nature) and physical data;
- it integrates aspects of tourism supply and tourism demand;
- it uses statistical sources from the National Accounts System, the Balance of Payments System and the statistical guidelines of the WTO.

Three main accounts are usually prepared:

- the production account which presents supply-side information;
- the consumption account highlighting information on utilisation;
- the commercial goods and services account reconciling supply and utilisation.

The three accounts are used in conjunction with each other to build a global system which encompasses all statistics relative to the consumption and production of tourism. The production account plays a major role in this global system. It is developed for each field of activity and reflects the production of goods and services used by tourists. However, the production account represents a system based on fields of activity and does not cover the concept of tourism exactly. For instance, when tourists consume products offered by non-tourism producers, this secondary supply of goods and services must also be accounted for.

The typical flow chart shown in Figure 1.2 is the basis of all tourism accounts systems. It brings together supply statistics with statistics on consumers and addresses several key questions:

- What types of goods and services are required by the tourism sector?
- Who are the main consumers of these goods and services?
- How has the National Accounts System been affecting the movement of commercial goods and services attributed to tourism?

In this way, it is possible to present the movement of commercial goods and services in the tourism sector and evaluate the economic role of tourism in the economy. However, certain problems of statistical

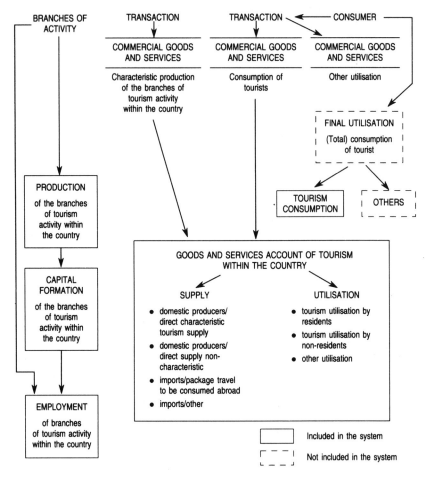

Source: OECD.

Figure 1.2 *Establishing a system of tourism statistics*

measurement do sometimes arise, mainly concerning the accounting unit (the country's currency expressed as an appropriate unit at current prices), the costing (supply at market prices minus value added tax (VAT)) and the classification of the fields of activity.

The creation of a tourism accounts system produces vital information on the economic impact of tourism on the economy. Using the system, it is possible to calculate:

• the added value at market prices in the fields of commercial activity involving tourism;

- the detailed expenditure on each category of goods and services consumed by tourists;
- the creation of gross fixed capital by the fields of commercial activity concerned with tourism;
- the volume of employment created by tourism in the fields of tourism commercial activity.

This combination of figures is used to establish a workable accounts system.

□ Economic indicators for international tourism

The role of economic indicators in international tourism is to establish bases for the comparison of tourism flow trends and to forecast future trends.

□ The departure rate

The departure rate is the ratio of the number of people travelling on at least one occasion to the total ordinary household population estimated from population surveys.

$$\text{Departure rate} = \frac{\text{Number of travellers} \times 100}{\text{Total population}}$$

The departure rate relates to trips away from home lasting four or more consecutive days (less than four months for domestic tourism) for motives other than those of professional activity, study or health. Periods of rest at the main place of residence are not included in this equation. It is, however, important to distinguish between the number of people travelling on at least one occasion on holiday and the number of different holidays taken (one traveller can take several trips). The concept of trips taken does not correspond to the concept of *departures*.

Hence, the general definition of *departure rate* is complemented by the *gross departure rate* and the *frequency of departure*:

The gross departure rate is the number of trips undertaken by travellers with respect to the total population during a specified period.

$$\text{Gross departure rate} = \frac{\text{Number of trips} \times 100}{\text{Total population}}$$

☐ The frequency of departure

The frequency of departure is the number of trips undertaken by each traveller during a specified period.

$$\text{Frequency of departure} = \frac{\text{Number of trips}}{\text{Number of travellers}}$$

The departure rate can be over 100, particularly in industrialised countries.

☐ Factors influencing the departure rate

The factors influencing the departure rate are age, socio-professional class of the head of the household, the size of the district where the main residence is located, income and lifestyle. The breakdown of departure rates by age group reveals that the young and the 30- to 39-year-old age group have the highest departure rate. However, the over-60-year-old age group stay abroad longer on average.

The departure rate is also influenced by *travel motivation*. Travel motivation in international tourism can be divided into three main categories: price, climate and personal motives.

- *Price* Cost is a major motivating factor in international tourism. The low prices for tourism products in certain countries explain their success in attracting tourists from countries that have a higher general price level. This is the case in several countries of Southern Europe, notably Spain, Greece and Portugal as highlighted in Table 1.1, 'The cost of living on holiday'. The survey carried out by American Express shows that of European countries, Spain, Greece and Portugal are relatively inexpensive, compared to France and Italy. This, and the favourable climate in these countries, explains their success as mass-market destinations. The USA and Thailand are popular long-haul destinations for Europeans and they are very competitive. The cost of travel to these destinations has fallen with the introduction of charter flights. In 1993, 1 million British tourists visited Florida.

  The differential in tourism prices between countries is a result of their different salary levels. Tourism is labour-intensive and salaries make up a large proportion of product costs. It follows that tourists from high-wage countries are attracted to the low tourism prices in low-wage countries. Price differential is an important factor in the motivation of Northern European tourists to visit Southern European destinations and the motivation of North American tourists to visit Mexico and Latin America.

- *Climate*   Climate is another determining motive for international tourism. Southern European countries, with their guarantee of sunshine, also benefit from this factor.
- *Personal motives*   Personal motives include:

Leisure and holidays – the main motivation for travel outside work-time and periods of professional activity: the motivation factors are rest, the lure of exotic surroundings, cultural discovery, visiting friends and relatives, sports etc.;

Business travel – trips taken within the framework of professional activities: this category includes commercial travellers, airline crews on short or extended stopovers, government and international organisation officials on assignments and equipment installation engineers staying less than one year and employed by companies outside the country of installation;

Congresses and other meetings – trips undertaken to attend a congress or other types of meetings (seminars, conferences, etc.) for non-profit motives;

Health – trips for medical reasons either to receive medical care or for health improvement by preventive medicine (fitness training, salt water cures etc.). This category also include all therapeutic treatments and visits to thermal resorts;

Study – visits abroad to attend courses or to undergo training in a study centre for one or more academic years;

Religion – pilgrimages and trips to holy shrines.

■ International tourism trends

Economic flows generated by international tourism have become essential factors of economic growth and international economic relations for a great many countries. With currently more than half a billion international tourist arrivals, the tourism sector has experienced rapid growth. Yet, it is apparent that is not the case in all of the world's regions. Indeed, the primary feature of world tourism trends is the unequitable distribution of international travel flows to the different regions of the world. Travel flows are concentrated towards a few regions and are mainly between countries within the same region.

Although demand for travel to developing countries is growing, the Third World only attracts one-third of the world's international visitors. Statistics compiled by the WTO show that developing countries receive

Table 1.1 *The cost of living on holiday (pounds sterling)*

	Meal for two with wine	Beer (bottle or glass)	Can of soft drink	Suntan lotion	Camera film	Sunbed hire	Souvenir T-Shirt	Postcard	Car hire (one week)	Petrol (litre)	Ave. entrance to a museum	Total
USA	24.81	2.84	0.31	3.10	4.65	2.48	4.96	0.31	68.32	0.37	3.10	115.28
Sweden	37.00	3.47	0.46	4.62	4.62	–	11.56	0.19	138.76	0.71	2.54	203.28
Spain	21.48	2.14	0.32	8.05	3.76	2.68	5.37	0.13	161.07	0.54	2.68	208.22
Thailand	23.00	1.00	0.25	5.00	2.35	1.05	3.15	0.13	184.00	0.25	0.50	220.68
Greece	21.37	1.22	0.41	2.44	3.66	2.44	4.58	0.30	186.00	0.61	3.66	226.69
Portugal	26.00	0.76	0.39	5.20	3.46	3.90	17.33	0.26	195.01	0.63	1.95	254.89
UK	30.00	1.50	0.50	3.99	4.00	1.00	9.99	0.10	210.00	0.50	5.00	266.58
Holland	29.53	1.01	0.55	2.95	5.16	5.53	9.22	0.73	221.48	0.68	3.69	280.53
Italy	31.93	1.87	0.68	3.64	3.87	3.47	5.47	0.29	296.52	0.72	2.28	350.64
France	30.81	3.70	0.61	4.31	4.93	6.16	9.86	0.24	314.31	0.65	4.93	380.51

Source: American Express Travellers Cheques (1993).

just 35 per cent of the world's total arrivals. Furthermore, the already considerable differences in travel flows between world regions are growing. The proportion of tourists received by the East Asian and Pacific region more than trebled between 1975 and 1992, passing from 3.89 per cent to 12.26 per cent of the world's total. Over the same period, South Asia's already very small share of world arrivals barely increased. In 1975, it was only 0.73 per cent. By 1992, it had progressed by only 0.03 per cent to 0.76 per cent.[8]

Europe is the largest receptor region and attracts 59.3 per cent of the world's tourists. Three-quarters of the international visits in the region are by European inhabitants. Europe therefore owes its dominant position to the *concentration* of travel flows to certain destinations in the region and to the effects of international travel within the region itself (the effects of *regionalism*).

Demand for world tourism is undergoing considerable quantitative and qualitative changes which are directly influencing the world tourism market. Several economic indicators are used to assess international tourism demand and its effect on the economy: the number of tourist arrivals at a destination; receipts from foreign tourists; expenditure by tourists travelling abroad; and the contribution made by tourism to a region's export earnings.

☐ *World and regional tourism trends*

The analysis of international tourism must focus on both tourist arrivals trends and on tourism receipts trends as they evolve differently.

☐ International tourist arrivals

The number of international journeys has doubled in fifteen years. WTO statistics show that there were 222 million international tourist arrivals in 1975. The volume of travellers steadily increased to 457 million by 1990. But international tourism suffered its first significant setback in 1991, registering a slight fall in arrivals of 0.32 per cent. The upward trend resumed in 1992, increasing by 4.5 per cent to reach a total of 481 million and 500 million in 1993.

The large growth in tourist flows since 1970 can be attributed to 'mass tourism'. Mass tourism has brought very high concentrations of tourists to certain zones, particularly costal regions, sometimes resulting in environmental and social damage such as water pollution, degradation of ecosystems, noise and confrontation with the local population.

Table 1.2   *International tourist arrivals and receipts worldwide, 1970–93*

Years	Arrivals (millions)	% change	Receipts (billions US$)	% change
1970	166	–	17	–
1975	222	34.08	40	127.38
1980	288	29.45	103	153.93
1985	330	14.54	116	12.38
1990	457	6.17	257	20.95
1991	456	−0.32	260	1.06
1992	481	5.51	296	13.75
1993	500	3.83	324	9.35

Notes: Totals for 1970 to 1991 are revised figures.
Figures on receipts exclude international transports.
Source: WTO.

However, domestic tourism rather than international tourism is generally responsible for bringing large volumes of tourists which exceed the carrying capacity of these areas.

Just under half of all international arrivals are by road, although arrivals by air have increased over the years. In 1992, 40 per cent of tourists travelled by air.

International arrivals by road are essentially intra-European where distances between countries and the highly developed road system makes this mode of transport easy and quick. Furthermore, immigration and

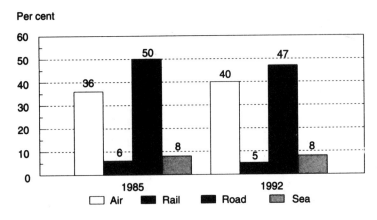

Source: WTO.

Figure 1.3   *Breakdown of arrivals by mode of transport, 1985–92*

customs procedure between European Union countries have been relaxed in recent years.

Only 5 per cent of travellers use the railway system to travel internationally (mainly to European destinations) and 8 per cent travel by boat, mainly on ferries (for example, between the UK and France and Belgium, between Italy and Greece, and between Sweden and Denmark).

☐ International tourism receipts

Revenue from international tourism (not including revenue from the transport sector) has increased significantly since 1980. In that year tourism generated US$103 billion. By 1993, this had reached US$324 billion annually. Tourism receipts have grown more rapidly and more regularly than world arrivals. Thus, during 1991, receipts increased by 1.06 per cent while arrivals fell. This halt in tourism growth can be considered the first major crisis of the tourism sector. It was caused on the one hand by the Gulf War and on the other, more especially, because of the fall in the economic growth in most of the industrialised countries.

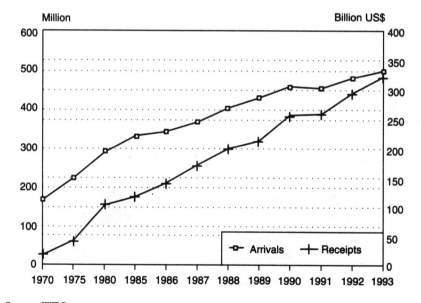

Source: WTO.

Figure 1.4 *Development of international tourism worldwide, 1970–93*

The sharp increase in international tourism receipts is not only the consequence of inflation in the 1970s, it is also a result of better-quality services being offered and better equipment being used.

☐ International arrivals and receipts by region

Europe is the world's main destination, although the number of international arrivals is growing at a slower rate than in other regions. It receives 59 per cent of the world's visitors who contribute only 50 per cent of total world receipts. In comparison, the East Asia and Pacific region (EAP) and the American region have proportionally higher revenues because they attract a greater number of high-spending tourists and business travellers.

Africa and South Asia are very weak tourism regions. Compared to the rest of the world, they receive few tourists and little revenue for tourism. South Asian and African countries do not have the necessary infrastructure and superstructure to develop their tourism sector and suffer many handicaps impeding them from competing against countries in other regions.

Recent trends in world tourism highlight the considerable changes that are taking place, particularly in international tourism receipts. Europe's share of world tourism receipts had fallen to 50 per cent in 1993 from nearly 53 per cent in 1985. During the same period, the East Asian and Pacific countries saw their share grow considerably from 11 per cent to 16 per cent. This situation demonstrates clearly that tourism is first and foremost an economic phenomenon. In 1993, the average receipt per tourist was US$547 in Europe and US$766 in East Asia and the Pacific.

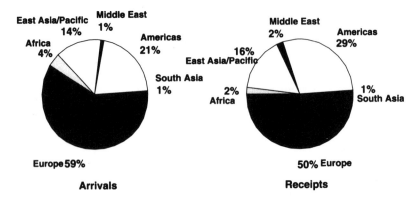

Source: WTO.

Figure 1.5   *Share of each region in total international tourist arrivals and receipts worldwide, 1993 (%)*

Table 1.3 *International tourist arrivals and receipts worldwide, 1985–93*

Regions		1985	Share of world total (%)	1993	Share of world total (%)	Ave. annual growth rate, 1985–92 (%)
World	A	329.6	100.00	500.1	100.00	6.1
	R	116.1	100.00	324	100.00	15.8
Africa	A	9.7	2.95	17.9	3.57	9.1
	R	2.6	2.24	6.4	1.96	13.6
Americas	A	66.5	20.17	106.5	21.30	7.0
	R	33.3	28.68	95.5	29.48	16.2
East Asia/Pacific	A	30.4	9.22	68.5	13.71	13.3
	R	12.8	11.06	52.6	16.23	22.3
Europe	A	214.2	65.00	296.5	59.29	4.7
	R	61.2	52.67	162.6	50.17	15.0
Middle East	A	6.2	1.89	7.2	1.44	2.1
	R	4.0	3.47	4.9	1.54	3.1
South Asia	A	2.5	0.77	3.4	0.69	4.3
	R	1.7	1.44	2.0	0.62	2.7

A = Arrivals (millions)
R = Receipts (billions US$)
Source: WTO.

Trends in the other regions of the world do not show great variations. There is a slight growth in the American region's market share from 28.6 per cent of total receipts in 1985 to 29.4 per cent in 1993. Africa is stagnating and there is a slight loss of market share for the Middle East and South Asia. For these three regions, political instability and more especially the problems created by slow economic development are the principle obstacles to increasing market share.

International tourism flows and the level of economic development

When countries are ranked by per capita GNP, great differences in the distribution of international arrivals and more especially receipts become apparent. According to the World Bank table of countries ranked by economic development, the industrialised countries receive 56 per cent of international tourism receipts while low-income countries (including India and China) receive just 1.5 per cent of receipts.

Table 1.4 *International tourist arrivals and receipts classified according to the World Bank groups of countries in 1991*

Groups of countries	Arrivals (000)	Receipts (millions US$)
Low-income economies	18,404	5,872
Including:		
• China and India	14,142	4,196
• Other low-income countries	4,262	1,676
Middle-income economies	130,315	54,163
Including:		
• Lower-middle-income	60,326	19,229
• Upper-middle-income	69,989	34,934
Developing countries	148,719	60,035
Oil exporters	28,264	11,390
Exports of manufactured goods	71,714	26,095
Highly indebted countries	34,124	14,574
Sub-Saharan Africa	5,540	1,639
Industrial market economies	262,376	182,353
Ex-USSR	6,895	250

Source: The World Bank.

Tourism receipts per capita GNP are very low in low-income countries, even when compared with other developing countries. According to studies by the WTO and the World Bank in 1991, per capita receipts average out at US$316[4] for lower-middle-income countries,[9] at US$500 for upper-middle-income countries[10] and at US$694 for industrialised countries.

Consequently, low-income countries are unable to finance tourism infrastructures. The services that they offer, particularly in the hotel trade, do not generate enough revenue to develop new units. Furthermore, the average price of their tourism products is generally much lower than that of other countries. Despite having to import many products, the cost of tourism production is lower than in industrialised countries (i.e. low labour costs). Many developing countries offer lower prices in their efforts to compete internationally but they are still unable to make up by increased volume the revenue they require for further development.

☐ The main destinations

Fourteen European countries feature in the top twenty receptor countries in the world. At the top of the list is the USA. It ranks first both in terms of receipts and expenditure. After the USA, France earns the most money from tourism and German tourists are the biggest spenders abroad.

Table 1.5 *World's top tourism earners (international tourism receipts)*

Country	Tourism receipts ($ US million)		% share of receipts worldwide	
	1992	1985	1992	1985
1 USA	53,861	17,937	18.17	15.54
2 France	25,000	7,942	8.44	6.84
3 Spain	22,181	8,151	7.48	7.02
4 Italy	21,577	8,756	7.28	7.54
5 UK	13,683	7,120	4.62	6.13
6 Austria	13,250	5,084	4.47	4.38
7 Germany	10,982	4,748	3.71	4.09
8 Switzerland	7,650	3,145	2.58	2.71
9 Hong Kong	6,037	1,788	2.04	1.54
10 Mexico	5,997	2,901	2.02	2.50
11 Canada	5,697	3,103	1.92	2.67
12 Singapore	5,204	1,660	1.76	1.43
13 Netherlands	5,004	1,661	1.69	1.43
14 Thailand	4,829	1,171	1.63	1.01
15 Belgium	4,053	1,663	1.37	1.43
16 Australia	3,992	1,062	1.35	0.91
17 China	3,948	979	1.33	0.84
18 Denmark	3,784	1,326	1.28	1.14
19 Portugal	3,721	1,137	1.26	0.98
20 Turkey	3,639	1,482	1.23	1.28
World total	296,375	116,149	100.00	100.00

Source: WTO.

Canada can claim unique characteristics. In relation to the size of its population, it generates the largest number of tourists who are among the biggest spenders per head abroad.

Some Eastern European countries (Hungary and Romania) are among the top twenty destinations for tourist arrivals but not in the top earners ranking. This is also the case for certain Asian destinations. Malaysia, although seventeenth in terms of tourist arrivals, does not appear in the top earners list.

Exchanges of money generated by tourism (receipts and expenditure) are predominantly *North–North* between a combination of industrialised and newly industrialised countries. There are five newly industrialised countries in the top twenty tourism earners: Hong Kong, Singapore, Mexico, Thailand and South Korea. There are no developing countries represented in this list. The twenty largest tourism spenders account for 45

Table 1.6 *World's top tourism spenders (international tourism expenditures)*

Country	Tourism expenditure ($US million)		% share of expenditures worldwide	
	1992	1985	1992	1985
1 USA	39,872	24,517	14.48	24.10
2 Germany	31,309	12,809	13.55	12.59
3 Japan	26,837	4,814	9.75	4.73
4 UK	19,831	6,369	7.20	6.26
5 Italy	16,617	2,283	6.04	2.24
6 France	13,910	4,557	5.05	4.48
7 Canada	11,265	4,130	4.09	4.06
8 Netherlands	9,330	3,448	3.39	3.39
9 Taiwan	7,098	1,429	2.58	1.40
10 Austria	6,895	2,723	2.50	2.68
11 Sweden	6,794	1,967	2.47	1.93
12 Belgium	6,603	2,050	2.40	2.01
13 Switzerland	6,068	2,399	2.20	2.36
14 Spain	5,542	1,010	2.01	0.99
15 Norway	4,081	1,772	1.48	1.69
16 Australia	3,994	1,918	1.45	1.89
17 Korea RP	3,794	606	1.38	0.60
18 Denmark	3,779	1,410	1.37	1.39
19 Finland	2,403	777	0.87	0.76
20 Singapore	2,340	613	0.85	1.60
World total	275,297	101,738	100.00	100.00

Source: WTO.

per cent of world tourism expenditure. In Asia, Japan, Taiwan and South Korea spend the most on tourism. In Europe, the largest expenditure is by British and German tourists.

The USA is the world's biggest spender on tourism, although its expenditure has recently declined sharply. In 1985, tourists from the United States accounted for 24 per cent of all money spent on tourism in the world. By 1992, this had fallen to just 14 per cent.

This introductory chapter has established that the distribution of international tourism flows (and how they evolve) is greatly influenced by economic conditions. The international exchange of services (such as tourism services) is more susceptible than the international trade of goods to levels of economic development.

World tourism flow trends clearly indicate the high growth rate of international tourism since the 1950s. For much of this period, until the economic downturn caused by the two petrol crises of 1974 and 1979, economic growth was the force behind the expansion of world tourism. Since the early 1980s, new factors specific to the tourism and air transport sectors are influencing and directing tourism development. The lengthening of statutory holidays, improvements in productivity, the competitiveness of tourism services and the liberalisation of air transport have all contributed to the high growth rate of international tourism arrivals.

Selecting the most advantageous tourism development approach (notably, methods for increasing expenditure per tourist) requires a thorough understanding of international tourism. This is based on accurate economic analyses comparing the tourism situation in each of the world's regional markets to determine the conditions that favour tourism development and those that impede it.

However, international tourism is not developing at the same rate in every region of the world. The distribution of tourist flows and more particularly of tourism receipts is uneven and highly concentrated in OECD and East Asian countries. Thus, the analysis of international tourism flows is the key to understanding the main economic characteristics of tourism.

References

1. WTO, *Recommendations on Tourism Statistics*. Madrid, 1993.

2. Ibid.

3. Ibid.

4. Ibid.

5. Ibid.

6. Ibid.

7. OECD, *The Manual of Tourism Economic Accounting*. Tourism Committee, 1991.

8. *WTO News*, no. 1, January–February 1994.

9. Included in these countries are the Republic of Korea, Argentina, Venezuela and Singapore.

10. Included in these countries are Indonesia, Morocco, the Ivory Coast, Thailand, Tunisia, Brazil and Mexico.

Further reading

WTO. *World Tourism Data*. Madrid, 1993–4.

WTO. *Compendium of Tourism Statistics*. Madrid, 1994.

Crompton, J. L. 'Motivation for Pleasure Vacation', *Annals of Tourism Research*, 6 (4), pp. 408–24, 1979.

Crowe, R. B. 'Recreation, Tourism and Climate – a Canadian Perspective', Weather, 30(8), pp. 248–54, 1975.

WTO. *Tourism Forecasting*, Madrid, 1981.

■ *Chapter 2* ■

The International Tourism Market in the Destinations of the World

International tourism demand in Europe: international tourist arrivals; tourism receipts; the main European destinations

International tourism demand in the America region: international tourist arrivals; tourism receipts; the main American destinations

International tourism demand in Africa: international tourist arrivals; tourism receipts; the main African destinations

International tourism demand in the Middle East: international tourist arrivals; tourism receipts; the main Middle Eastern destinations

International tourism demand in the South Asia region: international tourist arrivals; tourism receipts; the main South Asian destinations

International tourism demand in the East Asia and Pacific region: international tourist arrivals; tourism receipts; the main East Asian and Pacific destinations

The international tourism market is highly segmented by types of products, clientele and destinations. The analysis of tourism markets in each destination region of the world gives a general insight into current situations and past and future trends. For instance, it highlights the relative importance of intra-regional tourism in Europe, a consequence of the high concentration of international tourism in the region. Indeed, there are many country borders within a relatively small area and land communication (railway and road systems) is accessible and extensive. In contrast, the development of international tourism in other regions of the world such as Africa and South Asia is hampered by weak intra-regional flows, not just because of the low purchasing power of their populations but also because of the slowness of land transport and because access is restricted by poor networks of usable roads. Visitors to these areas tend to favour air transport although this is a far more expensive mode of transport.

The analysis of international tourism markets in each of the world's regions has three main objectives:

- identifying the regions where international tourism is increasing and those where it is declining;
- explaining the reasons behind the large differences in the geographic distribution of arrivals and receipts and how these differences evolved;
- and identifying countries where international tourism has the potential of becoming a significant element of economic development and job creation.

The six regions defined by the WTO are:

- Europe
- The Americas
- Africa
- The Middle East
- South Asia
- East Asia and the Pacific

For each of these regions, it is important to compare the international arrival trends with the international receipt trends.

■ International tourism demand in Europe

While European countries still receive the greatest proportion of tourists in the world, the current rate of arrivals is lower than the world average. In 1985, European countries received 65 per cent of the world's tourists. By 1993, this had fallen to below 60 per cent.

Several factors are behind the relative decline of Europe's dominant position:

- The falling trend in demand in Europe can be partly attributed to the growing popularity of countries which have only recently but successfully developed their tourism industry, particularly the South-East Asian countries.
- Some Eastern Europe countries (CIS and Romania) are experiencing difficulties adapting their tourism sector to the new environment of market economics. Furthermore, the conflict in the former Yugoslavia has also affected tourism in this European region.
- Some Western European countries, particularly in Southern Europe (Italy, Greece and to a lesser extent Spain and Portugal) have suffered a loss in competitiveness and a deterioration in the quality–price ratio of their products. This is a consequence of inadequate renovation of

existing structures. It is essential for these countries to adapt their tourism structures to today's market.

• Finally, several Northern European countries (Sweden, Denmark, Norway and to a lesser extent the United Kingdom) are very expensive for tourists. This is inevitably affecting their competitiveness.

However, despite the fall in Europe's market share of international tourism, it should be noted that arrivals and receipts have continued to increase year on year with the exception of 1991.

☐ *International tourist arrivals*

Table 2.1 shows that between 1970 and 1993, the number of international tourist arrivals in Europe more than doubled from 113 million visitors to 296 million. But, during the same period, Europe's share of total world arrivals declined from 68.16 per cent to 59.29 per cent.

Europe's share of world tourism is on a steady downward trend. There have been significant fluctuations in the average annual growth rate for arrivals to Europe, for instance it increased by 1.9 per cent in 1986 and 9 per cent in 1989 but fell 2.4 per cent in 1991. This instability can be partly

Table 2.1   *International tourist arrivals and receipts in Europe, 1970–93*

Year	Arrivals (000)	Change (%)	Share of total world arrivals (%)	Receipts (US$ millions)	Change (%)	Share of total world receipts (%)
1970	113,000	–	68.16	11,096	–	61.99
1975	153,859	36.16	69.22	26,310	137.11	64.64
1980	189,830	23.38	65.97	61,654	134.34	59.65
1985	214,264	12.87	65.00	61,181	−0.77	52.67
1986	218,320	1.89	64.06	77,028	25.90	54.80
1987	233,623	7.01	63.70	96,565	24.36	56.03
1988	251,237	7.54	62.48	106,788	10.59	53.71
1989	274,021	9.07	63.53	109,980	2.99	51.60
1990	286,651	4.61	62.59	139,700	27.02	54.19
1991	279,836	−2.38	61.30	135,768	-2.81	52.11
1992	290,304	3.74	60.27	153,815	13.29	51.90
1993	296,535	2.15	59.29	162,573	5.69	50.16

Source: WTO.

attributed to the economic situation in generating countries: 1989 was a year of economic growth whereas 1991 was a year of economic recession. However, the situation in receptor countries is equally as important, particularly variations in exchange rates. In 1991, the currencies of both Italy and Spain were very strong, which had negative implications on the competitiveness of their tourism products.

The decline is accelerating and Europe's dominant position will be challenged during the next decade. Between 1970 and 1980, Europe lost 2.2 per cent in market share; between 1980 and 1990, 3.4 per cent; and between 1900 and 1994, another 3.3 per cent. This is mainly a result of slow economic growth rates in generating countries.

A breakdown of nationalities arriving in Europe shows that more than 90 per cent of visitors were from European countries. German tourists travel the most within the region and account for 19 per cent of all international arrivals. British travellers represent 10 per cent of European arrivals, the French 7 per cent and the Dutch 6 per cent.

Since 1985, international travel by European tourists within the region has increased while visitor arrivals from the American region have fallen. In 1985, American tourists represented 11 per cent of visitors to Europe. By 1992, this had dropped to just 5.4 per cent largely because of the weakness of the US dollar against European currencies (see Figure 2.1).

These trends are even more disturbing in view of the economic recession in European countries during 1992 and 1993. The increasing dependency on the region's own tourists is having a significant impact on tourism expenditure in Europe.

The United States in seventh position is the only non-European country in the top ten tourist-generating countries.

□ *Tourism receipts*

The downward trend of tourism receipts in Europe has been even more pronounced than the falling trend in arrivals. There is now a 9-point differential in market share between arrivals and receipts. Table 2.1 indicates that in 1980, Europe's share of world tourism receipts was 59.6 per cent. By 1993, this had fallen to 50.1 per cent. Expenditure in European countries has been proportionally weaker than in other regions of the world.

As with the arrivals trend, the European tourism receipts trend is very irregular. Between 1980 and 1985, receipts stagnated with a 7-point drop in market share, whereas between 1985 and 1990 receipts doubled and regained 1.5 points in market share (see Figure 2.2) This instability shows

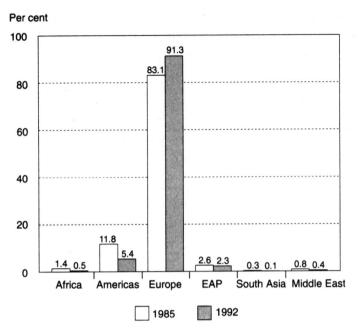

Per cent

Source: WTO.

Figure 2.1 *International tourist arrivals in Europe by country of origin, 1985–92 (%)*

how much international tourism is vulnerable to competition and to exchange-rate fluctuations. In 1984 and 1985, the US dollar fell sharply against European currencies, then between 1985 and 1990 the dollar exchange rate stabilised.

The proportion of revenue attributed to tourism in Europe's total export earnings is slightly higher than the world average. This is progressing at a good rate. In 1992, tourism receipts represented 8.7 per cent of Europe's total export earnings, up from 1985 when they represented just 6.4 per cent. This indicates that international tourism is an increasingly important sector in the economies of European countries.

☐ *The main European destinations*

Tourism flows to Europe are mainly to destinations in Western and Southern Europe. These areas account for 70 per cent of arrivals and 76 per cent of total European receipts. This tourism concentration is the result of European holiday-taking habits which mainly revolve around beach

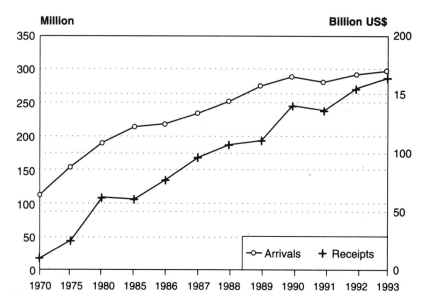

Source: WTO.

Figure 2.2   *Development of international tourism in Europe, 1970–93*

tourism during the summer months. Figure 2.3 shows that countries in Southern and Western Europe, principally France, Spain and Italy, benefit the most from these tourism flows. France, Spain and Italy are the main European tourist destinations both in terms of arrivals and receipts.

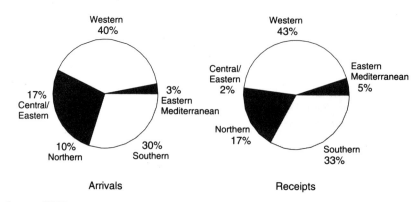

Source: WTO.

Figure 2.3   *Share of each sub-region in total international tourist arrivals and receipts in Europe, 1992 (%)*

However, green tourism to countries such as Ireland, Austria and the Scandinavian countries also accounts for a large proportion of tourists to Europe.

Flows to Central and Eastern Europe represent only 17 per cent of arrivals and 2 per cent of receipts. This is the result of the pricing policies in effect in these countries. The prices charged for their tourism products do not always correspond to the needs of market economics. Romania is one of the most extreme cases. In 1992, 6.2 million tourists travelled to Romania and spent US$262 million. Sweden on the other hand received US$3,086 million from just 0.6 million foreign tourists (see Table 2.2).

If Central and Eastern European countries are compared to Northern European countries, it is apparent that the contrast between them in arrivals and receipts is considerable. In 1992, the average receipt per tourist was US$66 for Central and Eastern European countries whereas it was US$925 for North European countries. In the countries of the ex-USSR, the unit receipt was just US$35 per tourist. In the United Kingdom, it was US$738 and in Belgium US$1258.

The considerable differences in tourism development between European countries are not only a result of their economic situation, they are also due to the varying levels of quality and modernity of their tourism infrastructure.

■ International tourism demand in the American region

The WTO defines the whole of the American continent as the American region which includes North, Central and South America and the Caribbean Islands.

☐ *International tourist arrivals*

With 21 per cent of the world's total international tourist arrivals, the American region ranks second behind the European region. In 1993, there were 106 million visits to the area. Its position is all the more important as the majority of arrivals are to the United States, Canada, Mexico and Brazil where domestic tourism is particularly well-developed. Consequently, the weight of tourism in the American region is more important than the number of international tourist arrivals it receives would imply. In fact, in terms of international tourism receipts, the American region's

Table 2.2   *International tourism in Europe, 1992*

Country	Tourist arrivals (000)	Tourism receipts (US$ millions)
Europe	290,304	153, 815
Central and Eastern	49,118	3,270
Bulgaria	3,750	49
Hungary	20,188	1,251
Poland	4,000	183
Romania	6,200	262
(Ex-)Czechoslovakia	8,000	1,280
(Ex-)USSR	6,900	245
Northern	27,702	25,634
Denmark	1,543	3,784
Finland	790	1,315
Iceland	143	129
Ireland	3,666	1,620
Norway	2,375	2,017
United Kingdom	18,535	13,683
Sweden	650	3,086
Southern	86,424	51,631
Gibraltar	136	116
Greece	9,331	3,268
Italy	26,113	21,577
Malta	1,002	568
Portugal	8,821	3,721
San Marino	583	–
Spain	39,638	22,181
Former Yugoslavia	700	200
Western	117,081	66,226
Germany	15,147	10,982
Austria	19,098	13,250
Belgium	3,220	4,053
France	59,590	25,000
Liechtenstein	72	–
Luxembourg	796	287
Monaco	246	–
The Netherlands	6,049	5,004
Switzerland	12,800	7,650
Eastern Mediterranean	10,042	7,054
Cyprus	1,992	1,539
Israel	1,502	1,876
Turkey	6,549	3,639

Source: WTO.

position is much higher. It accounts for nearly 30 per cent of the world's total receipts.

Between 1970 and 1993, the volume of international tourist arrivals increased at a slower rate than the world average (see Table 2.3). As a result, the American region's share of world tourism fell from 25.5 per cent in 1970 to 21.3 per cent in 1993 although it should be noted that since 1985 the rate of arrivals to the region has picked up. In 1985, the American share fell to its lowest percentage, 20.17 per cent.

The number of tourists visiting the region is dependent on the economic situation of the United States and Canada. These two countries provide half the international arrivals in the region. Fluctuations in the US dollar exchange rate have therefore a decisive influence on tourism demand in countries outside the dollar zone.

Tourist flows to the region are principally from tourists from the region itself. This percentage has decreased since 1985, when it stood at 85.8 per cent, to 78.6 per cent in 1993.

Tourism demand in American countries is much more diversified than tourism demand in European countries. There are seven European countries and Japan in the top sixteen generating countries. Nevertheless, the three largest tourist-generating countries are the United States, Canada and Mexico, all countries on the American continent. Argentina, Brazil and Venezuela are also important generating countries. Yet tourism

Table 2.3 *International tourist, arrivals and receipts in the Americas, 1970–93*

Year	Arrivals (000)	Change (%)	Share of total world arrivals (%)	Receipts (US$ millions)	Change (%)	Share of total world receipts (%)
1975	50,043	18.38	22.51	10,219	112.90	25.11
1980	61,387	22.67	21.33	25,503	149.56	24.67
1985	66,495	8.32	20.17	33,315	30.63	28.68
1986	71,771	7.93	21.06	37,629	13.04	26.79
1987	76,243	6.23	20.79	42,029	11.60	24.39
1988	83,462	9.47	21.76	49,830	18.56	25.06
1989	87,398	4.72	20.26	57,029	14.45	26.75
1990	93,424	6.89	20.40	67,138	17.73	26.04
1991	96,947	3.77	21.24	74,056	10.30	28.42
1992	101,080	4.26	20.99	83,595	12.88	28.21
1993	106,525	5.39	21.30	95,545	14.30	29.48

Source: WTO.

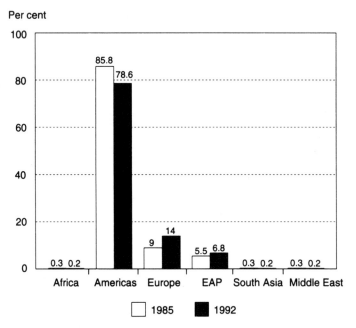

Per cent

Source: WTO.

Figure 2.4   *International tourist arrivals in the Americas by country of origin 1985–92 (%)*

flows are concentrated, with the top five countries accounting for 70 per cent of all international arrivals in the American region.

The arrival rate of European tourists in the American region is increasing. In 1992, it stood at 14 per cent compared with the arrival rate of East Asian and Pacific tourists, which was recorded at 6.8 per cent. The leading European market to the Americas is the United Kingdom which accounts for 4 per cent of all arrivals and the leading Asian market is Japan which also represents 4 per cent of all arrivals.

The growth of tourism to the region is largely due to the very favourable price of the American tourism product. Each element of the product is competitively priced: accommodation, transport and leisure. For example, the cost of one week's car hire in high season from Budget Rent-a-Car in 1994 was US$138 in California, US$185 in Portugal, US$303 in Greece and US$390 in Israel. Thus, because of the favourable prices and the fact that since deregulation of the airline industry, the cost of air transport has substantially fallen on North American routes, European Community and Japanese tourists are arriving in the region in constantly increasing numbers.

☐ *Tourism receipts*

The American region's share of world tourism receipts is significantly larger than its share of tourism arrivals. Table 2.3 reveals that in 1993, American countries received 29.5 per cent of the world's tourism earnings from only 21.3 per cent of the world's tourists. This clearly shows that visitors to the United States have a high level of expenditure. In contrast to international arrivals, the American region's international tourism receipts are increasing. The American share of world receipts progressed by more than three points between 1990 and 1993.

The increase in the receipts trend compared to the arrivals trend is a recent development. In 1970, the American region's share of world receipts (26.8 per cent) was approximately equivalent to its share of world expenditure (25.5 per cent) (see Figure 2.5).

The importance of the region's tourism receipts is also reflected in their contribution to the area's export earnings. They represented 11.5 per cent of total export earnings in 1993, proportionally the highest percentage contribution in the world. The relative importance of the tourism sector in the region's exports is a consequence of the recent competitiveness of

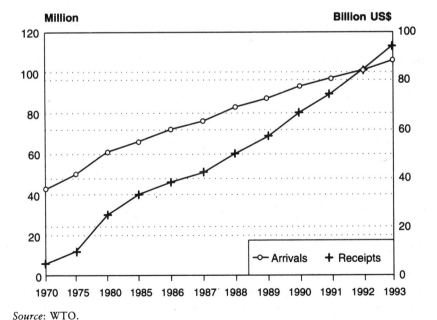

Source: WTO.

Figure 2.5   *Development of international tourism in the Americas 1970–93*

American tourism products in the world market and of the strong tourism specialisation adopted by certain countries of the region, notably the Caribbean Islands, Mexico and Canada.

☐ *The main American destinations*

North America (USA, Mexico and Canada) is the region's main destination with 76 per cent of arrivals and 78 per cent of receipts. The Caribbean also features strongly with 12 per cent of arrivals and 12 per cent of receipts. South America can only claim 10 per cent of arrivals and 9 per cent of receipts and Central America receives only 2 per cent of arrivals and 1 per cent of receipts (see Figure 2.6).

Tourism is highly developed in the Caribbean Islands which have a total population of around 30 million inhabitants (including Cuba) and receive more than 11.6 million tourists annually. On the other hand, tourism flows to South America remain weak with 10.4 million arrivals in total. Argentina is the exception and receives 3 million tourists annually. This situation arises from the economic difficulties (unstable exchange rates, hyperinflation) as well as political difficulties (security, drugs) which damage the tourism image of some countries of the region.

The United States is by far the largest tourism country in the region with 44 per cent of total arrivals and 64 per cent of total receipts in 1992. In fact, in terms of receipts, the United States ranks first in the world. Furthermore, the USA's tourism economy is supported by a vast internal market and highly developed infrastructure and superstructure such as its extensive domestic air transport industry and the largest hotel chains in the world.

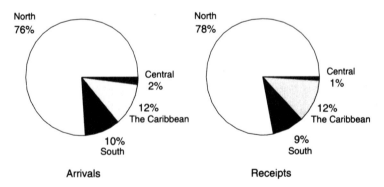

Source: WTO.

Figure 2.6 *Share of each sub-region in total international tourist arrivals and receipts in the Americas, 1992 (%)*

Table 2.4 *International tourism in the Americas, 1992*

Country	Tourist arrivals (000)	Tourism receipts (US$ millions)
Americas	101,080	83,595
The Caribbean	11,625	9,630
Anguilla	32	35
Antigua Barbuda	210	232
Aruba	542	443
Bahamas	1,399	1,244
Barbados	385	463
Bermuda	375	444
Bonaire	52	23
British Virgin Islands	117	100
Cayman Islands	242	439
Cuba	410	382
Curaçao	207	159
Dominica	47	25
Dominican Republic	1,524	1,054
Grenada	88	38
Guadaloupe	300	289
Haiti	90	40
Jamaica	909	858
Martinique	321	282
Monserrat	17	11
Puerto Rico	2,640	1,511
Saba	25	5
San Eustaquio	30	5
St Kitts/Nevis	90	67
St Lucia	177	173
St Martin	569	313
St Vincent	53	54
Trindad/Tobago	235	111
Turks Caicos Islands	52	41
US Virgin Islands	487	792
Central	2,378	1,079
Belize	225	96
Costa Rica	610	431
El Salvador	314	49
Guatemala	541	243
Honduras	230	32
Nicaragua	167	21
Panama	291	207
North	76,659	65,537
Canada	14,741	5,679
Mexico	17,271	5,997
United States	44,647	53,861

Table 2.4 cont.

Country	Tourist arrivals (000)	Tourism receipts (US$ millions)
South	10,418	7,349
Argentina	3,031	3,090
Bolivia	245	105
Brazil	1,470	1,307
Chile	1,283	706
Columbia	1,076	705
Ecuador	403	192
Guyana	93	30
Paraguay	334	153
Peru	217	237
Surinam	30	11
Uruguay	1,802	381
Venezuela.	434	432

Source: WTO.

■ International tourism demand in Africa

The African region includes all the African countries as well as the islands of the Indian Ocean, but excludes Libya and Egypt, which is classified by the WTO as part of the Middle Eastern region.

The volume of international tourism arrivals in Africa is very low. It accounts for only 3.57 per cent of the world's total. Africa is lagging behind the rest of the world in international tourism because many of its countries are economically underdeveloped. They lack sufficient air and road transport superstructures and the necessary financial means to invest in the hospitality and accommodation sector. As a result, most African countries are not able to introduce proper tourism development policies.

Despite the many difficulties facing Africa, the continent has exceptional assets and could participate more fully in the growth of world tourism. Besides its natural tourism heritage, Africa is close to Europe, the largest tourist-generating area, and lies mostly within the same time zone. Certain North African countries and East African countries (especially Kenya) have successfully exploited this situation. This has enabled them to develop their tourism industry. These countries lead the emergence of African tourism and are the force behind the 75 per cent increase in Africa's share of world tourists since 1985. In that year, African countries received 2.9 per cent of all arrivals in the world. By 1993, this had increased to 3.5 per cent.

□ *International tourist arrivals*

Although starting from the very low base of 4.7 million arrivals in 1975, international tourism demand trebled in fifteen years. During the same period, overall world demand only doubled. The increase in flow to Africa was particularly strong in 1988 and 1989. Even in 1991, despite the Gulf War which affected several North African countries, the tourism industry continued to grow.

Tourism flows between African countries are still very weak and this is a contributing factor to the slow development of tourism in that continent. In 1985, only 39 per cent of tourist arrivals were from other African countries. This pattern, however, may be changing. In 1992, 56 per cent of international visitors were African tourists (see Figure 2.7). Tourism activity between 1992 and the year 2000 could confirm this trend which may simply be a consequence of a decline in European arrivals after the Gulf War.

France is the main tourist-generating country and accounts for 8 per cent of all arrivals followed by Germany (under 7 per cent) and the United

Table 2.5 *International tourist arrivals and receipts in Africa, 1970–93*

Year	Arrivals (000)	Change (%)	Share of total world arrivals (%)	Receipts (US$ millions)	Change (%)	Share of total world receipts (%)
1970	2,407	–	1.45	400	–	2.23
1975	4,654	93.35	2.09	1,127	181.75	2.77
1980	7,337	57.63	2.55	2,711	140.55	2.62
1985	9,706	32.29	2.94	2,601	−4.06	2.24
1986	9,341	−3.76	2.74	2,970	14.19	2.11
1987	9,833	5.27	2.68	3,797	27.85	2.20
1988	12,940	31.60	3.22	4,601	21.71	2.31
1989	13,770	6.41	3.19	4,454	−3.19	2.09
1990	14,993	8.88	3.27	5,238	17.60	2.03
1991	15,842	5.66	3.47	4,830	−7.79	1.85
1992	17,552	10.79	3.64	5,855	21.22	1.98
1993	17,875	1.84	3.57	6,364	8.69	1.96

Source: WTO.

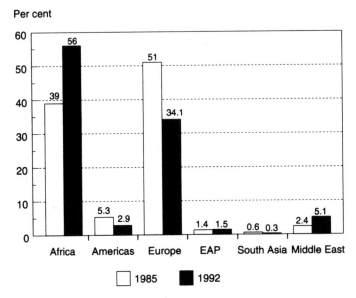

Source: WTO.

Figure 2.7   *International tourist arrivals in Africa by country of origin, 1985–92 (%)*

Kingdom (4 per cent). There are few tourists from the United States (just 266,000 in 1992) and their share of total arrivals is stagnating, even falling slightly. The is mainly because there are not enough air routes or airline companies prepared to fly between the United States and African countries.

☐ *Tourism receipts*

Tourism receipts in Africa are very low, accounting for less than 2 per cent of total world receipts. The trend in Table 2.5 shows that between 1975 and 1993 Africa's share of world tourism receipts fell from 2.77 per cent to 1.96 per cent. The diverging patterns between the receipts and arrivals trends is a consequence, on the one hand, of the lack of hotel and hospitality superstructures and, on the other, of the emergence of a form of low-expenditure mass tourism in Morocco and Tunisia which together account for 45 per cent of Africa's arrivals. In 1992, the average receipt per tourist was US$309 in Morocco and US$303 in Tunisia compared to US$355 for the rest of the African countries (US$892 for Mauritius).

The growth of international tourism in Africa is being hampered by financial constraints such as the high cost of promoting African destinations in generating markets. It is crucial to find ways of raising the average expenditure per tourist but this needs high investments to upgrade infrastructure and superstructure.

Since 1985, the trend in tourism receipts has been particularly erratic, with 1985, 1989 and 1991 recording sharp falls. The fluctuating financial contribution of tourism is very disturbing for countries with already weak economies. However, the contribution of tourism to Africa's total export earnings has increased considerably from 4.9 per cent in 1985 to 10.4 per cent in 1993.

□ *The main African destinations*

Tourism demand in Africa is mainly in North African countries, which receive more than half the total number of visitors to the region. Central Africa is particularly weak with 3 per cent of tourism flows and 1 per cent of receipts. Twenty-two African countries receive less than 100,000 visitors a year and thirteen less than 50,000 a year. However, some countries are experiencing rapid growth both in the number of visitors they receive and

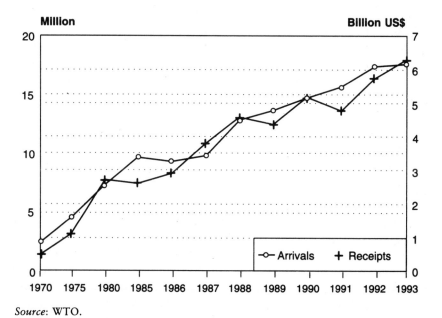

Source: WTO.

Figure 2.8 *Development of international tourism in Africa, 1970–93*

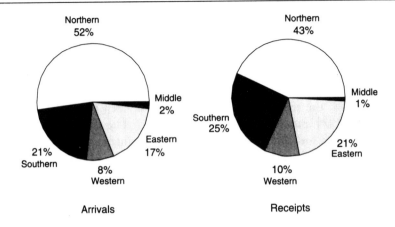

Source: WTO.

Figure 2.9 *Share of each sub-region in total international tourist arrivals and receipts in Africa, 1992 (%)*

Table 2.6 *International tourism in Africa, 1992*

Country	Tourist arrivals (000)	Tourism receipts (US$ millions)
Africa	17,552	5,855
Eastern Africa	2,963	1,238
Burundi	86	4
Comoros	19	8
Djibouti	40	5
Ethiopia	83	23
Kenya	699	442
Madagascar	38	39
Malawi	135	11
Mauritius	335	299
Reunion	217	–
Rwanda	43	4
Seychelles	99	117
Somalia	20	–
Uganda	50	10
Tanzania	202	120
Zambia	159	51
Zimbabwe	738	105
Middle Africa	396	69
Angola	40	–
Cameroon	119	23

Country	Tourist arrivals (000)	Tourism receipts (US$ millions)
Central African Empire	6	3
Chad	20	21
Congo	40	6
Equatorial Guinea	–	2
Gabon	130	5
Sao Tome Principe	1	2
Zaire	40	7
Northern Africa	9,067	2,514
Algeria	1,120	75
Morocco	4,390	1,360
Sudan	17	5
Tunisia	3,540	1,074
Southern Africa	3,765	1,433
Botswana	437	65
Lesotho	155	19
Namibia	–	91
South Africa	2,892	1,226
Swaziland	281	32
Western Africa	1,361	601
Benin	130	32
Burkina Faso	74	9
Cape Verde	–	7
Côte d'Ivoire	217	53
Gambia	95	56
Ghana	175	110
Mali	38	45
Mauritania	–	15
Niger	13	17
Nigeria	182	29
Senegal	246	172
Sierra Leone	91	17
Togo	100	39

Source: WTO.

in tourism receipts. Countries such as Morocco, Tunisia, South Africa, Mauritius and Senegal have pursued policies of tourism specialisation to which they can attribute their success.

Table 2.6 shows that South Africa is the leading tourism country in Sub-Saharan Africa with three million tourists a year. In 1992, it was ranked second in terms of receipts behind Morocco and in front of Tunisia with an average receipt per tourist of US$424. South Africa has a highly developed hotel industry and efficient internal and international transport systems. Furthermore, its tourism promotion policies have become particularly important. The International Tourism Fair in Durban is the largest tourism fair in Africa.

Mauritius is a good example of a country which has achieved its international tourism success by specialising in up-market and high-revenue beach tourism whilst still managing to protect its natural environment. Its success is based on providing high-quality service in luxury surroundings, for instance at the Sun and Beachcomber hotels.

▌International tourism demand in the Middle East

Tourism demand in the Middle East has been particularly erratic because of political problems and military conflicts in several countries of the region in the 1980s and 1990s. After a large fall of 17.7 per cent in 1986, international tourism grew in 1988 and 1989. However, 1991 saw another 10.2 per cent fall. Overall, the Middle East's share of world tourism declined from 2 per cent in 1980 to less than 1.5 per cent in 1993 (see Table 2.7).

The repercussions of the Gulf War have affected tourism not only in Iraq (63 per cent fall in arrivals from 1990 to 1991) but also in Saudi Arabia (−46 per cent) and in Jordan (−38 per cent). Egypt was also severely affected by the war, but it is the attacks on foreign tourists since the beginning of 1992 which have mainly caused the 33 per cent decline in arrivals in 1993.

☐ *International tourist arrivals*

There were 7.2 million international tourist arrivals in the Middle East in 1993. This was lower than in both 1989 and 1990 suggesting that tourism in the Middle East did not recover from the downturn caused by the Gulf War. Several countries still remain politically unstable.

The situation in the 1990s is very different to the situation during the 1970s. Despite the conflict in the Lebanon at the time, tourism arrivals trebled in the region from 1.8 million in 1970 to 5.9 million in 1980. Revenue from tourism doubled from 1.1 per cent to 2 per cent of the world total.

This relative deterioration of international tourism is particularly alarming for countries such as Egypt and Jordan. Tourism receipts are essential to these countries to service their foreign debt and maintain their foreign currency reserves.

The Middle East claimed only 1.5 per cent of world tourist arrivals in 1993. Tourists are returning to air transport as a mode of transport to the Middle East. In 1991, a year after the Gulf war, arrivals by air were just 38.1 per cent of all arrivals while arrivals by road had risen to 57.1 per cent. By 1992, arrivals by air increased rapidly to 55.9 per cent and arrivals by road fell back to 33 per cent of total arrivals (see Figure 2.10).

Figure 2.11 shows that the Middle East attracts tourists from a wide range of countries. The top nine generating countries supplied only 30 per cent of total arrivals to the region. The breakdown of arrivals by regions of origin reveals a diversified demand. European visitors mainly from the UK, Germany France and Italy account for 19 per cent of arrivals; 50 per cent come from other Middle Eastern countries and 18 per cent from East Asia and the Pacific region. However, tourism flows originating in the North American region are regressing and accounted for only 2.8 per cent of total arrivals in 1992. This situation can be mainly attributed to the political instability of the region. Moreover, the strong drop in arrivals from South Asia can be explained by the economic impact of the Gulf crisis.

Table 2.7 *International tourist arrivals and receipts in the Middle East, 1970–93*

Year	Arrivals (000)	Change (%)	Share of total world arrivals (%)	Receipts (US$ millions)	Change (%)	Share of total world receipts (%)
1970	1,864	–	1.12	404	–	2.26
1975	3,520	88.84	1.58	733	81.44	1.80
1980	5,992	70.23	2.08	3,470	373.40	3.36
1985	6,240	4.17	1.89	4,803	38.41	4.14
1986	5,132	−17.76	1.51	4,032	−16.05	2.87
1987	5,431	5.83	1.48	5,305	31.57	3.08
1988	6,961	28.17	1.73	5,051	−4.79	2.54
1989	7,519	8.02	1.74	5,434	7.58	2.55
1990	7,444	−1.00	1.63	5,127	−5.65	1.99
1991	6,674	−10.34	1.46	4,279	−16.54	1.64
1992	7,921	18.68	1.64	5,398	26.15	1.82
1993	7,200	−9.10	1.44	4,996	−7.45	1.54

Source: WTO.

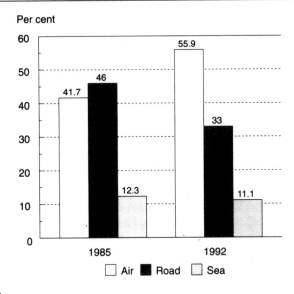

Source: WTO.

Figure 2.10   *Breakdown of arrivals in the Middle East by mode of transport,*
1985–92 (%)

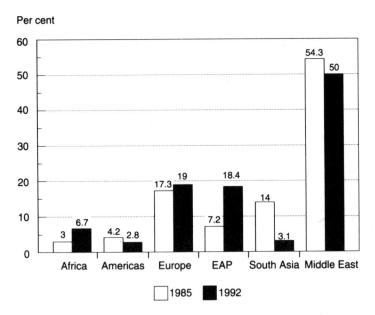

Source: WTO.

Figure 2.11   *International tourist arrivals in the Middle East by country of origin,*
1985–92 (%)

Egypt and Saudi Arabia are the largest tourist-generating countries in the region, respectively providing 12.2 per cent and 9.6 per cent of total arrivals.

☐ *Tourism receipts*

The problems of tourism development in the Middle East are linked to fluctuating trends in tourism receipts. Table 2.7 indicates that in 1993, tourism receipts were lower than in 1985. They have declined by 6 per cent since 1987. The year-by-year pattern of tourism receipts has been very irregular. Some years have shown strong increases (1985, 38.4 per cent; 1987, 31.5 per cent), others registered sharp falls (1986, −16 per cent; 1988, −4.7 per cent; 1991, −16.5 per cent; 1993, −7.4 per cent).

This instability has been responsible for the shortage of tourism development projects. Apart from a few investments in the business tourism sector, there is a reluctance to undertake ventures where return on investment cannot be guaranteed.

Figure 2.12 reflects the erratic nature of tourism flows to the Middle East and the general fall of tourism in the area which have resulted in an inconsistent contribution of tourism to the region's export earnings. In

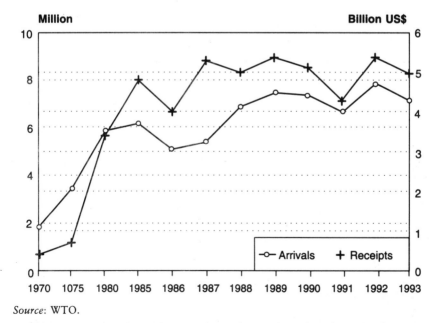

Source: WTO.

Figure 2.12   *Development of international tourism in the Middle East, 1970–93*

1987, 7.6 per cent of total export earnings were attributed to tourism. By 1991, this figure had fallen to only 4.11 per cent but then in 1992, it rose again to more than 8 per cent.

□ *The main Middle Eastern destinations*

Egypt and Saudi Arabia are the main destinations in the Middle East. In contrast to other regions of the world, their development has not been based on leisure and relaxation tourism. Egypt offers a cultural product and Saudi Arabia's tourism is based around religion. These unique products have ensured that, despite the political and military problems in the region, both countries continue to enjoy a high level of tourism development. Thus, Egypt and Saudi Arabia accounted for 69 per cent of total tourism receipts in the Middle East.

At US$681, the average expenditure per tourist is particularly high for Middle Eastern countries. The highest unit receipts are recorded in countries where business tourism is important, such as Kuwait (US$4200) and Saudi Arabia (US$1333). Egypt also has a high income per tourist (US$928) although flows have become erratic in the 1990s since the problems of traveller security.

Table 2.8 *International tourism in the Middle East, 1992*

Country	Tourist arrivals (000)	Tourism receipts (US$ millions)
Total	7,921	5,398
Bahrain	1,419	177
Egypt	2,944	2,730
Iraq	504	20
Jordan	661	462
Kuwait	65	273
Libya	89	4
Oman	192	85
Qatar	141	–
Saudi Arabia	750	1000
Syria	684	600
United Arab Emirates	400	–
Yemen	72	47

Source: WTO.

■ International tourism demand in South Asia

The South Asia region includes Afghanistan, Bangladesh, Bhutan, India, Iran, the Maldives, Myanmar (Burma), Nepal, Pakistan and Sri Lanka. The total population of the region is over one billion inhabitants. With a volume of 3.5 million, more than half of which visited India, the region accounted for only 0.69 per cent of the total world arrivals in 1993. Despite lagging behind the other regions of the world, tourism destinations in the region are responding to international tourism demand, particularly from Europe, by offering cultural tourism (India and Pakistan), beach tourism (Sri Lanka and the Maldives) and mountain tourism (Nepal).

As with the African region, tourism development in South Asia has been hampered by insufficient transport and hospitality superstructures. Tourism is growing, although at a much slower rate than in East Asia and the Pacific region. Between 1975 and 1992, international tourism arrivals increased by 142 per cent compared with East Asia and the Pacific region which progressed by 573 per cent.

Despite this, certain South Asian countries like the Maldives where tourism is the main economic activity are benefiting from the positive effect of international tourism. Sri Lanka has built on a tourism tradition and offers several products: cultural and discovery tourism in Kandy and Polonnaruwa, and beach tourism on the south coast. However, the civil war, although mainly located on the north-eastern side of the island, has had a considerable impact on international tourism arrivals which have progressed very slowly since 1983 (see Table 2.9).

Despite a great tourism potential, international tourism to Pakistan has fallen because of the conflict in Afghanistan which has had damaging effects on the whole region. Nepal, on the other hand, and more especially the Maldives have experienced strong tourism growth, particularly in the income they receive from tourism. Their success can be attributed to

Table 2.9 *Average annual growth rates, 1983–93*

Country/region	arrivals (%)	receipts (%)
World	5.5	11.7
South Asia	3.3	2.0
India	3.1	1.7
Sri Lanka	2.9	5.2
Pakistan	−0.03	−5.1
The Maldives	12.5	14.1
Nepal	4.7	12.6

Source: WTO, Tourism Market Trends, South Asia 1993.

specialisation policies. Nepal has developed a tourism image based around mountain sports and the Maldives has created a product that is virtually unique in the world: tourism on atolls offering the formula 'one hotel – one island'. This approach to beach tourism based on up-market and exclusive products is in complete contrast to the traditional beach product which tends to create great concentrations of tourists and urbanisation. Thanks to these policies, the Maldives' arrivals growth rate has been double the world's growth rate and tourism receipts have also marked a much stronger growth than the world average.

Bangladesh has also recently introduced policies to stimulate tourism development and one of their primary objectives is to increase the average receipt per tourist which is particularly weak at just US$72.

□ *International tourist arrivals*

The South Asian share of world tourism arrivals has always been very small but it has remained stable since 1975. From 1970 to 1990, South Asia's share of the world total has been constant at around 0.7 per cent (see Table 2.10).

Between 1975 and 1990, tourism flows doubled from 1.5 million to 3.1 million. The 1991 political and economic crisis did not affect South Asia as

Table 2.10   *International tourist arrivals and receipts in South Asia, 1970–93*

Year	Arrivals (000)	Change (%)	Share of total world arrivals (%)	Receipts (US$ millions)	Change (%)	Share of total world receipts (%)
1970	912	–	0.55	100	–	0.56
1975	1,557	70.72	0.70	329	229.00	0.81
1980	2,280	48.44	0.79	1,549	370.62	1.50
1985	2,540	11.40	0.77	1,400	−9.62	1.21
1986	2,731	7.52	0.80	1,677	19.07	1.19
1987	2,707	−0.88	0.74	1,875	12.48	1.09
1988	2,881	6.43	0.72	1,929	2.88	0.97
1989	3,054	6.00	0.71	2,022	4.82	0.95
1990	3,179	4.09	0.69	1,990	−1.58	0.77
1991	3,279	3.15	0.72	1,968	−1.11	0.76
1992	3,509	7.01	0.73	2,076	5.49	0.70
1993	3,459	−1.42	0.69	2,015	−2.94	0.62

Source: WTO.

much as it did other regions of the world and between 1990 and 1992 the rate of international tourist arrivals increased by 9.8 per cent. However, this promising upward trend is fragile, particularly in view of continuing political instability in Sri Lanka and in certain regions of India and Pakistan.

In 1992, 41.5 per cent of tourists to the region came from European countries. Tourism between South Asian countries was low and represented just 28.1 per cent of total visitors. East Asian and Pacific tourists made up 13.7 per cent of the total and American tourists 9.2 per cent (see Figure 2.13).

The United Kingdom is the largest generating country and provides 12 per cent of total arrivals. Recently, the Italian and Spanish markets have been very dynamic and between 1985 and 1991, their average arrival rate has progressed by 10 per cent annually. This is mainly due to the rising popularity of the Maldives with the Italian and Spanish clientele.

☐ *Tourism receipts*

Although South Asia has maintained its share of world tourist arrivals since 1980, its share of the world's income from tourism has been steadily

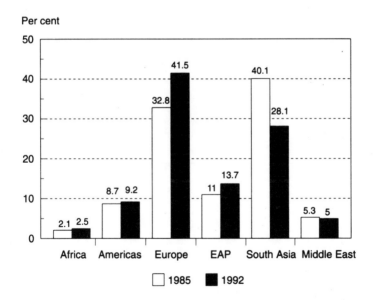

Source: WTO.

Figure 2.13 *International tourist arrivals in South Asia by country of origin 1985–92 (%)*

declining. Table 2.10 shows that in 1980 South Asia contributed 1.52 per cent of world tourism earnings. By 1993, this had fallen to 0.62 per cent. This means that per capita expenditure by visitors has fallen from US$679 in 1980 to US$582 in 1992, resulting in a deterioration of the economic impact of tourism.

The tourism receipts trend has been very erratic with some years recording large falls (1985 and 1993) and others showing strong increases (1986, 1987 and 1992). Therefore, it has been difficult to implement tourism development plans which require sustained investments over several years.

The contribution of tourism to the region's total export earnings is low at only 5 per cent. Between 1986 and 1991, tourism receipts increased by only 17 per cent while total exports for the region went up by 40 per cent, emphasising the dwindling impact of tourism in the economies of South Asian countries (see Figure 2.14).

In contrast to other regions in the world, 82 per cent of international tourists arrive by air. Road transport accounts for only 13.4 per cent of all international arrivals. Intra-regional tourism in South Asia is extremely weak because the region has few roads interconnecting the countries (see Figure 2.15).

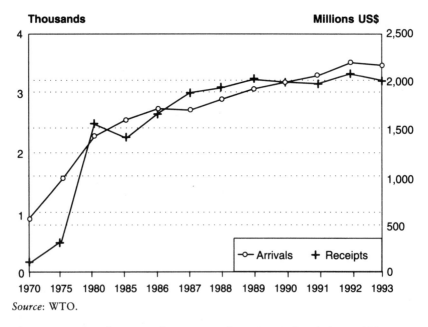

Source: WTO.

Figure 2.14 *Development of international tourism in South Asia, 1970–93*

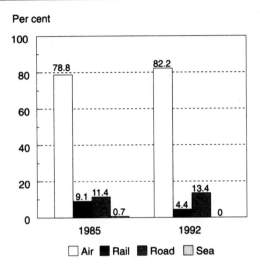

Source: WTO.

Figure 2.15 *Breakdown of arrivals in South Asia by mode of transport, 1985–92*

☐ *The main South Asian destinations*

There are distinct types of tourism flows to the region. The countries of South Asia fall into three categories:

- Afghanistan, Bangladesh, Bhutan, Iran and Myanmar (Burma) receive very few or no tourists at all because of military conflicts or internal policies;
- The Maldives, Nepal and Sri Lanka are committed to tourism development policies which play an essential role in their general development strategies;
- India and Pakistan receive close to two-thirds of the region's tourists yet their tourism has still not been exploited to its fullest potential.

Table 2.11 reveals that India is the main tourism country in the region with 53 per cent of total arrivals and 68 per cent of total receipts. Average expenditure per tourist was US$757 in 1993, distinctly higher than the region's average (US$591) and the world's average (US$648). Although, the development of tourism in India has been hampered by a lack of hotels and transport, particularly air transport, in the 1990s, the Indian government pursued policies which are favourable to foreign investment in the tourism sector to develop tourism supply particularly in recognised tourism zones. Furthermore, air transport deregulation allowing charter traffic also had a positive impact.

Table 2.11 *International tourism in South Asia, 1992*

Country	Tourist arrivals (000)	Tourism receipts (US$ millions)
Total	3,509	2,076
Afghanistan	6	1
Bangladesh	110	8
Bhutan	3	3
India	1,868	1,415
Iran	185	60
Maldives	236	113
Myanmar	21	8
Nepal	334	110
Pakistan	352	159
Sri Lanka	394	199

Source: WTO.

■ International tourism demand in the East Asia and Pacific region

Several countries in East and South-East Asia have only recently developed their tourism industries since the 1980s. Typically, these are also the newly industrialised countries, exporters of manufactured goods to Europe and North America. The 'new tourism countries' are Hong Kong, Singapore, Thailand, Malaysia, South Korea, Taiwan and Indonesia.

The similarity between the 'newly industrialised countries' with their exports of manufactured goods, and 'new international tourist receptor countries' can be largely explained by the complementarity that exists between the export of goods and the export of services. The development of these sectors is based on advancements made in international transport, particularly in air transport, in telecommunications and in the fields of financial facilities and international banking. Thus, a domino effect emerges: the export sector starts the process by stimulating the development of business travel which in turn stimulates the development of leisure tourism which creates a new economic growth and increases foreign currency reserves.

Japan and the new tourism countries region of East Asia, the European region (Northern Europe, Southern Europe) and the American region (North America, Caribbean, Central America) are the three most developed tourism areas in the world.

The Asian zone is endowed with unique features which should encourage further tourism development. It offers many different motivations for the traveller. The new industrial countries are particularly attractive for business travel. Leisure tourism is well-developed in the many coastal resorts of the region. Hong Kong and Singapore offer excellent shopping facilities and attract the 'commercial tourist'. Above all, the hospitality and accommodation superstructures of East Asian countries are highly specialised and of the highest quality. The Japanese, South Koreans and Taiwanese have taken to travelling for leisure and represent an enormous potential for tourism within the region.

Because of the many diverse motivations for travel to the area, tourism flows are less vulnerable to change than flows to other regions of the world. With 68 million tourist arrivals in 1993, the East Asia and Pacific region accounted for 13.7 per cent of the world total (see Table 2.12).

☐ *International tourist arrivals*

Between 1980 and 1993, the number of international tourist arrivals has more than trebled from 20 million to 68 million. The region's share of total tourist arrivals doubled over the same period. Tourist arrivals have

Table 2.12 *International tourist arrivals and receipts in East Asia and the Pacific, 1970–93*

Year	Arrivals (000)	Change (%)	Share of total world arrivals (%)	Receipts (US$ millions)	Change (%)	Share of total world receipts (%)
1970	5,331	–	3.22	1,100	–	6.15
1975	8,657	62.39	3.89	2,164	96.73	5.32
1980	20,961	142.13	7.28	8,469	291.36	8.19
1985	30,389	44.98	9.22	12,849	51.72	11.06
1986	33,505	10.25	9.83	17,200	33.86	12.24
1987	38,906	16.12	10.61	22,763	32.34	13.21
1988	45,092	15.90	11.21	30,640	34.60	15.41
1989	45,565	1.05	10.56	34,234	11.73	16.06
1990	52,263	14.70	11.41	38,617	12.80	14.98
1991	53,924	3.18	11.81	39,634	2.63	15.21
1992	61,306	13.69	12.73	45,636	15.14	15.40
1993	68,525	11.78	13.70	52,587	15.23	16.23

Source: WTO.

increased at a regular rate except for 1989 and 1991 when they increased more slowly. In contrast to the other regions of the world, since 1970 there has never been a fall in international tourist arrivals.

Japan, the largest tourist-generating market for the region, accounts for 14.8 per cent of total demand, followed by Singapore (9 per cent), Taiwan (6.9 per cent) and the United States (6.3 per cent). Tourism generated from visitors resident in countries of the region is particularly strong and provides 78 per cent of total tourism flows. Intra-regional tourism flows have increased significantly since the introduction of the 'Ten Million Programme' by the Japanese government. This policy is designed to stimulate the development of Japanese foreign holiday-taking, especially to Asian countries. Thanks to this programme and the active participation of Asian receptor countries, the number of Japanese travelling abroad for leisure has doubled in just a few years.

☐ *Tourism receipts*

Tourism receipts in the region have increased at a faster rate than international arrivals over the past few years. Table 2.13 shows that

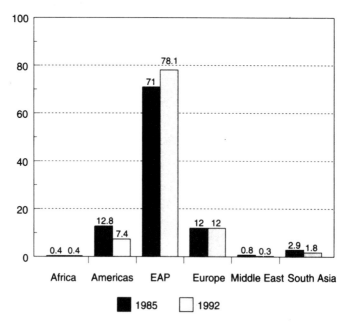

Source: WTO.

Figure 2.16   *Breakdown of arrivals by international tourists in East Asia and the Pacific by country of origin 1985–92*

between 1980 and 1993, the East Asia and Pacific region's share of world tourism receipts doubled from 8.3 per cent to 16.2 per cent but its worth increased over six times from US$8.5 billion to US$52.5 billion (see Figure 2.17). This is because many countries in the region have positioned their products to target the wealthier tourist. They offer an excellent quality–price ratio and lead the international competition.

Increasingly, the countries of Asia and the Pacific are receiving a proportionally larger share of the world's international tourism receipts (16.2 per cent) than of the world's arrivals (13.7 per cent). The average expenditure per tourist is US$764 compared to US$648 for the world average. In Japan, the average expenditure per tourist is very high at US$1706, in Hong Kong it is US$864 and Singapore US$955. On the other hand, expenditure per tourist is much lower in China at just US$239.

Despite the success of the tourism industry and the high receipts it brings East Asian and Pacific countries, the contribution of tourism to the region's economy is proportionally less than in other regions of the world. It accounts for only 5 per cent of total export earnings compared to the world average of 8.3 per cent. This is because Japan and the new industrial nations have been remarkably effective in exporting their manufactured products to the rest of the world (see Table 2.13).

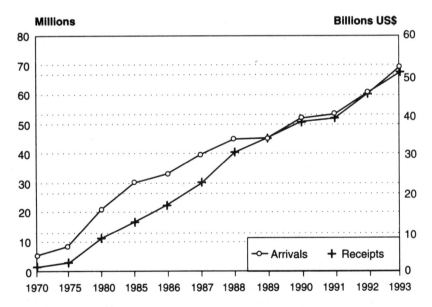

Source: WTO.

Figure 2.17 *Development of international tourism in East Asia and the Pacific, 1970–93*

Table 2.13   *Tourism and international trade in East Asia and the Pacific, 1985–92 (in millions of US$)*

Year	Exports f.o.b.	International tourism receipts	Share of receipts in exports
1985	393,796	12,849	3.26
1986	439,239	17,200	3.92
1987	524,344	22,763	4.34
1988	626,264	30,640	4.89
1989	677,018	34,234	5.06
1990	733,563	38,617	5.26
1991	817,719	39,634	4.85
1992	898,564	45,636	5.08

Source: WTO.

☐ *The main East Asian and Pacific destinations*

While East and South-East Asia are the main tourism areas in the region, tourism in countries of the Pacific is increasing; Polynesia, Melanesia and Micronesia together receive 4 per cent of the region's visitors; Australia and New Zealand 6 per cent. Despite their distance from other regions and their relative isolation, the small islands of the Pacific (except Hawaii) receive more than 2 million tourists per year (see Figure 2.18). This should be compared to other tropical island destinations. The islands in the Indian Ocean (Comoros, Mauritius, Réunion, the Seychelles and Madagascar) receive 0.7 million visitors, Sri Lanka and the Maldives 0.6 million and the Caribbean Islands 11.6 million. Proximity to the large generating countries definitely favours the Caribbean Islands. However, the Pacific Islands benefit from the relative proximity of the Australian and New Zealand market, and more importantly, they have a excellent quality image in the world, particularly in Europe. Additionally, air transport deregulation has meant that the cost of their tourism products has been reduced considerably.

The most developed tourist receptor countries, China, Hong Kong and Taiwan, receive 38 per cent of all the region's arrivals. The 'new tourism countries', Singapore, Thailand, Indonesia, Malaysia and South Korea, account for 40 per cent. They have successfully evolved powerful organisations and groupings based around hotel chains and airline companies. Because of the quality of their products, hotel chains like Mandarin, Shangri-La and Peninsula and airline companies like Singapore Airlines, Thai International and Korean Airlines are world leaders.

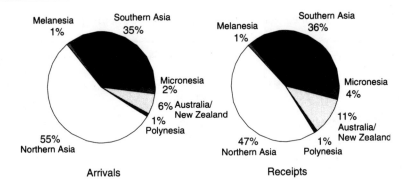

Source: WTO.

Figure 2.18   *Share of each sub-region in total international tourist arrivals and receipts in the East Asia and Pacific, 1992 (%)*

Thailand is one of the most important tourism countries in the region, particularly since it has developed (and continues to develop) new beach destinations in the south of the country (Phuket, Krabi, Koh Samui) and new cultural and discovery products in the north of the country in the Chang Mai area.

Vietnam, Cambodia and Laos have introduced new policies to develop tourism products and infrastructure which will complement the already existing products in the region.

The analysis of trends in the main tourism markets shows that tourism has become a major economic activity all over the world. In every region, it represents a significant proportion of international economic exchanges and has become one of the largest export activities.

However, because tourism needs investment, the growth of the tourism sector remains closely linked to global economic development. To operate successfully, tourism requires developed infrastructure such as airports, roads, telecommunication, potable water and energy. Without these, accommodation and leisure facilities cannot be developed. This explains why tourism first developed in the industrialised countries, then in the new industrial countries. International tourism is also growing at a rapid rate in many developing countries throughout the world, particularly in countries offering specialised tourism products. Tourism demand is evolving and the market is becoming increasingly segmented. Specialisation is the competitive strategic response to this demand.

International tourism flows and, more particularly, receipts are highly concentrated in a small number of countries which are generally both

Table 2.14   *International tourism in East Asia and the Pacific (EAP) 1992*

Country	Tourist arrivals (000)	Tourism receipts (US$ millions)
EAP	61,306	456,366
North-Eastern Asia	34,025	21,528
China	16,512	3,948
Hong Kong	6,986	6,037
Japan	2,103	3,588
South Korea	3,231	3,272
Macau	3,180	2,234
Mongolia	140	–
Taiwan	1,873	2,449
South-Eastern Asia	21,498	16,337
Brunei	500	35
Cambodia	88	–
Indonesia	3,064	2,729
Laos	25	18
Malaysia	6,016	1,768
Philippines	1,043	1,674
Singapore	5,446	5,204
Thailand	5,136	4,829
Vietnam	180	80
Australia/New Zealand	3,659	5,024
Australia	2,603	3,992
New Zealand	1,056	1,032
Melanesia	453	399
Fiji	279	223
New Caledonia	78	94
Papua New Guinea	41	49
Solomon Islands	12	6
Vanuatu	43	27
Micronesia	1,402	2,113
Guam	877	1,579
Kiribati	4	2
Mariana Islands	505	528
Marshall Islands	8	4
Pohnpei State	3	–
Truk State	4	–
Yap State	1	–
Polynesia	269	235
American Samoa	31	10
Cook Islands	50	27

Country	Tourist arrivals (000)	Tourism receipts (US$ millions)
French Polynesia	124	170
Niue	2	–
Samoa	28	19
Tonga	23	9
Tuvalu	1	–

Source: WTO.

tourist generators and tourist receptors. These are the United States and Canada in North America, the countries of the European Union and Switzerland in Europe and to a certain extent Japan and the new industrial countries such as Hong Kong, Singapore, South Korea and Taiwan in Asia. The geographic concentration of international tourism exchanges largely corresponds to the geographic concentration of commercial trade with, however, two important differences:

- Countries with the most favourable balances of trade have negative balances in their tourism exchanges, for instance Germany and Japan. Countries with negative balances of trade often have positive balances in tourism receipts. For example, the United States had a positive tourism balance of US$16.6 billion in 1993 but a negative balance of trade. Similarly, Portugal, Spain and Greece in Southern Europe traditionally have negative trade balances but strongly positive tourism balances.
- The exchanges of tourism services between industrialised countries with similar patterns of demand are not necessarily exchanges of the same types of products as with the commerce of goods. Indeed, exchanges of goods between industrialised countries are increasingly exchanges of products of the same categories which are differentiated rather than complementary (for example, the trade in cars between European countries). In tourism, exchanges of similar types of products also exist (for instance in the cultural tourism sector) but to a much lesser extent. The majority of exchanges are of traditional complementary products such as beach tourism products consumed by residents of North European countries in countries of the Mediterranean.

The factors which influence arrival and receipt flows and how these are distributed around the world can be explained by fundamental theories of international product exchanges. This chapter has concentrated on the worldwide trends of international tourism and has identified that tourism development is linked to economic development. The following chapter examines the mechanisms that influence the development of tourism (the determinants of international tourism) and adapts theories of specialisation in international economics to the tourism sector.

Further reading

Boerjan P. and Vanhove, N. 'The Tourism Demand Reconsidered in the Context of the Economic Crisis', *Tourist Review*, 38(2), pp. 2–11, 1984.

Boniface, B., Cooper, C. *The Geography of Travel and Tourism*, London: Heinemann, 1987.

Burton, R. *Travel Geography*, London: Pitman, 1991.

Calantone, R. J. and Johar, J. S. 'Seasonal Segmentation of the Tourism Market Using the Benefit Segmentation Framework', *Journal of Travel Research*, 23(2), pp. 14–24, 1984.

Mill, R. C. *Tourism: The International Business*. Englewood Cliffs, NJ: Prentice-Hall, 1990.

Richie, J. R. B. and Filiatraut, P. 'Family Vacation Decision-making – a Replication and Extension', *Journal of Travel Research*, 18(4), pp. 3–14, 1980.

Sauran, A. 'Economic Determinants of Tourist Demand: A Survey', *Tourist Review*, 33(1), pp. 2–4, 1979.

Smith, S. L. J. 'Room for Rooms: A Procedure of the Estimation of Potential Expansion of Tourist Accommodation', *Journal of Travel Research*, 15(4), pp. 26–9, 1977.

Uysal, M. and Crompton, J. L. 'An Overview of Approaches used to Forecast Tourism Demand', *Journal of Travel Research*, 23(4), pp. 7–15, 1985.

WTO, *WTO News*, no. 1, January–February 1994.

WTO, *International Tourism in Europe, 1970–1993*, January 1994.

WTO, *International Tourism in the Americas, 1970–1993*, January 1994.

WTO, *International Tourism in Africa, 1970–1993*, January 1994.

WTO, *International Tourism in the Middle East, 1970–1993*, January 1994.

WTO, *International Tourism in South Asia, 1970–1993*, January 1994

WTO, *International Tourism in East Asia and the Pacific, 1970–1993*, January 1994.

■ *Chapter 3* ■

The Theoretical Economic Determinants of International Tourism

The theory of factor endowments and international tourism: factor
  endowments in international tourism; the theory of factor endowments; the
  theory of factor endowments in international tourism; limitations of
  international tourism factor endowments
The theory of comparative costs and international tourism: the theory of
  comparative costs; the role of comparative costs in international tourism;
  exchange rates and comparative advantage
The theory of absolute advantage and technological advance
The theory of demand: the theory of demand; the role of demand in
  international tourism

The determinants of international tourism are factors which, with respect
to the international exchange of tourism services, continually influence the
position of each country in the international division of labour.

Basing the study of determinants on an empirical analysis of
international tourism trends helps to explain the mechanism of
international tourism. Certain influential factors particularly stand out:
the variations from country to country in inflation, interest rates and
prices, the availability of leisure time and relative household incomes. This
method of analysis highlights the major differences between regions of the
world and case studies of sectors and of countries can be developed. In
order to adopt concrete tourism policies, the role and scope of each
determinant must be examined separately. From their economic analysis,
the factors (or causes) of international tourism and how they influence
economic and social growth and development become apparent.

The balance of international tourism services has become as important
in most countries' international exchanges as the balance of international
commerce, the balance of the movement of capital and the balance of other
invisible exchanges. In some countries, international tourism exchanges are
extremely influential. The contribution of international tourism has helped
Spain, for instance, become the tenth industrial power in the world.

Spain's balance of trade deficit in 1994 will have been completely offset by its international tourism earnings.

To formulate an international tourism policy, it is essential to analyse the most important determinants individually. This isolates the determinants that must be acted on to achieve the planned employment and balance of payment objectives, or to conceive and implement an overall policy in countries where tourism represents an important part of the national product.

The economic study of international tourism determinants is based on a theoretical method of analysis supported by empirical studies. For this purpose, economic theories such as the theory of international specialisation are very effective. Four determinants, based on theories of international trade, explain the position of a country in international tourism exchanges:

- The theory of factor endowments
- The theory of comparative costs
- The theory of absolute advantage and technology
- The theory of conditions of demand

These four determinants can, to a large extent, explain the international distribution and trends of tourism flows.

The theory of factor endowments and international tourism

The theory of factor endowments was formulated by E. Heckscher in 1919 and developed in the work of B. Ohlin in 1933. It influenced the fundamental analysis of international trade theories to a considerable extent. It is based on the distribution of factor endowments in each country to explain the comparative advantage which any country may have over its commercial partners. Countries with an abundance of a certain resource will benefit from a comparative advantage for the production and export of products requiring this resource. For example, according to Heckscher and Ohlin, countries endowed with large amounts of capital will export goods that are capital-intensive and will import goods that are labour-intensive. This is also true for natural resources which are very important for international tourism because many tourism products use comparative advantages provided by its natural resources. Therefore, the international tourism specialisation of a country will be directly linked to an abundance of the resource necessary to develop the supply of tourism products to be aimed at the international clientele. This analysis, traditionally only applied to the international commodities exchange sector, was brought into question by the paradoxical results obtained by Leontief's empirical tests on international trade in the United States. The application of factor endowments to the analysis of international tourism exchanges appears, from this point of view, much more significant.

Indeed, factor endowments are the resources or factors available to ensure a country's production of international tourism services. The relative abundance of these resources seem to have a decisive influence in explaining a country's position in international tourism.

☐ *Factor endowments in international tourism*

Factor endowments are the basic components of the production of tourism products. They correspond to the general factors required for the functioning of the whole economy, and to factors specific to the tourism sector such as certain natural and cultural resources.

Factor endowments can be divided into three categories:

* natural resources, historic, artistic and cultural heritage;
* human resources in employment and skills;
* capital and infrastructure resources.

☐ Natural resources, historic and cultural heritage

Natural resources consist of land, space and natural features: landscape, climate, sea, rivers and lakes, flora and fauna. The value of these resources depends on their characteristics and their accessibility (without which they remain just potential resources). With a means of access and an organisation in place to exploit them for tourism ends, natural resources become economic resources as they satisfy a demand for international tourism. However, this exploitation should not degrade or destroy them. Therefore, effective measures for the protection of the ecological equilibrium must be established and the limits of exploitation must be calculated and recognised.

Historic and cultural resources are equally very important to evaluate the factor endowments of a country in the tourism sector. Historical monuments and works of art can be essential motivations for international tourist visits. However, it should be noted that these factor endowments will only have an impact on tourism flows if they are developed and made accessible to tourists which often means considerable investments. Furthermore, endowments in natural and artistic factors are not fixed, they can be increased with the import of collections from other countries. For example, Europe and the United States have some of the best museum collections in the world. Thus, acquiring factor endowments can also have a determining role.

☐ Human resources – employment and skills

Labour can be considered as the factor of production which has the most crucial role in the theory of international specialisation while possibly being the most controversial. The role of labour is all the more important in tourism because it is a service sector which requires much manpower. Consequently, the comparative advantage of tourism firms lies in its labour resources, particularly in the skills level of their workforce.

Human resource employment

Demography determines trends in international tourism supply and demand. The analysis of a country's demography must appraise population volume, the percentage of active population, its geographical distribution and the apportionment by age band. The importance of employment and its contribution to tourism economics has clear and definite influences on international tourism flows between countries and regions. For instance, tourism development on the French Côte d'Azur and on the Italian Riviera has not only been a consequence of the natural resources of these areas. It has also been dependent on the high demographic density available to provide a workforce. The Balearic Islands and Corsica have similar natural resources but the make-up of their population is very different. There are fewer than 200,000 inhabitants in Corsica and a large proportion of the population is retired. The Balearics, on the other hand, have more than 600,000 inhabitants and a much younger population. Therefore, the Balearics have a larger population available for employment in the tourism sector.

There are also important considerations not directly concerned with economics. The *tolerance threshold for foreigners* can be defined simply as the maximum number of foreign visitors which will be accepted by the local population. But there are several factors which will determine this tolerance threshold: the similarity or differences between the two groups (cultural, linguistic, social, ethnic and religious); length of stay; where tourists are accommodated (isolated or integrated); visitor behaviour and respect for local values; the degree of receptivity of the local population and so on. The local population of the Balearics has a much higher tolerance threshold for foreigners than that of Corsica.

Human resources skills in the tourism industry

The labour endowment of a country is defined by the skill level of its workforce which determines the country's position in the international division of labour. Skills in the international tourism industry have been influenced by training needs.

There is little need for skilled workers in most sectors of the tourism industry. A distinction must be made between permanent and seasonal employment, which is generally less skilled. In northern countries seasonal employment is usually undertaken by the young, by women and by immigrant workers.

The availability of skilled labour has two different effects. First, it influences tourism flows and their geographical distribution according to the specialisation of the destination country and, second, it influences the mobility of the workers. Because of the lack of skilled managers in their hotel industry, developing countries are forced to employ managers (usually foreign), who have been trained abroad, to manage and maintain hotels used by the international clientele.

☐ Capital resources and infrastructure

International tourism is extremely capital-intensive and therefore capital resources are one of the most important determinants of tourism production. Tourism needs developed infrastructures, superstructures and equipment for transport, accommodation, area development and site development. Investments therefore necessitate large capital sums. In this respect, tourism production is similar to heavy industry.

Hence, the relative capital resources of a country have a determining influence on the economic importance of international tourism to that particular country. A country which has very important natural resources, but limited capital, will not be able to develop its international tourism sector sufficiently, because it will not be able to acquire the necessary equipment. This situation exists in most developing countries, hence the importance of financial aid and capital and technological transfers.

The combination of the three main factor endowments (natural, cultural and historical resources; human resources; and capital and infrastructure resources) form the basis of the international specialisation of some countries in the export of tourism services (see Figure 3.1). It corresponds to the theoretical model of factor endowments as applied in international economics.

☐ *The theory of factor endowments*

The theory of factor endowments explains the international specialisation of different countries. It is based on the relative international differences in the production factors of each country. The quantitative differences of production factors between countries are the principal cause of international exchanges. This theory is also applicable to international tourism. It is based on a number of hypotheses relating to the basic model.

☐ Hypotheses of the factor endowments model

The main hypotheses of the theory of factor endowments are very restrictive. They correspond to the characteristics of pure and perfect competition where there are no obstacles to international exchanges, such as customs barriers and exchange restrictions. Consequently, in the case of tourism products, no restrictions concerning the movement of foreign tourists and the transfer of currencies for tourism purposes are taken into account.

There are six hypotheses in the basic model:

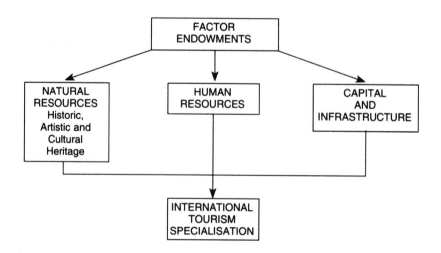

Figure 3.1   *Factor endowment model*

Hypothesis 1

Two countries, A and B, differ only in the importance of their relative factor endowments. International exchanges between these countries involve goods and services required by tourism.

- Countries A and B produce and consume two types of homogeneous goods X_1 and X_2.
- The factors of productions used are homogeneous; they are limited to two in the basic model, L (labour) and K (capital). However, this limitation of the number of factors can only be considered for developing the basic model, after which it becomes too restrictive and does not correspond to the reality of international exchanges. In particular, natural resources on the one hand and labour skills on the other must be taken into account.

Hypothesis 2

Whichever system is adopted, each good X_i is produced with a different relative level of capital (or labour). For example, the production of good X_1 will be relatively more capitalistic with respect to labour than that of good X_2.

$$X_i = X_i(K_i, L_i) \qquad i = 1, 2 \tag{3.1}$$

Hence

$$k_i = \frac{K_i}{L_i}$$

$K_1 > K_2$ is true for all price systems for the factors.

Hypothesis 3

The factors of production available in fixed quantities are fully used in production and in the most efficient way.

$$K = K_1 + K_2 \tag{3.2}$$
$$L = L_1 + L_2$$

Each country produces both the goods and there is incomplete international specialisation.

Hypothesis 4

The functions of production for each product are internationally identical, homogeneous, of degree 1, with a constant level of output and decreasing marginal productivity.

$$X_1 = F(L_1, K_1) = L_1 f(k_1) \tag{3.3}$$

$$\text{with } k_1 = \frac{K_1}{L_1}$$

$$X_2 = G(L_2, K_2) = L_2 g(k_2) \tag{3.4}$$

$$\text{with } k_2 = \frac{K_2}{L_2}$$

The factor intensities are not reversible whatever the relative price of the factors.

$$l_1 - k_2 > 0 \tag{3.5}$$

Hypothesis 5

Consumer preferences are identical in each country. These are characterised by the marginal use of each good, constantly decreasing.

Hypothesis 6

Only products or services are exchanged internationally. However, the factors of production cannot be moved from country to country.

From these hypotheses, certain theoretical conditions required for international specialisation can be identified.

☐ The abundance of factors

Countries are characterised by differences in their factor endowments. If they have the same technology (the required techniques to manufacture products), in technical terms, they have the same production function for each good. Then, they are differentiated by their respective factor endowments which allows them to produce more or fewer goods.

Figure 3.2 represents a situation where both countries have an equal level of technology to produce good X. Fixed capital stocks as well as the differences in labour endowment L' or L^* are considered to manufacture X' for country A and X^* for country B.

The abundance of factors in themselves can be measured in real or financial terms. In the first case, the relative factor endowment of a country can be the following ratio: K/L, capital divided by available labour in the country.

The ratio can be used to compare both countries; for instance, country A will be relatively more abundant in capital if the following inequality is obtained:

$$KA/LA > KB/LB$$

Country B will then be relatively more abundant in labour than country A.

The relative abundance of factors will determine their cost: factors of production which are relatively rare are relatively expensive.

☐ The conditions of international exchange

The main determinant of exchange is in the relative differences in domestic prices within each country in a self-sufficient situation.

$$P_A = \frac{P_{1A}}{P_{2A}} \neq P_B = \frac{P_{1B}}{P_{2B}} \tag{3.6}$$

This difference in relative prices of tourism products between two countries can only come from the difference in relative factor endowments

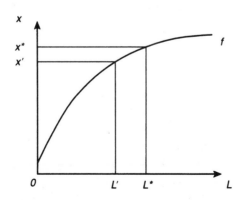

Figure 3.2 *Endowments and production*

between them. For example, the relative price of a labour-intensive product is lower in a country where the factor is relatively abundant. Hence, the Heckscher–Ohlin theory can be applied in the following manner: a country will have an comparative advantage in the production of the good that uses most intensively the factors which the country has in relative abundance. It will export this good and import a good intensive in the factor of production for which it has the least availability.

The basis of the country's advantage and of its international specialisation lies in the fact that the production of the exported good uses a greater quantity of productive factors which the country has in relative abundance. According to Ohlin, the abundance of a factor of production is measured by its price within the country. Consequently, if $W_a > W_b$, labour is relatively more expensive in country A compared to country B. As a result, the workforce is in relatively short supply in country A and abundant in country B.

If the theory of factor endowments is tested, country A will, in a commercially isolated situation, produce a greater quantity of good X_1 and a smaller quantity of good X_2 because the production of X_1 requires more capital than that of X_2. Thus, country A uses more capital (which is its abundant factor) in exchanges. Conversely, country B will produce more good X_2 because it has a large workforce.

The international specialisation of both countries can be described graphically (see Figure 3.3). Each point on these curves represents a combination of more or less intensive production in capital or in labour,

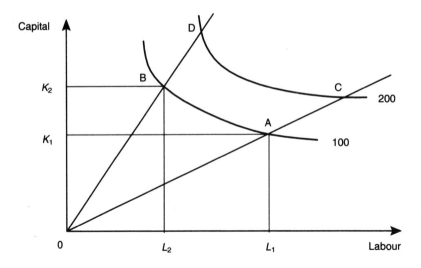

Figure 3.3   *Factor intensity and specialisation*

according to the K/L ratio. Thus, point A representing the K/L ratio indicates a production more intensive in capital than point B, which will use for the same level of production a more capitalistic ratio K_2/L_2.

The hypothesis of factor intensity expounded by Hechscher and Ohlin indicates that a good is always more intensive in capital than another even if the cost of the factors change. Thus, when good X_1 is more intensive in capital than good X_2 for a given w/r, it will remain so whatever the w/r ratio. This is the hypothesis of factor intensity irreversibility.

Thus, there are, in the world's production and therefore in the international exchange of goods and services, goods and services that are capital-intensive and goods and services that are labour-intensive in such a way that a chain of factor intensity can be established between all the goods i: $(i = 1, ..., n)$.

Therefore:

$$k_1 > k_2 > k_3, ... > k_n \tag{3.7}$$
$$\text{with } k = K_i/L_i, \forall \, w/r$$

The main condition of international exchange stems from the difference in the relative prices of products (P^1 and P^2) in each country in an isolated situation. This difference in relative prices cannot be just a result of differences between both countries in factors. Indeed, the relative price of a product intensive in labour, for instance, will be lower in the country where this factor is relatively abundant and vice versa.

The theory of factor endowments in international tourism

The theory of factor endowments defines the basis of international tourism flows between countries. Indeed, international exchanges, be they commercial flows or tourism flows, can be defined as the difference in the proportion of factors of production of each product exchanged. A country will tend to specialise in the production and sale of goods and services which it has in abundance and which are cheap. On the other hand, it will tend to purchase goods and services which are unavailable in the country. In international tourism flows, goods exchanged are tourism services.

Countries which have an abundance of tourism resources will tend to develop an international specialisation in the tourism sector. There is a greater likelihood that they will export their international tourism services which results in a positive balance in the travel account. This situation is found in many of the Mediterranean countries (for instance, Spain with the Balearics and the Canaries, Greece and its islands, Turkey, Tunisia and Morocco) which have an abundance of tourism resources such as beaches, the sea, the sun and many resorts.

However, international tourism specialisation does not just imply that tourism countries are solely receptors. They can also be tourist generators. As a general rule, the higher their GNP the more likely they are to be tourist-generator countries. Amongst the Mediterranean countries, France and Italy are both generators and receptors. Many industrialised countries such as the UK, Germany and the United States are also both generators and receptors of tourists. This interchange of tourism products corresponds to the demand for difference which exists for manufactured products from different countries.

Thus, to apply the factor endowment model to tourism, new hypotheses already present in neo-factor analyses of international commerce must be integrated into the model. These hypotheses include natural resources and the increase in the number of factors of production.

☐ The importance of natural resources

Natural resources are the most important tourism factor. They are unique to each country, they cannot be moved and are a major motivation for tourism. The importance of natural resources, already commented on by Buchanan,[1] Brown[2] and Leontief,[3] completes the factor endowment model and adds to its significance. However, from an empirical point of view, international comparisons between the natural endowments of different countries are particularly difficult. Indeed, natural resources are heterogeneous and therefore almost impossible to evaluate, but, nonetheless, they play a decisive role in international tourism specialisation.

☐ The role of job skills

To examine the quality of the factors of production, capital and labour must be broken down into several distinct sub-factors.

The labour factor is subdivided according to skill. The comparative advantage of countries depends on the amount of available skilled and unskilled labour. This distinction plays a crucial role in international tourism, which relies largely on manpower.

☐ Limitations of international tourism factor endowments

The factor endowment model advances an accurate explanation of international tourism flows. However, it does have certain limitations which cannot take into account:

- demand based on the search for 'something different' which can be a result simply of the existence of international borders;
- availability and absolute non-availability.

☐ Differentiation

It is possible to demonstrate that the mere existence of international borders can stimulate demand based on the need for 'something different'.[4] This explains certain types of international economic relations. In international tourism, it constitutes an important modifier to factor endowments. In this case, it is not the conditions of supply which explain the causes of international tourism but the conditions of demand. Tourists are motivated to cross borders because they want to experience something different, a need they cannot satisfy by staying in their own country. The need for a change accounts for the reciprocal international tourism exchanges between neighbouring countries, despite the possession of similar resources.

☐ Availability or non-availability

Kravis, continuing the debate begun by Adam Smith, demonstrated that a certain number of international exchanges can be explained by absolute availability and non-availability.[5] This can also be applied to international tourism. Tourism sites classified as 'unique' create flows that are not in direct competition with, for instance, seaside or climatic resorts. Similarly, the absence of a coast for landlocked countries such as Austria and Switzerland constitutes an important factor for international demand for tourism products on the coast of other countries.

Thus, to consume the tourism product that they desire, tourists may have to travel to other countries. Belgian and Dutch demand for ski holidays can only be satisfied in countries which have skiing facilities. Japanese or German tourists who want beach holidays in winter must also travel abroad. In these cases, non-availability modifies potential tourism demand and international tourism demand because of the fact that it is impossible to satisfy the demand with their own country.

Consequently, it is not the relative resources that are the basis of international exchanges but the absolute resources.

■ The theory of comparative costs and international tourism

An analysis of comparative costs reveals that a country will specialise in producing the goods and services that can be produced at a better price than in other countries.

The analysis of comparative costs is not just a case of comparing international prices as they bring a qualitative quality to the determinants of international exchanges. Whilst factor endowments are concerned with quantitative data, comparative costs are concerned with qualitative factors, especially the price–quality ratio, which plays an essential role in the comparison and the choice of tourism supply offered by competing countries or destinations.

□ *The theory of comparative costs*

First expounded by David Ricardo in 1817, the theory of comparative costs explains a great number of international tourism exchanges.

Even if a country is in the position of producing the entirety of the goods and services it consumes at a better relative cost than other countries, it is in its interest to limit its production to goods and services which have a relatively low production cost compared to their production cost abroad. If it can acquire goods at a lower cost abroad, then it is in its financial interest to do so.

This theory suggests that countries specialise in the production and export of their most competitive goods and services. However, this specialisation is rarely exclusive. The analysis of international commercial exchanges only indicates a tendency towards specialisation in relation to comparative costs. This also happens in international tourism. Although there are wide fluctuations in costs, it is difficult to determine what a country specialises in by price alone. Nonetheless, comparative costs can be considered as one of the determining factors in the distribution and trends of international tourism.

The comparative cost model adapted from Ricardo explains bilateral exchange of tourism products as a result of differences in prices between two countries.

Ricardo used two countries in his example, Great Britain and Portugal, and two products, wine and sheets. Portugal has a cost advantage in the manufacture of both products. If we generalise, we assume that Portugal is advantaged in the manufacture of all products. The manufacture of wine and sheets is more expensive in Great Britain, which, if we generalise, would suggest that Great Britain is disadvantaged in all productions. This situation does not constitute, as one may think, an exception in international exchanges. It is the situation of all countries with national economies competing with the rest of the world. In this case, Great Britain represents the country facing the rest of the world. Therefore, it is disadvantaged in all manufactures except for some absolute advantages (for the trade of goods, absolute advantage can be a natural or technological advantage, for tourism it can also be from natural or artistic resources). Portugal, on the other hand, represents the rest of the world.

Ricardo's example demonstrates that international exchanges are profitable for all countries whatever their situation, each will gain quantitatively in the exchange. Thus, to manufacture one unit of wine, Great Britain needs 120 man-years and Portugal needs 90 man-years. To manufacture one unit of sheets Great Britain needs 100 man-years and Portugal 90 man-years.

The unit cost of production is higher in Great Britain than in Portugal for both products. Therefore Portugal has an absolute advantage for each of the two goods. However, the comparative cost of sheets with respect to wine is lower in Great Britain than it is in Portugal:

$$100/120 < 90/80 \Rightarrow 0.83 < 1.12$$

Conversely, the comparative cost of wine with respect to sheets is lower in Portugal than it is in Great Britain:

$$80/90 < 120/100 \Rightarrow 0.88 < 1.2$$

Therefore, in the hypothesis of constant costs, it is in Portugal's interest to specialise in the production of wine and for Great Britain to specialise in the manufacture of sheets. Each country can then take part in the exchange and specialise in the good that it can produce best which is the good that it can produce at a lower comparative cost and for which it has the best productivity.

By specialising internationally, both countries will gain in the exchange.

This example can be represented by the following simple model which includes the following hypotheses:

1. Two countries (A and B)
2. Two goods (1 and 2)

Table 3.1 *Comparative advantages*

Unit labour cost for each good (man-years)	GB	Portugal
Wine (1)	120	80
Sheets (2)	100	90

3. A homogeneous factor of production (labour) which is mobile between the sectors
4. Constant cost whatever the level of production

If we assume that $a_{L_i} = L_i/X_i$ and $i = (1, 2)$, (the inverse ratio represents labour productivity such as $A_{L_i} = X_i/L_i$), we can calculate the internal supply prices which are equal to the input-output coefficient multiplied by the wages rate:

$$p_1 = wa_{L1} \text{ and } p_2 = wa_{L2} \tag{3.8}$$

thus

$$\frac{p_1}{p_2} = \frac{wa_{L1}}{wa_{L2}} = \frac{a_{L1}}{a_{L2}}$$

In the same way for the foreign country:

$$\frac{p_1^*}{p_2^*} = \frac{a_{L1}^*}{a_{L2}^*} \tag{3.9}$$

In Ricardo's numeric example, the following ratios are obtained:

$$\frac{a_{L1}^*}{a_{L2}^*} < \frac{a_{L1}}{a_{L2}} \tag{3.10}$$

or,

$$\frac{a_{L1}^*}{a_{L1}} < \frac{a_{L2}^*}{a_{L2}}$$

Portugal has a comparative advantage in the manufacture of wine (product 1) and Great Britain has a comparative advantage in the manufacture of sheets (product 2). By pursuing policies of international specialisation, labour can be employed in the sectors in which the country has a comparative advantage. Thus, international specialisation is a consequence of the best apportionment of activities throughout the world and its effects engender a global gain. The comparative cost theory is particularly apt to explain the international distribution of tourism flows and receipts.

☐ *The role of comparative costs in international tourism*

The importance of comparative costs in international tourism is increasing. There is a great diversity in tourism products. Comparing them is very difficult and often impossible. Furthermore, tourism products are generally services that cannot be repeated in an identical way every time. Therefore, the study of comparative costs must be orientated towards the specific attributes of international tourism. It cannot merely analyse the components of cost (transport, accommodation, associated services). It must also take into account the quality-price ratio and technological advances.

☐ The quality–price ratio

The concept of quality implies more than just price. Switzerland and Germany, for instance, are amongst the world's leading tourism countries and yet their tourism prices are relatively high. This shows that service quality is the best way to compete and to have the best comparative advantage.[6]

A country competes internationally by improving the quality–price ratio of its products. It generally adopts a policy of differentiating its tourism sector from that of its competitors.

☐ The cost of transport

Trends in transport costs affect the cost of tourism products. Transport costs depend on different elements, notably technology (adapting means of transport to the needs of international tourism), the structure of transport companies, the cost of fuel and government policy. In particular specific policies aim at lowering the cost of transport for international tourism.

- The cost of road transport in tourism can be reduced by 'petrol bonds' or motorway toll concessions for foreign visitors
- The cost of rail transport can favour tourists with concessionary fares (France, Italy, Germany, Canada)
- In air travel, international agreements on lowering fares for regular flights and the liberalisation of charter flights are crucial in developing the flow of tourism towards destinations which cannot be served by terrestrial transport.

☐ Accommodation costs

Accommodation costs directly influence tourism movements, especially in periods of economic crisis and high energy costs. In fact, when transport costs are high because of high energy costs, the tourism cost often 'compensates' by putting constraints on the price of accommodation so that the package is within the purchasing power of the tourist (in other words adapting to demand). Accommodation cost is influenced by several factors:

- The use of new technology in construction, equipment and fittings. For example, certain new two-star hotel chains, using new building techniques and installing innovative receptions and customer service, have succeeded in reducing accommodation costs.
- Labour costs and productivity are important when comparing international accommodation costs. By using new techniques, certain developed countries are experiencing a 'return to comparative advantages' despite high labour costs, and can compete again with countries with low labour costs. This phenomenon, already observed in the textile industry, can be explained by the rapid progress of technology.

☐ The cost of tourism services

The cost of tourism services, excluding transport and accommodation, are those relating to hospitality, catering and various leisure services. These costs are difficult to compare from country to country because tourism supply is extremely diverse. Nonetheless, they should be taken into account when analysing the distribution and development of international tourism flows.

☐ The role of the state

Economic policies (such as labour policy, prices policy and credit policy) influence tourism supply both directly and indirectly, thus affecting international tourism flows even though it is not their main objective. There are, however, certain selective fiscal policies which are designed to act directly and specifically on the tourism sector. For example, two fiscal policies specifically concerned with the tourism sector were introduced in France in the 1980s:

- The first policy (in 1981) imposed a rise in VAT on luxury hotels (four-star and five-star), thus directly affecting the cost of accommodation. The impact of this policy has been largely negative for the luxury hotel sector and for the image of France in general. Indeed, luxury hotels were obliged to increase their prices to cover the extra taxation and as a result lost competitiveness. To compensate, many four-star hotels were downgraded to three-star hotels in order to lower their tax liability. This has had the effect of reducing the French supply on the international luxury hotel market, resulting in a loss of the international clientele that usually stay at this category of hotel.
- The second (in 1984) granted tax relief on certain tourism investments in France's overseas territories. Investment expenditure can, in certain circumstances, be deducted from the investors' taxes on profits. The construction of the Sofitel hotel in St Barthélemy and the Marine apartment–hotel complex in Martinique and in St Martin have both benefited from this policy and, although the investment cost was lower, the sales price of the products was not affected.

☐ *Exchange rates and comparative advantage*

Variations in exchange rates have a decisive effect on comparative cost trends of international tourism and therefore on tourism flows and distribution.

Along with a number of other factors (such as variations in the GNP and the balance of payments), fluctuations in exchange rates are largely responsible for the diverging trends in tourism expenditure by the main OECD countries.

The period spanning 1963 to 1994 can be subdivided into three phases, which correspond to fluctuations in the dollar exchange rate against other currencies.

• From 1963 to 1968, the international monetary system in force was the Bretton Woods system, which was characterised by a fixed convertible rate of US$35 dollar to one ounce of gold and by fixed exchange rates between all other currencies.

Table 3.2 shows that dollar exchange rates with other currencies did not change during this period. Similarly, the major countries' share of international tourism expenditure varies very little: it is unchanged for Germany (15 per cent), slightly down for the United States and increasing for France and Japan. These last variations are a consequence of differences in the rate of economic growth. Between 1963 and 1968, the growth rate of the GNP and the National Income was stronger in Japan and France than it was in the United States and Germany.

• From 1968 to 1980, the international monetary system abandoned fixed exchange rates and adopted flexible exchange rates. As a result, fluctuations in exchange rates, dominated by the currency markets, were very erratic. From 1968 to 1978, the dollar fell against the Deutschmark by more than half of its value and the DM value increased considerably against the currencies of the Mediterranean countries (favourite destinations for German tourists).

The German share of international tourism expenditure doubled in the OECD between 1968 and 1978 because of the increased purchasing power of German tourists. Meanwhile, the American share of international expenditure declined along with the weakening of the dollar.

In 1968, the United States share was 28 per cent and the German share was 15 per cent. By 1978, the American share had decreased to

Table 3.2   *Trends in exchange rates*

Exchange rates	1963	1968	1973	1978	1982	1990	1994
DM/$	4.0	4.0	2.62	2.00	2.37	1.62	1.67
Y/$	360.0	360.0	271.22	210.47	232.77	144.80	103
FF/$	4.93	4.93	4.45	4.51	6.72	5.45	5.90
DM/FF	1.22	1.24	1.62	2.24	2.83	–	3.39

DM = Deutsche Mark
Y = Yen
FF = French Frank

Sources: OECD, World Bank.

15.5 per cent whilst German expenditure was now 26.7 per cent of total tourist expenditure in OECD countries.
- From 1980 to 1994, the fluctuations again transformed the breakdown of international tourism expenditure. The value of the dollar increased, which resulted in a sharp rise in tourism expenditure by American tourists and a relative decline in German expenditure.

On the other hand, Japan's share of international departures has increased considerably because of the rise in the value of the yen, the higher spending power of the population and the lengthening of holidays. Thus, in 1991, Japanese tourists were the third highest spenders in international tourism and accounted for 12 per cent of tourism expenditure in OECD countries (see Table 3.4).

Table 3.3   *Nominal exchange rate against the dollar*

	Exchange rate (unit per dollar)		
	1989	1991	1992
Austria	13.23	11.67	10.99
Belgium–Luxembourg	39.40	34.16	32.15
Denmark	7.31	6.40	6.04
Finland	4.29	4.04	4.49
France	6.38	5.64	5.29
Germany	1.88	1.66	1.56
Greece	162.08	182.06	190.47
Iceland	57.11	59.10	57.62
Ireland	0.71	0.62	0.59
Italy	1,371.69	1,240.65	1,232.03
Netherlands	2.12	1.87	1.76
Norway	6.90	6.48	6.21
Portugal	157.10	144.35	134.82
Spain	118.40	103.93	102.40
Sweden	6.45	6.05	5.82
Switzerland	1.64	1.43	1.41
Turkey	2,119.96	4,168.91	6,860.59
United Kingdom	0.61	0.57	0.57
Canada	1.18	1.15	1.21
United States	1.00	1.00	1.00
Australia	1.26	1.28	1.36
New Zealand	1.67	1.73	1.86
Japan	137.97	134.50	126.67

Source: OECD.

Table 3.4   *International tourism receipts and expenditure, 1992 (in millions of US$)*

	Receipts	Expenditure
Austria	14,830.6	8,370.7
Belgium–Luxembourg	4,053.4	6,604.2
Denmark	3,782.4	3,777.7
Finland	1,270.5	2,346.5
France	25,052.8	13,866.4
Germany	10,891.0	36,782.2
Greece	3,211.9	1,156.7
Iceland	128.5	287.6
Ireland	1,615.3	1,356.6
Italy	21,461.8	16,532.3
Netherlands	5,193.8	9,527.5
Norway	1,973.5	3,867.3
Portugal	3,680.1	1,155.1
Spain	20,734.5	4,709.0
Sweden	3,041.4	6,692.6
Switzerland	7,722.0	6,125.0
Turkey	3,639.0	776.0
United Kingdom	13,493.7	19,467.2
Europe	145,796.2	143,400.6
Canada	5,663.7	11,219.7
United States	53,861.0	39,872.0
North America	59,524.7	51,091.7
Australia	4,089.6	3,988.3
New Zealand	1,469.8	979.0
Japan	3,589.2	26,809.7
Australasia–Japan	9,148.6	31,777
OECD	214,469.5	226,269.3

Source: OECD.

☐ Foreign exchange policies, comparative costs and international tourism

The comparative costs of tourism products from country to country are subject to exchange rates and at times, this greatly influences international tourism flows greatly. For certain countries, especially those around the Mediterranean, foreign exchange policy is the basis for their international tourism policy (for instance, the devaluation of the peseta in 1992 resulted in a rise in arrivals to Spain). It allows these countries to sustain and even improve competitive tourism prices despite often high inflation rates. They are anxious to maintain comparative cost advantages at the expense of exchange-rate fluctuation by, for instance, devaluing the currency.

Although international tourism can be sensitive to exchange-rate fluctuations, this is curtailed by consumer habit. Price fluctuation will primarily influence the length of stay rather than the number of departures.

The theory of absolute advantage and technological advance

This theory is a development of Adam Smith's analysis of international trade. Today it corresponds to the export monopolies of certain countries, which either arise from unique natural advantages or from technological advances. This analysis explains, for instance, the export successes of countries like Japan in the electronic and information technology sectors.

Absolute advantage plays a crucial role in international tourism. Indeed, certain countries have unique tourism resources which can be either exceptional natural sites, like the Grand Canyon, or, more usually, architectural or artistic resources known all over the world.

These man-made resources motivate tourists to visit a country. Their importance in terms of international tourism factors is determined by their 'uniqueness' which gives a country a monopoly or a near-monopoly (the Mona Lisa, the Sistine Chapel, Windsor Castle, the Acropolis, the Pyramids, the Colosseum, the Taj Mahal, the Forbidden Palace, Macchu Pichu, etc.).

Created by man, their advantage is that they can be renovated, developed, adapted and, if necessary, improved (the Pompidou Centre in Paris, the British Museum in London, the Valley of the Kings in Egypt). Their unique qualities allow countries to create specific tourism products very different from those offered by other countries.

Innovation is another aspect of a differentiation policy which reinforces a country's absolute advantages. It ensures a better long-term international specialisation. Developed countries are finding it increasingly difficult to offer a standard tourism package based on the hotel–restaurant–beach formula at a competitive price. Until now, the improvement of tourism quality has allowed countries to pursue successful differentiation policies whilst still commanding relatively high prices. However, considerable progress is being made by countries which consider high quality the primary objective of their tourism policy. Developing countries adopt policies of innovation and technological progress in order to maintain and increase their comparative advantage.

Technical innovation in the tourism sector mainly involves super-structures, information and promotion, product development and market-ing. Tourism superstructures increasingly use new technology, particularly in the accommodation, catering and reservations sectors. Innovation can bring down costs (new materials, energy savings, electronic data transmission, new management, reservations and payment techniques) but also create new tourism products (leisure centres, holiday centres).

In the most developed countries, technological progress has meant that tourists can *automatically produce* certain services that they used to purchase, thereby saving on labour costs. These include minibars in hotel rooms, kitchenettes, automatic services, studio hotels or hotel clubs.

Tourism marketing is probably the area which has benefited the most from advances in technology with the development of real-time manage-ment software for information, availability, reservations, invoicing and payment using smart cards.

Thus, determinants in international tourism are adequately explained by the absolute advantages theory as well as by the comparative cost and the quality–price ratio theories.

■ The theory of demand

Demand theories explain the reasons behind both the development and the intensity of tourism flows between countries. Tourism demand represents the quantity of goods and services that consumers require at a given moment. It is a direct function of per capita income as well as the population's interest in international tourism.

Trends in the number of holidays taken and the percentage of total holidays taken abroad are international tourism indicators.

The theory of demand applied to international tourism

The theory of demand describes the international specialisation of countries with respect to internal, regional and international demand. It describes the international distribution of tourism flows and the importance of tourism in national economies particularly well. Different levels of demand also describe characteristics of the development of international tourism, notably, tourism exchanges between similar countries of high economic development. The theory of demand was formulated by Linder in 1961.

☐ Linder's analysis

S.B. Linder (1961) noticed that the difference in the levels of factor endowments between countries did not always reflect international exchanges. Indeed, often the greatest number of exchanges are between economies which have similar factors. For instance, in Europe, the most important tourism exchanges are between neighbouring countries. This observation led Linder to reject the theory of factor endowments and to develop a new theory of international exchanges based on interior demand or representative demand.

According to Linder, the international specialisation of a country depends on a high level of domestic demand. In the main tourist-receptor countries (France, the United States, Canada, Germany, Switzerland and the United Kingdom), international tourism demand complements a domestic demand which is very high. In fact, the development of international tourism is a result of the conditions created by domestic demand. A country's comparative advantage stems from the quality of its infrastructure and superstructure and also from its tourism know-how, its level of technology and its favourable environment.

Therefore, the volume of international tourism will be greater between countries which have similar domestic tourism structures. Does this mean that the more similar the countries are, the greater their tourism exchanges? This question is central to the theoretical analysis of demand. Indeed, in addition to the quantitative aspect, there is a qualitative aspect which demonstrates that the basis of international exchange is primarily a 'demand for difference' between partner countries.

☐ The demand for difference

International exchanges depend on both the volume of demand and the differentiation of the products. Even if products are similar, there will always be a difference in quality or brand which will prompt an international exchange. This 'demand for difference' is particularly significant in international tourism. It is based on geographical, cultural and linguistic differences which induce exchanges between neighbouring countries with similar levels of economic development.

Consequently, geographically close countries with resources that are relatively similar will benefit from greater tourism flow exchanges than countries with quite different resources which are located far from each other, although tourism flows will only occur between countries with similar resources if the tastes of the consumers differ, however slightly.

It is clear that demand not only explains the cause of international tourism but also its intensity. The volume of international exchanges will be greater between countries which also have a high level of domestic tourism and a similar structure. The volume of international tourism is greater and increases faster in geographical areas comprising developed countries with high spending-power.

☐ *The role of demand in international tourism*

The role of demand in international tourism can be measured quantitatively by statistical analysis and qualitatively by research into motivation.

☐ Measuring demand

Demand in international tourism comprises three elements which, depending on the country, play more or less important roles. However, together they explain most of the differences in international tourism flows.

First element: domestic tourism demand

The level of domestic tourism demand determines the level of international tourism in a country. Indeed, in accordance with Linder's theory, a high domestic tourism demand creates an environment and conditions favourable for the development of international tourism. Transport and accommodation superstructures are established and natural, historic and cultural sites are developed to satisfy this demand. Therefore, countries which can handle strong domestic tourism demand are ready to satisfy international demand.

To measure domestic demand, several indicators are used: the per capita GNP of the country, the population and the number of domestic tourism nights in all types of accommodation.

France and the United Kingdom are industrialised countries with the highest domestic demand. Developing countries such as Senegal and Togo have very low levels of domestic demand (see Table 3.5).

Second element: intra-regional tourism demand

Intra-regional tourism can be defined by the demand of tourists from other countries within the same region or within the same continent.

There are two types of flows:

- the arrival of tourists *resident* in other countries of the region (both nationals of these countries and foreigners residing in the country);

Table 3.5 *Domestic tourism demand in selected countries*

Country	Population (million), 1990	GNP per capita in US$	Domestic tourism nights for all types of accommodation (000), 1991
Industrialised countries:			
Germany	80.4	23,650	248,014
Denmark	5.1	23,660	13,440
Spain	38.9	12,460	68,079
France	56.6	20,600	727,052
Italy	57.1	18,580	167,496
The Netherlands	15.2	18,560	39,141
Poland	38.3	1,830	55,857
Portugal	10.6	5,620	13,404
UK	56.5	16,750	396,000
Developing countries:			
Morocco	27.6	1,030	11,953
Myanmar	42.6	188	295
Syria	13.0	1,000	1,935
Tanzania	28.4	120	744
Senegal	7.6	720	68
Sri Lanka	17.2	500	494
Togo	3.6	410	31
Tunisia	8.4	1,510	1,350

Source: OECD.

- the arrival of *foreign* tourists from other countries in the region on a tour of the region.

Intra-regional tourism relates mainly to trips taken by residents within the zone. There are great differences in tourism demand between industrialised zones and zones consisting of developing countries. Most international tourism is concentrated in regional tourism within Europe and North America. In 1991, the proportion of tourism which was regional in Europe as against international tourism was 93 per cent in Europe and 79 per cent in North America. However, it was less than 30 per cent in South Asia.

Intra-regional tourism is vital for the development of international tourism. Unfortunately, developing countries suffer a great disadvantage.

Europe and North America continue to be the receptor regions for international tourists (82 per cent of the world total in 1992), although South-East Asia and the Pacific are gaining ground with a higher growth rate than the world average.

Third element: international tourism demand

This category includes both intra-regional and inter-regional international tourism.

International tourism demand is mainly orientated towards countries which have a large domestic demand (for instance, the United States, France and the United Kingdom). In developing countries with virtually non-existent domestic demand, the demand for international tourism is often very weak. Consequently, the analysis of tourism flows generally confirms the theories of demand. However, some countries (Spain, for instance) have succeeded in developing the international aspect of their tourism industry without relying, initially at least, on domestic demand.

☐ Demand motivation

International tourism demand motivation depends on the motives for travel, economic and social factors, and personal factors. Tourism demand can be assessed qualitatively by analysing travel motives.

Travel motives

International tourism demand can be segmented into different travel motives. A good understanding of demand segments is important in order

Table 3.6 *Domestic and international tourism demand in selected industrialised and developing countries, 1991*

	Domestic tourism nights (000)	International tourism nights (000)
Industrialised countries:		
Germany	248,014	37,426
Denmark	13,440	10,431
Spain	68,079	77,128
France	727,052	372,175
Italy[1]	167496	84,720
Netherlands	39,141	17,206
Poland	55,857	4,551
Portugal	13,404	21,957
UK	39,600	18,800
Developing countries:		
Morocco	11,953	13,400
Myanmar[2]	295	137
Syria[2]	1,935	1,715
Tanzania[1]	744	1,265
Senegal	68	1,016
Sri Lanka[2]	494	2,560
Togo[3]	31	257
Tunisia[3]	1,350	12,443

[1] 1990.
[2] Hotels and similar establishments.
[3] 1- and 2-star hotels only.
Source: OECD.

to forecast future demand and to adapt the supply to the requirement of the demand.

According to the WTO, 70 per cent of international travel motives are *'holiday purposes'*. *'Business travel'* accounts for 13–14 per cent of the total and the remaining 16 per cent is attributed to a variety of reasons: *religious purposes, visiting friends and relatives, sports* and so on.

The trends show that more travellers in the American region travel for holiday purposes than elsewhere, whereas in other regions there is a higher percentage of people travelling to visit their family and friends (Europe, for instance). Increases in the disposable income of households now means that the use of free time is becoming more and more important. People with high earnings are taking more holidays even if the length of stay of each holiday is shorter. Supply has had to adapt to these trends in tourism demand by increasing the number of short breaks (less than one week) to both long-haul and short-haul destinations.

Economic and social factors

These can be summarised as 'time and money', or, in other words, the amount of free time available and the level of income.

- *The availability of free time* is a primary condition of tourism demand. The shrinking working week and the increase in the length of paid holidays are determining factors of the development of tourism demand. As a result of these factors there is more available free time. The 'long weekend' (Friday afternoon or evening, Saturday, Sunday and official days off) has greatly influenced domestic tourism as well as international tourism, particularly intra-regional tourism. However, it is chiefly the increase in allowed holiday time (the French labour force, for instance, enjoy five weeks of statutory holiday) and the fall in retirement age which have contributed greatly to the recent development of international tourism demand.
- *Income* is the second motivating factor for international travel and creates tourism demand. From an international point of view, there appears to be a correlation between the Gross National Product (GNP) and the departure rate. Countries with the highest GNP per inhabitant have a proportionally higher tourism demand. The influence of income on tourism demand also depends on its distribution.

Furthermore, international tourism demand is also affected directly by *fluctuations in exchange rates*.

Personal factors

Personal factors are the individual tastes and preferences which influence tourism demand. These factors are very important and tourism producers must research the tastes and preferences of the generating market, notably by conducting market surveys.

☐ Factors limiting demand in international tourism

International tourism demand is further influenced by geographic, political and cultural factors:

- *Geographic factors* This essentially relates to the proximity of countries to each other. Countries with similar demand conditions tend to be geographically close, often bordering each other. This factor increases the use of the more economical means of transport; this is the case in Western Europe, the main zone of international tourism.
- *Political and administrative factors* These factors relate to agreed measures for easing the movement of people travelling for holiday purposes, notably border-crossings with lax controls (police and customs). Inadequate 'facilitation' measures can hinder the conditions of demand between countries geographically close to each other. Political instability and upheaval are also strong dissuading factors.
- *Cultural factors* These factors can both cause and obstruct international tourism development. A great difference in cultural environment between two countries is a motivating factor but can also limit international tourism and prevent mass tourism. Bypassing this obstacle depends on the services and equipment available to tourists who speak a different language than that of the population at the destination.

These three elements are essential to understanding the influence of demand as a determinant of international tourism. However, if demand is the main determinant of international tourism, it must be examined in conjunction with conditions of supply (factor endowments and comparative costs) in the destination country, in order to explain international tourism flows comprehensively.

Theories of international specialisation explain the fundamental mechanisms of the international exchanges of services. While theories of supply are often criticised in international commerce, they play a central role in international tourism, particularly the theory of factor endowments and the theory of comparative costs. Certain resources are essential to the development of tourism flows, particularly:

- *natural resources* to which must be added *cultural and artistic heritage*;
- *capital* given the high financial investment required for tourism development;
- *labour* which constitutes the basis of economic activity in the services sector.

It is possible to explain why certain countries are highly specialised in the export of tourism services by comparing internationally the relative abundance of each of these factors. Similarly, comparing costs internationally provides valuable insight on tourism specialisation. Although comparative costs are often a result of the different levels of factor endowments, they are also influenced by specific determinants such as exchange rates and labour productivity.

Thus, the main supply determinants can, to a large extent, explain the causes of international tourism flows. However, this explanation should be completed by the influence exerted by the determinants of demand. According to Linder, *representative demand* has an equally important role. It reinforces the concentration of international tourism flows to certain regions and countries of the world by increasing the role of the industrialised countries which are both generators and receptors of international tourists.

These international economics theories based on the determinants of supply and demand are particularly adaptable to tourism and offer rationales for the international tourism specialisation of each country. However, conclusions drawn from these theories must be subjected to the reality of the world's current tourism market. Thus, the structures of world tourism supply, notably accommodation, tourism products and transport (principally air transport), are analysed in the following chapters to determine how their quality and quantity are influencing world tourism flows.

References

1. Buchanan, N. S. 'Lines on the Leontief Paradox', *Economia Internazionale*, no. 8, November 1955.

2. Brown, A. J. 'Professor Leontief and the Pattern of World Trade', *Yorkshire Bulletin*, no. 9, November 1957.

3. Leontief, W. 'Factor Proportions and the Structure of American Trade: Further Theoretical and Empirical Analysis', *R.E.S.*, November 1956.

4. Lassudrie-Duchêne, B. 'La Demande de Différence et l'Échange International', Cahiers de l'ISEA, *Economies et Sociétés*, juin 1971.

5. Kravis, I. 'Availability and Other Influences on the Commodity Composition of Trade', *Journal of Political Economy*, April 1956.

6. Report to the Economic and Social Council, *The Economic Aspects of the Tourism Industry*, 21 July 1984.

Further reading

Bull, A. *The Economics of Travel and Tourism*. London: Pitman, 1991.
Linder, S. B. *An Essay on Trade and Transformation*, New York: John Wiley & Sons, 1961.

Papadopoulus, S. I. 'The Tourist Phenomenon: An Examination of Important Theories and Concepts', *Tourist Review*, 40(3), pp. 2–11, 1986.

Vaughan, R. 'Tourism as a Generator of Employment: A Preliminary Appraisal of the Position of Great Britain', *Journal of Travel Research*, 21(2), pp. 27–31, 1982.

Vellas, F. 'Economie et Politique du Tourisme International', *Economica*, Paris, 1985.

WTO. *Economic Effects of Tourism*. Madrid, 1980.

■ *Chapter 4* ■

Supply in the Accommodation Sector

The hotel trade in the world: growth in the number of rooms from 1987 to 1992; hotel supply in Europe; hotel supply in the Americas; hotel supply in Africa; hotel supply in Asia

Hote chains: hotel consortia; integrated hotel chains; hotel franchising; Club Méditerranée

Tourism lodgings: second homes; furnished rented accommodation

Restaurant chains

The accommodation sector is central to international tourism. Tourism flows are directly influenced by the size of this sector, by the way it adapts to demand and by the quality of the accommodation on offer. Three characteristics are associated with accommodation:

- *Seasonality* Its economic activities are seasonal which implies a great flexibility in structures.
- *Manpower planning* The industry is labour-intensive, which further compounds the problems caused by seasonality. It requires accurate forward planning of temporary employment.
- *Perishability* Accommodation production cannot be stocked. As with transport, accommodation products that are not consumed cannot be stored for use at a future date. Non-utilisation is expensive.

The superstructures needed to operate in high season are generally underutilised in low season. The problems of the accommodation industry (design, management, financing, etc.) are at the core of the economic analysis of tourism. The quality of accommodation, the hospitality and customer service provided by staff and the efficiency of the operation all contribute to the success of international tourism. Since the advent of mass tourism, many forms of accommodation have been developed. These can be classified according to different criteria:

- *built accommodation or alternative accommodation*: hotels, second homes and holiday centres or campsites, caravans and cruise liners;

- *individual or collective accommodation*: second homes or holiday villages;
- *profit- and non-profit-making accommodation*: hotels or holiday camps for children and social tourism.

The economic analysis of the hotel sector is based on analysing the investment involved in accommodation supply: profitability, depreciation, price and clientele. First the international hotel industry as a whole will be analysed, then hotel chains and independent hotels. Other types of accommodation will also be examined: timeshares, second homes, camping, social tourism accommodation and accommodation on cruise ships and yachts.

■ The hotel trade in the world

The hotel is the traditional form of tourist accommodation. As a major economic activity, it creates direct and indirect employment and provides an important source of foreign currency. The growth of the hotel trade has come about as a result of the traditional industry adapting to current conditions and modernising (for instance, the creation of integrated hotel chains and of new concepts in commercial accommodation, catering for different segments of tourism demand).

Accommodation supply is determined by the specific nature of the tourism industry. The hotel trade displays features associated with both heavy and labour-intensive industries:

- Investments in hotel construction tie up large amounts of capital for medium- to long-term periods, a typical feature of heavy industries;
- The activities connected with running a hotel are those of a service industry which is labour-intensive. The ratio of employees to the number of rooms is very high, particulary in superior-category establishments.

Industrialised countries have a competitive advantage, since sources of finance for investments are generally more easily available to them. Although developing countries have plenty of manpower, they often lack the necessary resources to develop tourism adequately and to manage their services in a competitive manner.

World capacity of hotels and similar establishments was 11 million rooms in 1992.

▢ *Growth in the number of rooms from 1987 to 1992*

Between 1985 and 1992, the number of available rooms increased at a slower rate than the number of tourist arrivals, 13.5 per cent compared to 46.2 per cent. As a result, there has been a growing demand for tourist lodgings other than the traditional hotel (rented furnished accommodation or lodging with friends and relatives). These types of lodgings are not represented in official tourism statistics.

The growth in hotel supply has been strongest in East Asian countries with a 49.8 per cent increase between 1985 and 1992. European hotel supply actually fell over the period, resulting in a decline of Europe's share of world supply (see Table 4.1).

Table 4.1 *Trends in the capacity of hotels and similar establishments worldwide, 1985–92*

		Number of rooms		
Sub-regions		1985	1992	% change
World total		9,759,002	11,075,261	
	%	100	100	+13.5
Africa		264,625	344,410	
	%	2.71	3.11	+30.1
Americas		3,540,412	4,416,712	
	%	36.28	39.88	+24.7
East Asia and pacific		897,247	1,343,746	
	%	9.19	12.13	+49.8
Europe		4,906,993	4,731,405	
	%	50.28	42.72	−3.6
Middle East		132,116	149,204	
	%	1.35	1.35	+12.93
South Asia		101,713	89,678	
	%	1.04	0.81	−11.83

Source: WTO (adapted table).

▢ *Hotel supply in Europe*

In 1992, 42.2 per cent of the world's hotel capacity was in Europe. Nearly 79 per cent of this capacity is found in Southern and Western Europe. On the other hand, since 1985, the hotel supply in Central and Eastern Europe has been contracting. Indeed, between 1985 and 1992, 66.1 per cent of rooms in hotels and similar establishments have disappeared. This explains the overall slow growth rate of Europe's hotel supply. In fact, in some areas it is increasing, for instance, supply in Western European countries grew by 10.7 per cent between 1985 and 1992.

Table 4.2   *Trends in the capacity of hotels and similar establishments in Europe, 1985–92*

		Number of rooms		
Sub-regions		1985	1992	% change
Europe total		4,906,993	4,731,405	
	%	100	100	−3.6
Central/Eastern		636,136	215,751	
	%	12.96	4.56	−66.1
Northern		718,290	616,049	
	%	14.64	13.02	−14.2
Southern	%	1,916,520	1,956,727	
	%	39.06	41.36	+2.1
Western		1,604,530	1,776,872	
	%	32.70	37.55	+10.7
Eastern Mediterranean		–	166,006	
	%	–	3.51	–

Source: WTO (adapted table).

☐ *Hotel supply in the Americas*

The hotel supply in American and Caribbean countries amounts to 39.88 per cent of world supply and is the second largest concentration of hotel accommodation. However, the supply is not distributed equally throughout the region. South America represents only 11.63 per cent of total American capacity whereas North America has 84.24 per cent of the region's supply.

The Caribbean countries attract mainly leisure tourism and have limited hotel space, just 3.21 per cent of total American capacity. Nevertheless, the growth rate of this sector is high, 41.6 per cent from 1985 to 1992. The average of all American countries was 24.8 per cent over the same period.

Table 4.3   *Trends in the capacity of hotels and similar establishments in the Americas, 1985–92*

Sub-regions		Number of rooms		% change
		1985	1992	
Americas total		3,540,412	4,416,712	
	%	100	100	+24.8
Caribbean		100,264	141,971	
	%	2.83	3.21	+41.6
Central America		28,192	40,638	
	%	0.79	0.92	+4.2
North America		2,702,104	3,720,615	
	%	76.32	84.24	+37.7
South America		409,852	513,439	
	%	11.58	11.63	+25.3
Western		1,604,530	1,776,872	
	%	32.70	37.55	+10.7

Source: WTO (adapted table).

Table 4.4   *Trends in the capacity of hotels and similar establishments in Africa, 1985–92*

Sub-regions		Number of rooms		% change
		1985	1992	
Africa total		263,268	344,410	
	%	100	100	+30.8
Eastern Africa		38,490	45,815	
	%	14.62	13.30	+19.3
Middle Africa		19,820	35,737	
	%	7.53	10.38	+80.3
Northern Africa		101,080	161,170	
	%	38.39	46.79	+59.5
Southern Africa		53,619	50,687	
	%	20.37	14.72	−5.5
Western Africa		47,790	51,001	
	%	18.15	14.81	+6.7

Source: WTO (adapted table).

☐ *Hotel supply in Africa*

Hotel supply in Africa is concentrated in certain areas. North African countries (mainly Morocco and Tunisia) have 46.79 per cent of total African hotel capacity whereas Central African countries have just 10.38 per cent (although from this low base there has been a high growth rate of 80.3 per cent between 1985 and 1992).

The prominence of North African countries is increasing. Between 1985 and 1992, North African hotel capacity grew by 59.5 per cent compared to 30.8 per cent for the whole of Africa.

☐ *Hotel supply in Asia*

South-East Asian countries register the highest growth rate in hotel capacity, particularly Thailand, Malaysia, Singapore and Hong Kong. In contrast, the hotel supply in South Asia is growing at only half the speed and represents less than 1 per cent of the total capacity in the world.

Table 4.5 *Trends in the capacity of hotels and similar establishments in East Asia and the Pacific (EAP), 1985–92*

Sub-regions		Number of rooms		% change
		1985	1992	
Total EAP		813,143	1,343,746	
	%	100	100	+65.25
North Eastern Asia		364,811	682,076	
	%	44.86	50.76	+87.0
South Eastern Asia		364,811	432,600	
	%	44.86	32.19	+18.6
Australia/New Zealand		144,375	205,927	
	%	17.76	15.32	+42.6
Melanesia		8,054	9,834	
	%	0.99	0.73	+22.1
Micronesia		5,930	8,644	
	%	0.66	0.64	+45.8
Polynesia		4,190	4,665	
	%	0.52	0.35	+11.34

Source: WTO (adapted table).

Table 4.6   *Trends in the capacity of hotels and similar establishments in South Asia, 1985–92*

Year	Rooms	Bed-places
1985	101,713	200,278
1986	100,843	203,596
1987	96,288	183,384
1988	99,979	189,222
1989	107,996	203,476
1990	111,431	210,494
1991	114,045	215,673
1992	89,878	220,487

Source: WTO.

■ Hotel chains

In the economic analysis of international tourism, a hotel must be differentiated from other forms of lodgings used by tourists. Thus, a hotel is a commercial establishment offering rooms or furnished apartments to a market which is either passing through the area or staying for several nights. It may offer a catering service, bar and complementary services. It can operate all year round or seasonally. The hotel trade constitutes the principal accommodation capacity in industrialised countries. However, there is a relative decline in its importance with respect to other types of accommodation and the whole structure of the hotel trade is undergoing profound change. The number of small independent and family-run hotels is falling, while the number of hotel chains is growing rapidly.

There are two main kinds of hotel chains: *hotel consortia* which group together independent hotels, and *integrated chains*, which are made up of homogeneous units.

□ *Hotel consortia*

Independent hotels are grouped together by hotel consortia, in order to compete with integrated and franchised chains. They promote an image of quality and aim at providing comparable standards of service, buildings and furnishings in order to build up customer loyalty from a domestic and international clientele.

Hotel consortia benefit from economies of scale when it comes to purchasing and marketing. A study of the UK hotel sector reveals that in terms of profitability per room, hotel chains are seven times more profitable than non-affiliated hotels.[1] The main benefits of joining a consortium are:

- joint production of guides and brochures, which advertise all the hotels in the chain and are distributed at each hotel through tour operators and travel agencies;
- joint national and international publicity campaigns;
- links into computer reservation systems (CRS) which allow agents to book directly from a screen;
- centralised purchasing of hotel equipment to achieve economy of scale;
- technical assistance and management consultancy.

This enables the small hotel to be represented on the international market while still keeping its managerial independence. The concept of the hotel consortium has become very popular and their numbers have expanded considerably.

In Europe, France has one of the most important hotel consortia supply. They represent a quarter of all registered hotels in the country with, in 1989, 6,187 hotels and 125,263 rooms. There are some twenty consortia of differing sizes. By far the largest, Les Logis de France accounts for 73 per cent of all hotel members of a consortium and 61 per cent of total room supply in the country (4,548 establishments and 76,570 rooms). Some hotel consortia have very few members and cannot offer all the advantages of a hotel chain. Hexagone hotels is a consortium grouping together only six hotels.

In the United Kingdom, unaffiliated hotels still provide 60 per cent of total room supply. However this market is declining and large integrated hotels chains now make up 25 per cent of the market. To compete, single independent hotels are increasingly grouping together in hotel consortia. They now make up 7 per cent of the market and membership grew 29 per cent between 1988 and 1991. This reflects a realisation by some smaller hoteliers that in order to survive in the market, it is necessary to share costs.

The largest hotel consortium in the world is the Best Western chain with 3,000 hotels and more than 250,000 rooms. The cost of membership of a large international hotel consortium is 1 per cent of turnover after tax (Best Western).

☐ Integrated hotel chains

Integrated chains develop and commercialise hotel products that are consistent and homogeneous. They exert their control either directly, by complete ownership of the hotel, or indirectly, through a franchise system or a management contract. All hotels in the chain carry the name and insignia of the chain. The main integrated hotels originate from the United States, although the French group Accor is ranked fifth in the world in terms of size, and the British group Forte is ranked ninth (see Table 4.7).

☐ French hotel groups

Accor, the leading hotel chain in France, has considerably strengthened its position by acquiring the Pullman International Hotel group from Wagon-Lits in 1991. They also have a large interest in the Barrière group through the Hotel et Casinos de Deauville (20 per cent) and the SA Cannes Balnéaire (15 per cent).

Accor manages the following hotels:

- Sofitel (4-star)
- Novotel, Mercure (3-star)
- Ibis (2-star)
- Formula 1 (1-star)

and the resort hotels PLM Azur and Marine Hotels.

Table 4.7   *The twenty largest hotel groups (number of rooms) 1992*

Group	Rooms	Hotels
Hospitality Franchise Systems	354,997	3,413
Holiday Inn Worldwide	328,679	1,692
Best Western International	273,804	3,351
Accor Group	238,990	2,098
Choice Hotels International Inc.	230,430	2,502
Marriot Corporation	166,919	750
ITT Sheraton Corp.	132,361	426
Hilton Hotel Corp.	94,653	242
Forte	76,330	871
Hyatt Hotels/Hyatt International	77,579	164
Carlson/Radisson/Colony	76,069	336
Promus Cos	75,558	459
Club Méditerranée SA	63,067	261
Hilton International	52,979	160
Sol Group	40,163	156
Inter-Continental Hotels	39,000	104
Westin Hotels & Resorts	38,029	75
New World/Ramada International	36,520	133
Canadian Pacific Hotels	27,970	86
Société du Louvre	27,427	398

Source: Hotels (adapted table).

☐ British hotel groups

In the United Kingdom, the major chains are publicly quoted companies (plc). They make up nearly 25 per cent of the industry, recording an 11.8 per cent increase between 1988 and 1991. The largest group is Forte with 338 hotels in the UK (29,530 rooms) followed by Mount Charlotte Thistle Hotels with 109 hotels (14,263 rooms) and Queen Moat Houses with 102 hotels (10,434 rooms). Almost 40 per cent of plc rooms are in the five primary UK cities and are concentrated in the middle and upper level of the market.

Privately owned chains are, in general, much smaller. It is more difficult for them to raise large amounts of capital. There are, however, some notable exceptions. Imperial London Hotels is ranked eleventh in the league with 7 hotels (3,046 rooms), Jarvis Hotels thirteenth with 33 hotels (2,750 rooms) and Edwardian Hotels nineteenth with 9 hotels (1,766 rooms). This sector has 8.3 per cent of the market and expanded by 10.9 per cent between 1988 and 1991.

European groups are also taking a market share. The French Accor group, ranked ninth in the league of the top 50 hotel groups in the UK, has 25 hotels (3,639 rooms). One factor that makes Britain attractive to foreign investors is that wage costs are lower than on the continent.

☐ *Hotel franchising*

Hotel franchising is largely responsible for the expansion of the integrated hotel chain sector. In France, franchising has developed particularly in the one- and two-star hotel sector. This system benefits both the franchiser and the franchisee:

- *The franchiser* brings his standards, his brand name, his experience and his reputation. The franchise company is a commercial enterprise (generally a public limited company) and the hotelier is both a client and an associate. The company contributes its technical expertise and financial help to set up the investment and it assists the franchisee's management by putting the marketing services and computerised central reservation system at its disposal. The franchise company will give support in publicity campaigns and provide advice on management matters and equipment-purchasing.
- *The franchisee* contributes personal funds normally amounting to around 30 per cent of the investment. He also undertakes the whole financial risk of the hotel investment. He benefits from the

standardisation and the profitability of the group and from the commercial and promotional advantages brought by belonging to a group. Franchisees are charged 3–4 per cent of turnover depending on the franchise company. Furthermore, a membership fee, amounting to approximately 10 per cent of the investment, is charged to cover feasibility studies and financial packages.

The franchise contract concentrates on the management of the enterprise. It encompasses the rights of the franchisee to use the chain's brand name, promotion and marketing, central reservation, monitoring and reporting of operations and eventual total managerial control for investors who require it. The franchisee undertakes to comply with the criteria set by the franchising company, to maintain its standards of service and comfort and to pay the agreed royalties.

By operating the franchise system, the French two-star hotel chains Campanile, Climat de France, Arcade and Ibis, and the one-star hotel chains Formule 1 and Balladin built hundreds of 40- to 50-room hotels in the 1980s. The success of the system can be attributed to the policy of franchising hotel chains. To attract franchisees, they ask for low initial investments ranging from US$270,000 to US$540,000 depending on the size of the unit.

☐ Club Méditerranée

Usually placed in the hotel and holiday village category, the Club Méditerranée is considered one of the world's greatest successes in the leisure and tourism industries. It was developed from a new tourism product concept (a large range of activities and entertainment, top-quality equipment, furnishing and catering, a break from the constraints of daily life) which has remained unique. This is mainly a result of the professionalism of the staff (the GOs or Gentils Organisateurs), the quality of the resorts and areas where they have been developed, and the constant search for innovation. The Club Méditerranée's tourism product is a technologically advanced product. To quote Gilbert Trigano, the chief executive of the Club: 'the originality of the Club, still unequalled, will continue to make our enterprise a fact of society'. These factors have protected it from the effects of recessions and from the repercussions of the Gulf War. The Club Méditerranée was the eleventh largest hotel chain in the world with 100,000 beds and 190 accommodation units in 1990. It complements rather than competes with other hotel chains because it offers a separate and unique product.

The Club Méditerranée group is made up of:

- the *Club Méditerranée SA* which is the head office and manages the activities of the European and African zone;
- and the *Club Med Inc.* subsidiary which has 20 per cent of its shares quoted on the New York stock exchange. This section manages the activities of the American, Caribbean and Pacific areas.

The structure of the company allows Club Méditerranée to take advantage of opportunities in American financial markets to continue its development, for instance, by increasing company funds when interest rates are abnormally high.

Its continuing expansion and its resilience are a result of the wide geographic distribution of Club Méditerranée villages and its many sales offices in all the main tourist-generating countries. These are essential for spreading the risk tourism companies face by their involvement in areas in economic crisis (Europe), areas in growth (North America, Japan) and those affected by political, financial and climatic risk.

However, if Club Méditerranée's potential to further develop is considerable, the market segment that consumes its top-of-the-range tourism products constantly requires new ideas and is vulnerable to economic and political changes. For this reason, Club Méditerranée has diversified into cruising with the Club Med One liner in the Caribbean and Club Med Two in the Pacific. It has also moved into air transport and has acquired the airline companies Minevre and Air Liberté which constitutes the second largest air transport grouping in France after the Air France Group.

The Club is concerned with maintaining its autonomy especially now that the Air France Group is following diversification policies and European deregulation of the airline industry is in process. For this reason, Club Méditerranée has increased its promotional efforts in the American and Japanese markets by emphasising its technological advances on other companies and its differentiation. In some villages, new activities are being offered (for instance, a video and computing workshop in the Opio village in France – an insight on leisure in the twenty-first century).

■ Tourism lodgings

These are second homes, rented furnished apartments, timeshares, camp sites, holiday villages, holiday centres and holiday camps.

☐ *Second homes*

Second homes include homes wholly owned by the tourist, apartments in a co-owned block with shared collective services (condominiums) and timeshare properties.

☐ Second homes wholly owned by tourists

These are lodgings in addition to their main residence which they use for tourism purposes. The strong growth in the number of second homes (33 per cent growth from 1975 to 1992, more than 2.2 million units in France) has important economic consequences, particularly in secondary effects. They help maintain and sometimes boost the economic activities of different industrial sectors such as the handicrafts trade, security services, the retail trade, and the construction industry in rural, mountain and seaside areas which previously have had poorly developed manufacturing industries. Furthermore, the purchase of second homes by foreigners brings in currency, which affects the balance of payments and generates and fixes future visits to the area by the purchaser. Finally, the growth in the number of second homes in an area increases accommodation capacity, particularly if these are rented to other tourists when the owners are not using them.

☐ Second homes with shared collective services

They are usually apartments in blocks which are serviced by a management company. These services include: maintenance of the apartments; laundry and linen hire; management of common equipment such as swimming pool, tennis courts and sports complexes and sometimes entertainment. Owners usually use the apartment themselves or put them in the hands of the management company for rental. They receive a proportion of the rent net of all charges. This system was developed in the United States, Spain and France, mainly in mountain resorts and some seaside resorts. It increases the profitability of the real estate investment but requires a high initial investment. The economic benefits (particularly in employment) are very positive, since the management of the apartment block operates all year round.

☐ Timeshare

Timeshare can be defined as the purchase of a holiday accommodation divided into one- or two-week periods. Each period is sold separately. This system is very cost-effective as the cost is shared between several proprietors (up to 52) although the purchase value of the apartment is higher in peak season.

There are many economic benefits directly attributable to the timeshare industry. The system increases the utilisation of a property considerably and the management of timeshare blocks creates many permanent jobs. Selling property in many sections has meant that it has been possible to erect new buildings in areas where the land cost is very high, such as the Côte d'Azur in southern France and in locations where conditions are technically difficult, such as the new high-altitude ski resorts.

The timeshare industry developed in the early 1970s from home exchange programmes in the United States. By the 1990s, it has become a worldwide industry. In 1992, there were 2.4 million timeshare owners in 3,050 timeshare resorts. This was an increase of 600 per cent since 1980. The total sales volume was US$3.74 billion in 1991 and is predicted to reach $30 billion by the year 2002. There are timeshare resorts in 75 countries and timeshare owners reside in 157 countries.

The United States is the largest timeshare area both in terms of the number of resorts (43.6 per cent of the world total) and in terms of the number of owners (1.4 million). Europe is the second largest area with 27.5 per cent of resorts and 424,000 owners. In Europe alone, timeshare sales were worth around US$1.5 billion in 1992. The biggest timeshare market

Table 4.8 *Resort timesharing market by area of world, end 1991*

Area	Resorts		Owners	
	Number	% of total	Number	% of total
United States	1,329	43.6	1,411,000	59.7
Europe	839	27.5	424,000	17.9
Mexico	201	6.6	124,000	5.2
South Africa	135	4.4	120,000	5.1
Caribbean	131	4.3	5,000	0.2
South America	115	3.8	29,000	1.2
Australia	106	3.5	78,000	3.3
Japan/SE Asia	92	3.0	66,000	2.8
Canada	84	2.8	94,000	4.0
Elsewhere	18	0.6	12,000	0.5
Total	3,050	100	2,363,000	100

Source: European Timeshare Federation Study, *The Worldwide Timeshare Industry and its European Perspective*, 1992.

in Europe is the United Kingdom with 1.5 per cent of all UK households owning a timeshare.[2]

A study by the Ragatz Associates of the economic impact of the timeshare industry worldwide estimated that direct consumer expenditure at timeshare resorts amounts to US$3 billion annually. An additional US$6 billion is generated in the resort areas due to the multiplier effect. Thirty thousand permanent jobs and 10,000 temporary jobs have been created in on-site resort operation and management with an additional 45,000 permanent jobs in the resort area due to the multiplier effect (see Box 4.2).

☐ *Furnished rented accommodation*

Furnished accommodation rented on a seasonal basis has become an important type of tourism lodging particularly in countries where 'bed and

---

Box 4.1   *RCI – holiday exchange*

RCI (Resort Condominiums International) is the world's largest and oldest holiday exchange network, with over 1.6 million member families worldwide. It emerged in the 1970s after the oil crisis which severely affected the holiday home market. Originally an 'apartment swap system' between friends in Indiana, USA, the company was incorporated in January 1974.

RCI has 2,400 affiliated resort properties in 72 countries. In 1992, it organised over 1.1 million exchanges. In total six million people travelled to RCI-affiliated resorts.

The company employs more than 2,400 staff worldwide in 49 offices located in 22 countries. The turnover for the European region alone was £65 million in 1992.

As well as its core business of organising exchanges, RCI offers a range of associated travel facilities to its members. These include flight and hotel reservation, car hire, travel insurance, a holiday rental programme and a programme of up-market tours and cruises which may be added on to exchange holidays.

The company produces a number of publications to advertise its services:

- *The World of RCI Holidays* – the annual directory for members in eleven different language versions lists all resorts;
- *Holiday* – a quarterly magazine for members in ten language versions;
- *Review* – a monthly magazine in English for developers;
- *Endless Vacation* – an annual American directory listing all resorts.

Source: RCI Europe Ltd.

Box 4.2 *The economic impact of timeshare*

Puerto Vallarta, Mexico

- About US$125 million of timeshare sold in 1992;
- 55,800 households have purchased at projects in Puerto Vallarta;
- of these, 33,500 are Mexican and 22,300 from other countries, the majority from the USA;
- 29 timeshare projects containing 2,616 units and 133,416 intervals;
- 82,429 intervals sold at an average price of US$7,600;
- total sales volume is US$626 million;
- average occupancy was 75 per cent (compared with 46 per cent for the local hotel industry);
- over 2.6 million visitors generated by the timeshare industry;
- this involved more than 330,000 timeshare holiday-makers;
- US timeshare owners are three times as likely to return than if they did not own timeshare;
- US$630 million annual contribution to the local economy;
- equivalent to US$241,000 per timeshare unit;
- 2,325 direct jobs created;
- 1,625 indirect jobs created;
- annual payroll in excess of US$32 million.

Canada

- Over US$100 million of timeshare sold in 1992;
- 55,200 households purchased at Canadian projects;
- of these, 49,700 are Canadian households;
- 66 timeshare projects containing 1,444 units and about 73,650 intervals;
- 57,000 intervals sold;
- total sales volume of US$400 million;
- average occupancy rate almost 80 per cent;
- over 800,000 visitor days generated in Canada by the timeshare industry;
- this involved over 100,000 timeshare holiday-makers;
- timeshare owners are four times as likely to holiday in the community where their resort is located than if they did not own timeshare;
- US$64 million of direct consumer expenditures to the Canadian economy;
- US$64 million of indirect consumer expenditures;
- US$20 million of travel expenditures;
- US$18 million of maintenance fees;
- US$2.9 million property taxes and US$29 million of sales taxes;
- US$124,000 of expenditure and taxes per unit;
- 938 ongoing full-time jobs and 537 ongoing part-time jobs on-site;
- 3,397 ongoing and short-term full-time and part-time jobs on-site and elsewhere in the community;
- US$100 to US$150 million in payroll.

Source: European Timeshare Federation.

breakfast' is common, like the United Kingdom. This sector brings the advantage of elasticity to the tourism supply. Indeed, furnished rented accommodation (furnished apartments, guest houses and rural cottages) do not bear the high fixed costs of the hotel trade. They constitute complementary lodging in the high season and, more importantly, generate supplementary income for the local population.

☐ Seasonally rented furnished accommodation

These are self-catering apartments, studios and villas rented to tourists for periods ranging from one week to three months. The rapid growth of this sector has persuaded tour operators to develop new tourism products (transport + accommodation) at a lower cost than those using hotels. These products are better adapted to mass tourism. The most buoyant markets are in the Mediterranean resorts (France, Spain). Tour companies like the German firm Anton Götten combine coach travel to the resorts with the provision of rented accommodation.

☐ Cottages and farmhouse accommodation

Rural cottages (or 'gîtes') divert tourism flows towards rural areas by providing new and inexpensive accommodation. They provide additional income for the population of rural communities and help to maintain country buildings.

Rural cottages and guest houses have seen rapid growth recently, particularly in France. According to the *Fédération Nationale des Gîtes Ruraux de France*, the official body, in 1990 there were 58,584 gîtes in France. These are houses or rooms in guest houses for rent on a seasonal basis in a country setting. A favourable commercial, fiscal and social environment would encourage the development of the sector. However, no such incentives are being offered and, in some instances, businesses are incurring higher taxation.

☐ Guest lodgings

This form of lodging is particularly well-developed in Great Britain (bed and breakfast), Austria, Ireland, Portugal (estalagem), Italy (pensione) and Greece. Rooms are rented in private houses with breakfast provided. As with the rural cottages and farmhouses, the bed and breakfast sector does not benefit from incentives to encourage its development. This type of accommodation was, mainly found in industrialised countries. Today, it exists in most countries of the world (for instance purpose-built cottages on Thai, Caribbean, Indian and Philippine beaches; mountain lodges in Nepal and Peru). However, quality is difficult to control in these types of lodgings. This is why quality charters have been established in many countries to guarantee the quality level of equipment, facilities and services in this sector.

☐ Social accommodation

Social accommodation includes holiday villages, holiday centres and family holiday camps, youth hostels and accommodation provided by associations and staff clubs in firms. The accommodation is provided on a non-profit basis. In France, the main accommodation organisations are the VVF (Villages Vacances Familles), l'OCCAJ (Organisation central des camps et d'activités de jeunesse), Tourisme et travail, staff clubs at public and private firms such as EDF (Electricité de France), SNCF (the French Railways) and Renault, Trade and Craft Associations etc.

In 1990, holiday villages supplied most social accommodation (715 villages with 242,026 beds in total). There were 341 youth hostels with a total of 21,007 beds and 152 family holiday camps with 13,847 beds.

Camping can be either on designated sites or in the wilderness (with the permission of the landowner). In France, there are four categories of campsite ranging from one- to four-star. There were 8,352 sites in 1989 with 824,768 spaces. The greatest concentration of sites is in the Languedoc-Roussillon region with 109,237 spaces followed by the Provence–Alpes–Côtes d'Azur region with 90,768 and the Aquitaine region with 99,961 (statistics from the Ministry of Tourism, 1989).

■ Restaurant chains

There has been a remarkable increase in the number and size of restaurant chains, primarily in the United States, but also in the rest of the world. According to a survey conducted by the *Nation's Restaurant News*, the top ten restaurant chains in the world accounted for 87 billion dollars in 1990. Burger and pizza chains have been the fastest growing type of restaurant chain, particularly in the United States.

Hamburger chains are the largest segment in the market with a turnover of US\$39.4 billion, followed by contractors (US\$14.8 billion) and pizza chains (US\$13.8 billion). McDonald's has by far the highest turnover

(US$21.8 billion in 1992). Although 7-Eleven has the greatest number of units, it ranks twenty-ninth in terms of turnover (see Table 4.9).

If holding companies are compared, the ranking of restaurant chains is different. Indeed, certain groups own several brand names, for instance the

Table 4.9   *Top 30 restaurant chains in the USA classified by number of units*

Rank 1992	Rank 1989	Chains	Total units (1992)	Type of concept
1	3	7-Eleven	13,760	Convenience stores
2	1	McDonald's	13,093	Burgers
3	2	Pizza Hut	9,450	Pizza
4	7	Kentucky Fried Chicken	8,729	Chicken
5	6	Subway	7,327	Sandwiches
6	5	Burger King	6,648	Burgers
7	8	Dairy Queen	5,381	Sweets
8	4	Domino Pizza	5,300	Pizza
9	–	Gardner Merchant Food Services	4,600	Contractors
10	12	Little Caesars	4,300	Pizza
11	11	Taco Bell	4,000	Mexican
12	10	Wendy's	3,962	Burgers
13	15	Baskin-Robbins	3,425	Sweets
14	22	Holiday Inn Hotels	3,385	Lodging
15	9	Hardee's	3,365	Burgers
16	13	ARA Services	2,767	Contractors
17	18	Dunkin' Donuts	2,754	Sweets
18	14	Arby's	2,603	Sandwiches
19	16	Marriot Management Services	2,519	Contractors
20	–	Army and Air Force Services	2,189	Military
21	21	Canteen Corp.	1,862	Contractors
22	–	Choice Hotels	1,707	Lodging
23	–	Sheraton	1,510	Lodging
24	24	Denny's	1,460	Family dining
25	23	Long John Silver's	1,449	Seafood
26	26	Hilton Hotels	1,200	Lodging
27	28	Sonic Drive-in	1,191	Burgers
28	27	Jack in the Box	1,155	Burgers
29	26	Big Boy	940	Family dining
30	–	Shoney's	855	Family dining

Source: Adapted from *NRN Research* and *Restaurants & Institutions*.

PepsiCo Inc. owns Pizza Hut, Taco Bell and Kentucky Fried Chicken; TW Holdings include Denny's, Hardee's, Quincy's, El Pollo Loco and Canteen Corp (see Table 4.10).

Competition is particularly intense in the sandwich market which accounts for more than 40 per cent of sales by restaurant chains.

According to the classification adopted *by NRN Research*, sandwiches include hamburgers like those served at McDonald's, French-style like those of the Subway chain and Tex/Mex like those of Taco Bell. It appears that large restaurant chains are following two commercial strategies: on the one hand, the short-term strategy is to bring down prices by reducing margins in order to maintain and capture market share; on the other, the long-term strategy concentrates on offering services in the evening with a greater added value. Furthermore, restaurant chains are diversifying into the pizza sector which has grown considerably since 1990. The pizza market in the United States has become very concentrated, with three chains: Pizza Hut (9,450 units), Domino's (5,300 units) and Little Caesars (4,300 units) accounting for 85 per cent of the market.

Analysing the international distribution of hotels enables us to understand why there are such strong concentrations of tourism flows to certain destinations. The sale of tourism products is reliant on hotel capacity, especially accommodation intended for the international market. The success of the Balearics and the Canaries which receive more tourists than all the countries of South Asia or of West Africa is based on their large

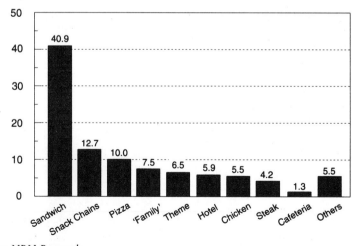

Source: NRN Research.

Figure 4.1 *Market share of the top 100 by restaurants by sector (%)*

Table 4.10   *Top 25 holding companies in the USA classified by number of units*

Rank 1992	Holding companies	Concepts	Sales 1990 (millions US$)
1	PepsiCo Inc.	Pizza Hut, Taco Bell, Kentucky Fried Chicken	5,555.0
2	Marriot Corp.	Marriot hotels, contract feeding, Host Intern.	4,927.3
3	McDonald's Corp.	McDonald's	4,048.0
4	TW Holdings Inc.	Denney's Hardee's, Quincy's, El Pollo Loco, Canteen Corp.	3,700.0
5	General Mills Inc.	Red Lobster, Olive Garden	2,000.0
6	ARA Services Inc.	ARASERVE, ARA Leisure Services	1,709.0
7	Servam Inc	Service America Food Service	1,360.0
8	Imaco Ltd	Hardee's, Roger's	1,295.0
9	Wendy's Int. Inc.	Wendy's	1,128.0
10	Foodmaker Inc.	Jack in the Box, Chi-Chi's	1,100.0
11	Carlson Cos.	TGI, Friday's, Dalt's, Radisson Hotels, Country Kitchen	1,040.0
12	Morrison Inc.	Morrison cafe., contract feed., Ruby Tuesday	1,025.0
13	Rest. Enter. Grp	El Torito, Casa Gallardo, Carrow's, Coco's, Reubens	900.0
14	Grand Met. plc	Burger King	815.0
15	Tennesse Rest. Inc.	Perkins Family Rest., Friendly Ice Cream	779.0
16	Shoney's Inc.	Shoney's, Lee's Famous Recipe Chicken, Captain D's	775.3
17	Greyhound Dial	Dobbs Int., Greyhound Food Mgmt, Burger King	770.0
18	Domino Pizza Inc.	Domino's Pizza	733.0
19	S&A Restaurant	Bennigan's, Steak and Ale	705.0
20	Caterair Int.	Marriot In-flite	656.0
21	Jerrico Inc.	Long John Silver's	608.6
22	Walt Disney Co.	Disney theme parks, hotels	604.6
23	Collins Foods Int.	Sizzler, Kentucky Fried Chicken	509.6
24	Sodexho	The Seiler Corp, Boatel, Food Dimensions Inc.	503.1
25	Al Copeland Inv.	Popey's, Church's, Copeland's, Super Popeye's	499.0

Source: Adapted from *NRN Research*.

hotel capacity. Accommodation trends reflect changes in tourism flows. Indeed, South and East Asian countries have greatly increased their accommodation capacity thanks to heavy investment by local hotel chains. This increase in hotel supply is attributed to the increase in tourism flows and receipts. Tourism development in the new industrial countries of Asia has been a result of high quality and advanced technology linked to strong competitiveness through low wage costs. These countries have attracted multinational hotel chains and have succeeded in increasing their market share. Large hotel chains not only possess the know-how, they have also established vast marketing networks throughout the world. By developing high-quality tourism in the area, the international tourism chains have created conditions for local chains to develop and also to become international, such as the Regent, Mandarin and Oriental chains.

Accommodation supply statistics show that the strategies pursued by international hotel chains follow and even reinforce international tourism trends. Thus, the strong growth in tourism supply is supported by a large range of accommodation. However, to achieve a congruous development of tourism flows, transport structures must develop in a similar way by adapting to certain situations such as mass tourism which inevitably comes with increased tourism flow volumes.

References

1. Slattery P., 'Unaffiliated Hotels in the UK', *EIU Travel Tourism Analyst*, No. 1, p. 99, 1992.

2. European Timeshare Federation Study, *The Worldwide Timeshare Industry and its European Perspective*, 1992.

Further Reading

Boschken, H.L. 'The Second Home Subdivision, Market, Suitability for Recreational and Pastoral Use', *Journal of Leisure Research*, 7(1), pp. 63–72, 1975.

Clout, H.D. 'Second Homes in the USA', *Tijdschrigt voor Economische en Sociale Geografie*, 63, pp. 393–401, 1972.

Coppock, J.T. *Second Homes: Curse or Blessing?*. London: Pergamon, 1977.

Jones, P. and Pizam, A. *The International Hospitality Industry: Organisational and Operational Issues*. London: Pitman, 1993.

Lockwood, A.L. and Jones, P. *Management of Hotel Operations*. London: Cassell, 1989.

Richie, J.R.B. and Goeldner C.R. *Travel, Tourism and Hospitality Research*. New York: Wiley, 1987.

Teare, R. and Olsen, M. *International Hospitality Management*. London: Pitman, 1992.

■ *Chapter 5* ■

Air Transport and Tourism

International air transport demand: the international air transport market; international non-scheduled air traffic

Airline companies: ranking airline companies

The geographic distribution of airline companies: the North American region; the European region; the Asia–Pacific region; the Latin American region; the African and Middle Eastern region

Cost structures of airline companies: comparing cost structures of scheduled and charter airlines; direct operating costs; indirect operating costs; labour costs

The fleet of airline companies

Deregulation and international competition

The 'Open Skies' policy and the United States

Air transport liberalisation in EU countries

Strategies adopted by airline companies: mergers, acquisitions and market concentration; partnership agreements; diversification strategies; privatisation strategies

The role played by air transport in international tourism development: comparative international analysis of the air transport and tourism sectors; problems of equipment and infrastructure associated with international tourism development

The different modes of transport in existence are significant to the growth of international tourism. The cost of transport often determines the total cost of tourism products and directly influences the choice of tourism destination. Air transport has contributed to the creation of new tourism markets far from tourist-generating countries which are not accessible either by road or by sea. The air transport industry occupies an important part of the tourism industry and the world economy. In 1990, air transport contributed US$700 billion to the world economy and the industry employed 21 million people worldwide. Despite a very rapid growth rate, higher than the world's GNP growth rate, international air transport is a difficult industry to manage, and both business and leisure traffic are susceptible to economic crises.

Three conditions characterise air transport in the 1990s: an exceptional growth, increasingly competitive markets and extreme vulnerability to international economic and political crises.

- *Exceptional growth* The growth of the air transport sector has been more than 6 per cent annually since the 1970s. However, this growth has been geographically concentrated in the industrialised regions and in the newly industrialised countries. Third World countries, particularly the least advanced ones, are not included in the main international air transport routes.
- *Intense competition* The intense competition in the air transport industry causes difficulties in the management of airline companies, even during periods of high demand. The worldwide policy of deregulation, following the experience of the United States, has transformed the market by creating competition between the carriers. This development has proved beneficial to the consumer and has resulted in a restructuring of airlines.
- *Vulnerability* Vulnerability to economic and international political shifts is the third feature of the air transport industry. The Gulf crisis and the economic recession at the beginning of the 1990s resulted in a decline in air traffic. In fact, according to statistics compiled by the ICAO (International Civil Aviation Organisation), world airline traffic fell by 3.5 per cent. The industry was particularly unstable throughout the 1980s; consequently, several major airline companies have disappeared, including the American companies Pan Am and Eastern.

In 1990, the ICAO estimated that world demand for scheduled domestic and international air transport amounted to a total of 235,870 million tonne-kilometres. Statistics show that world traffic grew on average 6.4 per cent annually between 1981 and 1990.

Comparing the annual growth rates of the three categories of traffic (passenger, freight and airmail) between 1981 and 1990 highlights the particular buoyancy of freight traffic which grew at an average annual rate of 7.5 per cent (see Table 5.1).

The annual growth rate of world air traffic is double that of the world's GNP. It is predicted that, barring major incidents like the Gulf War, the industry will continue to grow, although at no more than 5 per cent annually throughout the 1990s.

Table 5.1 *Average growth rate of air transport demand, 1981–90*

Passengers carried	4.9%
Passenger-kilometres	6.0%
Tonne-kilometre for freight	7.5%
Tonne-kilometres for air mail	3.7%

Source: ICA.

The demand for air transport increased considerably with the introduction of the first jet aircraft. Since 1950, passenger receipts from commercial aviation have multiplied 60 times, a much greater growth rate than that of other modes of transport. This also implies a change in the travel pattern of tourists.

The economic analysis of passenger traffic and freight traffic reveals that their exceptional growth can be attributed to the elasticity of demand with respect to price. The fare structures adopted by airline companies prove that there is a strong price elasticity for leisure travel demand and weak price elasticity for business and, to a lesser extent, personal travel demand.

■ International air transport demand

International air transport demand is concentrated in three areas: North America; Europe; Japan and the newly industrialised countries of Asia. Air traffic between these areas accounts for 75 per cent of world passenger traffic. The USA has the largest scheduled domestic market which represents 56 per cent of the world's domestic travel. EU countries account for 22 per cent of world domestic traffic.

□ *The international air transport market*

Two countries provide 30 per cent of the world's international services: the United States (20 per cent) and the United Kingdom (10 per cent). This also corresponds to international tourism flows in the world. According to WTO statistics, the United States, Europe and East and South Asia receive more than 80 per cent of all international tourist arrivals.

The North Atlantic is the busiest route in the world and accounts for 22.3 per cent of the world's passengers. However, forecasts of the growth of demand for the North Atlantic route show that the annual rate will be lower than the average demand for other world routes.

In its *World Market Outlook* publication (1994), Boeing predicts that world air travel will grow at a rate of 5.9 per cent annually until the year 2000 and at 4.9 per cent from 2000 to 2013. Between 1980 and 1990, the average annual growth rate of 5.9 per cent added 51 billion RPM (revenue passenger miles) each year to the world's air traffic. Because the base is so large, Boeing predicts that between 1990 and the year 2000, 74 billion RPM will be added annually to the system and 119 billion RPM each year between 2000 and 2010. In effect, passenger traffic will almost triple between 1994 and 2013.

Table 5.2   *The international air transport market, 1990 (millions of RPK)*

Region	1990
North Atlantic	197,153
Europe–Asia	130,470
North and Central Pacific	126,865
Intra-Asia	105,074
Intra-Europe	88,500
Europe–Africa	46,193
North America–Central America	32,848
Other routes	26,235
South Pacific	24,619
Europe–Middle East	22,497
North America–South America	19,417
Central Atlantic	19,063
South Atlantic	18,065
Intra-North America	10,195
Intra-Middle East	5,541
Intra-South America	5,025
Intra-Africa	3,946
Intra-Central America	1,957
Total international	883,663

Source: McDonnell Douglas.

The busiest international routes are increasingly towards Asia which is also the region experiencing the strongest growth in tourism and international trade. Figure 5.3 shows that over 40 per cent of future growth will come from the Intra-Asia–Pacific, Trans-Pacific and Asia–Europe travel markets travelling to, from and within this region of the world.

The busiest European routes start from London and include: London–Paris (route with the most seats on offer in the world), London–New York and London – Amsterdam (see Table 5.3).

☐ *International non-scheduled air traffic*

Non-scheduled air traffic represents approximately 17 per cent of total international passenger traffic. Charter companies and regular carriers have equal shares of the international non-scheduled air transport market. Europe has most of the traffic, principally to the tourism destinations in Southern Europe. Non-scheduled traffic between countries of the ECAC

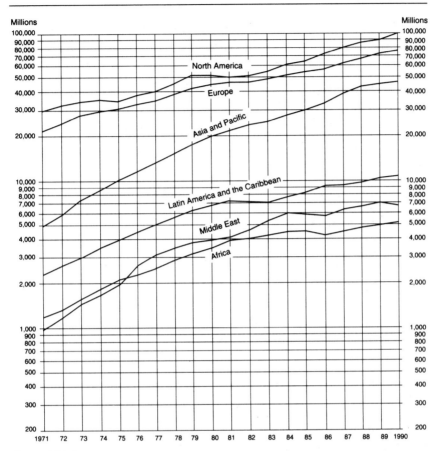

Source: ICAO.

Figure 5.1 *Air traffic trends according to major regions, 1971–90*

(European Civil Aviation Commission) represents 60 per cent of the total number of passenger-kilometres.

Charter airlines are particularly well-adapted to air transport demand in periods of crisis. Between 1988 and 1992, non-scheduled transport increased its market share by 5 per cent in Europe to account for 43 per cent of international intra-European traffic. In the UK, the growth of the charter company Britannia owned by Thomson is a remarkable example of the success of non-scheduled air transport used exclusively for tourism. In 1992, Britannia declared a profit of US$45 million. Britannia's fleet of Boeing 747s and Boeing 737s fly to destinations attracting a high proportion of leisure traffic. It is the largest charter airline in the world, serving 100 destinations. In 1991, it carried 6 million passengers on its fleet of 39 aircraft (by 1994, its fleet was reduced to 36 aircraft).

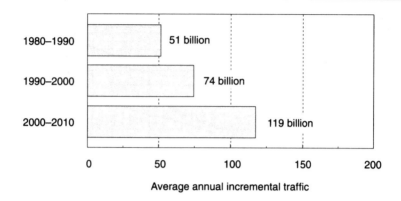

Source: Boeing, *Current Market Outlook*, 1994.

Figure 5.2   *Annual growth in air travel (average annual incremental traffic: RPMs in billions)*

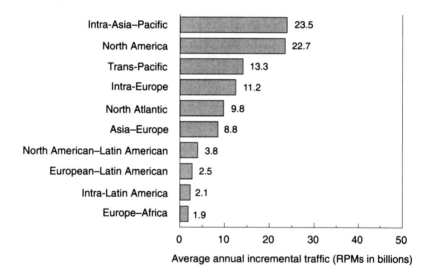

Source: Boeing, *Current Market Outlook*, 1994.

Figure 5.3   *Major air travel markets, 1994–2013 (average annual incremental traffic: RPMs in billions)*

■ Airline companies

Air transport supply is very concentrated with North American companies playing a determining role in its distribution. In 1993, six North American companies featured in the list of the world's ten largest companies:

Table 5.3   *The world's busiest routes (scheduled traffic, March 1993)*

Route	Seats offered (000)	Number of flights	SKO (millions)	Number of companies
London–Paris	492.4	2,987	170.4	8
Hong Kong–Taipei	465.9	1,473	376.0	7
Jakata–Singapore	351.3	1,616	313.7	15
Bangkok–Hong Kong	322.0	1,049	552.2	10
London–New York	320.7	1,119	1,779.6	8
Honolulu–Tokyo	278.8	643	1,728.6	6
Amsterdam–London	273.8	1,995	101.6	8
Kuala Lumpur–Singapore	286.4	1,543	82.6	5
Bangkok–Singapore	261.2	999	378.2	20
Seoul–Tokyo	237.3	681	290.7	7

SKO = Seat-kilometres Offered.
Source: *Resabook Transporteurs*, Edition 1994.

United Airlines (in first place), American Airlines (second), Delta (third), NorthWest (fourth), Continental (seventh) and USAir (eighth).

North American companies are dominant, not only in terms of world air traffic and market share, but also in CRS (Computer Reservation Systems) which are essential to international tourism.

The general ranking is based on Revenue Passenger Kilometres (RPK). This unit of measurement corresponds to the transport of one passenger for a distance of one kilometre. To calculate the traffic on a given route or network of routes, the number of carried passengers on each flight is multiplied by the distance travelled.

The greatest international routes are over the North Atlantic and Europe to Asia and to the North and Central Pacific.

☐ Ranking airline companies

Depending on the criterion chosen, the ranking of airline companies can be very different.

Table 5.4, based on passenger-kilometres, confirms the dominance of North American companies, particularly for domestic traffic.

The United States provides more than half the domestic air transport in the world. Consequently, North American companies usually have a solid base to develop links with the rest of the world and the top five companies internationally in terms of volume transported are also the top domestic carriers: United, American, Delta, Continental and NorthWest.

Table 5.4   *Airline performance, 1990 (revenue passenger kilometres)*

Rank	Airline company	Millions of RPK
1	UAL– United Airlines	162,954
2	AMR Corp. – American Airlines	156,302
3	Delta Airlines	133,454
4	Northwest Airlines	94,466
5	British Airways	92,713
6	Lufthansa Group	67,018
7	Continental Airlines	64,587
8	USAir	56,681
9	Japan Airways	56,667
10	Air France Group	55,393
11	Singapore Airlines	42,328
12	Qantas	40,603
13	KLM Royal Dutch Airlines	38,606
14	ANA All Nippon Airways	36,881
15	TWA Trans World Airways	36,673
16	Southwest Airlines	30,299
17	Cathay Pacific	29,097
18	Alitalia	28,386
19	Korean Air Lines	25,937
20	Iberia	22,814

Source: Airline Business.

If only international figures are considered, several European and Japanese companies carry more travellers than North American companies. British carries the most international traffic, followed by United, Japan Airlines and Lufthansa. This situation is changing and developing very quickly with approaches being made for international links by United, American and Delta.

The table of company turnover reveals the vulnerability of certain North American companies to European and Asian airline groups. Nevertheless, North America still dominates the ranking with five companies in the top ten (see Table 5.5).

If airline company profitability is ranked, the list looks quite different. Although Table 5.6 shows that four American companies were ranked in the top twenty most profitable airlines in 1993, in reality the Asia–Pacific companies are the most profitable in the world with seven companies in the top twenty.

Both Continental and TWA at the top the ranking were declared bankrupt earlier in the year. The Chapter 11 bankruptcy law in the United States allows an airline to suspend its long-term debt. The objective of the

Table 5.5 *Airline performance, 1991 (turnover)*

Rank	Airline company	Sales (US$ millions)
1	American Airlines	15,816.0
2	United Airlines	14,511.0
3	Delta Group	12,375.6
4	Lufthansa Airlines	10,723.1
5	Air France	9,732.0
6	British Airways	9,478.2
7	Japan Airlines	8,542.0
8	Federal Express	8,479.5
9	NorthWest Airlines	8,448.0
10	ANA All Nippon Airways	7,950.0
11	US Air Group	7,083.0
12	Continental	5,775.3
13	SAS Group	5,022.0
14	Alitalia	4,675.7
15	KLM Dutch Royal Airlines	4,611.5
16	Swissair	4,326.1
17	Qantas	4,111.7
18	Singapore Airlines	3,974.8
19	Korean Airlines	3,316.1
20	Iberia	3,316.1

Source: *Airline Business.*

law is to get the company up and running again. Management proposes a re-organisation plan and the creditors and public stockholders appoint a committee to represent their interests. If the court rules that the plan is acceptable, the airline can continue to operate. This leaves it free to discount prices allowing it to compete without having to cover the full cost of operations. Although Continental and TWA registered the larger profits for the year (US$2,601.6 million for Continental and US$623.8 million for TWA), both carriers suffered operational losses.

European Airlines lost ground in 1993. Swissair ranked tenth in 1991 did not feature in the top twenty ranking and KLM ranked ninth in 1991 fell to sixteenth position in 1993. British Airways was the only Western European company ranked in the top ten although its profits fell from US$623.8 million in 1991 to US$430 million in 1993.

In 1993, the difference in profitability between European airline companies was even more pronounced than in 1992, with US$430.1 million profits for British Airways (US$298 million in 1992) but a loss of US$1,495.5 million for Air France (US$617 million in 1992).

According to the Comité des Sages report commissioned by the European Union in 1994, European airlines' operating costs are about 48

Table 5.6 *Airline performance, 1993 (profitability)*

Rank	Airline company	Profits (US$ millions)
1	Continental Airways	2,601.6
2	TWA Trans World Airlines	623.8
3	Singapore Airlines	510.5
4	British Airways	430.1
5	Cathay Pacific	296.4
6	Federal Express	204.4
7	Southwest Airlines	169.6
8	Aeroflot RIA	146.7
9	China Airlines	115.4
10	Air India	114.7
11	China Eastern Group	114.6
12	China Southern Group	95.2
13	Northwest Airlines	81.2
14	Air New Zealand	75.3
15	Thai Airways International	55.0
16	KLM Royal Dutch Airlines	54.8
17	Atlantic Southeast Airlines	50.5
18	Tunis Air	45.9
19	LTU Group	45.4
20	Austrian Airlines	43.2

Source: *Airline Business.*

per cent higher than those of their US counterparts, measured per available tonne kilometre (ATK). Total labour costs per ATK are nearly 37 per cent higher, leading to much lower productivity than in the US, according to the study.

The geographic distribution of airline companies

There are 24 North American companies, 34 European companies, 21 from the Asia–Pacific region, 10 from Latin America and 11 African and Middle Eastern companies in the top 100 companies ranked according to their turnover. Together, North American companies form the largest economic and financial bloc accounting for 39.5 per cent of world sales in 1991. European companies represented 33.5 per cent, Asian–Pacific companies 20.8 per cent, Latin American companies 3.2 per cent. Just 3.0 per cent is attributed to African and Middle Eastern companies. The high geo-

Table 5.7   *European airlines: winners and losers*

	Profits[1] 1992 (US$ millions)	Productivity[2] 1992	Productivity rise 1988–92 (%)
British Airways	298	298,939	6.9
Sabena	12	n/a	n/a
Alitalia	−12	279,617	7.6
Aer Lingus	−196	144,136	7.8
TAP	−200	132,557	3.1
Olympic	−225	n/a	n/a
Lufthansa	−250	291,196	2.9
KLM	−319	325,635	6.4
Iberia	−340	172,244	5.2
Air France	−617	289,170	1.5

[1] Pre-tax profits.

[2] Productivity is stated in terms of available tonne kilometres per employee, a way of measuring output per employee. Apart from BA and KLM, most gains came from low bases.

Source: The 'Comité des Sages' report.

graphical concentration of airline companies in the USA and Europe reflects the distribution of world demand for air transport.

☐ *The North American region*

The impact of deregulation in North America has been to strengthen the dominant position of the largest companies. The disappearance of Pan Am and Eastern has further increased the sales figures of the three major companies: American Airlines, United and Delta.

☐ *The European region*

European airline companies have either expanded by internal growth (Lufthansa, KLM) or by merging national carriers (British Airways and British Caledonian or Air France, UTA and Air Inter). However, potential mergers are limited and companies are now joining in alliances or acquiring controlling shares in airline companies in different countries of the world. British Airways is extensively involved in the French and North American markets.

The list of European airlines ranked by turnover does not correspond to the list ranked by passenger-kilometre. For instance, in 1993 British Airways was the leading European company with 92,713 million RPK, whereas Lufthansa reported 67,018 million RPK and the Air France Group 55,393 million. However, in terms of turnover, British Airways was in third position with US$9 billion in sales behind Lufthansa (10.7 billion) and the Air France Group (US$9.7 billion). Therefore, despite a smaller turnover, British Airways claims the dominant position in the European air transport market. This situation is a result of strategic differences between the companies: British Airways concentrates its activities principally on air transport while Air France and Lufthansa also use other modes of transport to carry passengers and freight.

□ *The Asia–Pacific region*

Airline companies in the Asia–Pacific region have the highest growth rate and the best financial performances in the world. The sales figures for Singapore Airlines, for instance, increased by 15.4 per cent in 1992–93, compared with a 2.9 per cent average increase for all the airline companies. Singapore Airlines is most profitable airline in the world (excluding Continental and TWA who have being given Fresh Start accounting gains under chapter 11 bankruptcy level). Its profit margin was 12.8 per cent in 1993 and a total profit of US$510.5 million. Airlines from the new industrial countries are some of the best performers in the world: Cathay Pacific from Hong Kong, China Airlines from Taiwan and Korean Air from South Korea.

The turnover of Asia–Pacific airlines is lower than that of North American and European companies, which benefit from a market with a high spending-power. However, all the forecasts by international organisations (ICAO and IATA) and by aeroplane manufacturers agree that the distribution of international traffic will shift towards Asian companies in the next few years.

□ *The Latin American region*

Airline companies in Latin America have developed from highly regulated domestic markets. The main airline companies are in the largest and most populous countries: Brazil, Argentina and Mexico.

Today, important privatisation programmes are being implemented in many Latin American countries. These have been based on grouping together airlines regionally as well as internationally (for instance Iberia's interests in Aerolíneas Argentinas, Viasa and Dominicana).

☐ The African and Middle Eastern region

The airline companies of the African and Middle Eastern region show clear contrasts. Some are amongst the most profitable in the world: for instance, Tunis Air with a profit margin of 10.4 per cent. On the other hand, Saudia (with a turnover of US\$2,490 million and US\$78.8 million loss) and Egyptair (US\$430 million turnover, a fall of 20.4 per cent on 1992) are among the companies who have declared the highest losses in the world. It should be noted, however, that both these airlines are required to provide a public service by covering unprofitable domestic routes.

Most African airlines have insufficient volume to properly develop strategies that will lead to growth. For this reason some countries have pooled their resources to create companies such as Air Africa.

However, a few of the most successful companies have adopted other strategies for growth:

- creating a hub and spoke system (like Royal Jordanian covering Europe, the Near and Far East);
- developing multiple stopover links, taking advantage of the fifth freedom (the right to operate commercial transport between two states other than the airline company's own country), as Ethiopian Airlines has done, with its links with East and West Africa.

■ Cost structures of airline companies

The total operating cost of airline companies is made up of direct operating costs and indirect operating costs. Scheduled and charter airlines have different cost structures.

☐ Comparing cost structures of scheduled and charter airlines

The growth of non-scheduled air transport (or charter) is a result of the low prices charged for its services. If

q_0 is the quantity of seat-km on offer and

c is the load factor in percentage and

the price system is represented by different tariffs: $p_1, p_2, p_3 \ldots p_i \ldots p_n$

the load factor corresponds to different tariffs: $c_1, c_2, c_3 \ldots c_i \ldots c_n$

for each tariff, total receipts will be:

$$R_1 = (q_0/c_1)p_1$$
$$R_2 = (q_0/c_2)p_2$$
$$R_3 = (q_0/c_3)p_3$$
$$R_i = (q_0/c_1)p_i$$
$$R_n = (q_0/c_n)p_n$$

Total receipts will be:

$$RT = (q_0 \cdot c_1)p_1 + (q_0 \cdot c_2)p_2 + \dots (q_0 \cdot c_1)p_1 + \dots (q_0 \cdot c_n)p_n$$
$$RT = q_0(c_1p_1 + c_2p_2 + \dots c_ip_i + \dots c_np_n)$$

$$RT = q_0 \sum_{i=1}^{n} c_np_n \text{ corresponds to receipt per passenger}$$

As an example, a 300-seat Airbus breaks even on a given trip at US\$30,000.

1. For a charter airline (load factor near 100 per cent)

Passenger tariff will be: $\dfrac{US\$30,000}{300} = US\$100$

2. For a scheduled airline (load factor 60 per cent)

Passenger tariff will be: $\dfrac{US\$30,000}{180} = US\$166$

The scheduled company can compete with the charter company by creating a low-cost tourist class. However, to make the flight profitable, it needs to maintain a high load factor in economy or business class charged at full tariff.

- *Scenario one*   high load factor in business class.

First class:	$c_1 = 3\%$	$p_1 = US\$500$
Business class:	$c_2 = 36\%$	$p_2 = US\$200$
Tourist class:	$c_3 = 21\%$	$p_3 = US\$110$

$$RT = (q_0 \cdot c_1)p_1 + (q_0 \cdot c_2)p_2 + (q_0 \cdot c_3)p_3$$
$$RT = (300.3\%)500 + (300.36\%)200 + (300.21\%)110$$
$$RT = 4,500 + 21,600 + 6,930$$
$$RT = US\$33,030$$

The scheduled service is profitable.

- *Scenario two* low load factor in business class.

First class:	$c_1 = 3\%$	$p_1 = US500$
Business class:	$c_2 = 12\%$	$p_2 = US200$
Tourist class	$c_3 = 45\%$	$p_3 = US110$

$$RT = (q_0 . c_1)p_1 + (q_0 . c_2)p_2 + (q_0 . c_3)p_3$$
$$RT = (300 . 3\%)500 + (300 . 12\%)200 + (300 . 45\%)110$$
$$RT = 4,500 + 7,200 + 14,850$$
$$RT = US26,550$$

The scheduled service is making a loss.

Therefore, the main difficulty for scheduled airlines competing on routes used by charter airlines is determining the price levels which will satisfy tourism demand while ensuring a high enough load factor to guarantee the profitability which will allow the company to develop.

They must also take into account a number of variables: competition, differences in inflation rates with competing destinations, fluctuations in the exchange rate, costs, political risks, the success of promotional and marketing efforts, client satisfaction with the tourism product, the destinations and so on.

The difference between the pricing policies of charter and scheduled airlines shows that, for the same overall cost, the charter airline can offer lower fares as long as they achieve a high load factor and enough flight-hours.[1]

☐ *Direct operating costs*

There are two categories of direct cost:

- The direct cost of the flight, which includes the cost of flight crews, fuel and oil, insurance and airport costs.
- The variable cost of material, for instance, maintenance and overall costs, depreciation and amortisation, and rental of equipment.

These costs constitute approximately half the total cost. Fluctuations will come from changes in the price of fuel which is dependent on the price of oil and the type of aeroplane and engine used. The latest technologically advanced aircraft are economical in fuel.

☐ *Indirect operating cost*

These are mainly marketing and administrative costs, which for the larger companies can be very high. Their spending on marketing and public relations includes promotional and publicity campaigns, points of sale at major commercial outlets in large cities around the world and rental and maintenance of exclusive areas at airports.

There are four types of indirect operating costs:

- *Stopover cost* which includes station and ground costs, handling fees and airport taxes;
- *Passenger service cost* which includes in-flight catering, cabin crew salaries and expenses, overnight accommodation costs for cabin crew and transit passengers and the cost of insurance;
- *Reservation cost* which includes ticketing, the cost of retail shops and offices and commissions paid to travel agencies;
- *General and administration costs.*

Gradually, the stopover cost and the marketing cost have increased significantly while airline companies have been following a policy of reducing general and administration costs.

The cost structure of airline companies is heavily dependent on the price of fuel. Fuel is the largest expenditure incurred in operating an airline (traditionally 30 per cent), followed by the stopover cost (15.5 per cent). However, since the fall in oil prices, fuel and oil costs can be lower than 20 per cent, particularly when new aircraft are operated.

Direct operating costs amount to 53 per cent of total cost and indirect operating costs to 47 per cent. It should be noted, however, that Table 5.8 represents average cost which can vary from one airline company to another.

☐ *Labour costs*

Labour is an increasing cost for the airline companies. This is partly a result of the high wages paid to flight crews, particularly pilots, but also due to the restructuring of companies which has increased the number of administrative staff.

Comparing the labour force and wage costs of large airline companies in the five main industrialised countries reveals that there are great differences in both productivity and salaries. The United Kingdom and the United States are much more competitive than other countries in Western Europe and even Japan.

Table 5.8 *Airline operating cost distribution, ICAO airlines, 1991*

Direct operating costs	
Flight operation	12.7%
Fuel	15.0%
Depreciation	7.1%
Maintenance	11.5%
Indirect operating costs	
Landing fees	3.9%
User charges and station expenses	12.4%
Ticketing, sales and promotion	16.6%
Passenger service	10.3%
General and administrative	10.5%

Source: Boeing, *Current Market Outlook*, 1993.

Table 5.9 *Workforce of the top airline companies, 1993*

Rank	Airline company	Number of staff
1	AMR Corp – American Airlines	118,900
2	Federal Express	91,449
3	UAL – United Airlines	85,000
4	Delta Airlines	69,537
5	Air France Group	61,759
6	Lufthansa Group	60,514
7	British Airways	49,628
8	USAir	45,400
9	NorthWest Airlines	43,489
10	SAS Group	37,871
11	Continental Airlines	34,871
12	TWA – Trans World Airlines	28,620
13	Varig	25,152
14	Iberia	24,476
15	Singapore Airlines	24,377
16	KLM	24,048

Source: *Airline Business*.

According to Lord King, the chairman of British Airways until 1992, the success of the company both in terms of growth and in terms of profits stems from a significant reduction in wage costs and a large increase in productivity.

The strategies pursued in the 1990s for turning around the financial situation of airline companies are generally based on reducing wage costs.

These were first adopted in the United States by NorthWest, Continental and TWA in the 1980s after deregulation and more recently SAS and Lufthansa in Europe have followed suit. These policies have been implemented to bring European and North American companies into line with the world average. For instance, in 1984, the cost of the crew by tonne-km ranged from 3.5 per cent for the French company UTA and 2.8 per cent for Pan Am to 2 per cent for Qantas, 1.7 per cent for Cathay Pacific and just 0.4 per cent for Korean Airlines.

The cost of fuel also plays a crucial role in the management of airline companies. At the beginning of the 1970s, the fuel cost was just 10 per cent of the total operating costs. In 1992, for a scheduled airline whose main activity is carrying passengers, the fuel cost represented 25–30 per cent of total operating costs. However, this percentage can differ according to the airline company and will depend on the composition of each company's fleet.

■ The fleet of airline companies

The dominant position of North American companies is also reflected in the capacity of their fleet. The top American companies own an enormous capacity with fleets of over 500 aircraft. European companies' fleets number around 100 aircraft on average and those of the regions in the rest of the world less than 100.

The consequence of deregulation in the United States has been a change in the capacity of American airlines. Within less than five years after deregulation, two of the best-known companies have ceased trading: Eastern and Pan Am.

Table 5.10   *Number of aircraft in airline fleet (jets and turbo), 1992*

North America		Europe		Asia–Pacific	
America	667	Lufthansa	301	ANA	130
Delta	563	British Airways	253	Qantas	123
United	544	Air France	225	JAL	111
Federal Express	458	SAS	169	Malaysian Airways	94
USAir	441	Alitalia	161	Japan Air Service	74
Northwest	358	Iberia	121	Garuda	73
TWA	186	KLM	101	Singapore	64
Southwest	178	Swissair	62	Thai Airways	62
United Parcel	148	Sabena	54	China Airlines	61

Source: Airline Business.

Box 5.1   *Job losses in the airline industry*

Since 1991, more than 80,000 jobs in the airline industry have disappeared worldwide. This has been a direct result of the financial losses incurred by airline companies because of the recession of the early 1990s, the recent policies of mergers and alliances adopted by the most successful airline companies and the policy of contracting out jobs to cheaper labour markets (such as in the Philippines and China) embraced by some airlines.

The merger of Air France and UTA in 1991 resulted in 3,000 job losses and the announcement of further job cuts at Air France triggered a crippling strike led by the unions in 1993. The demise of Pan Am in December 1991 cost 16,000 jobs and a further 36,000 jobs were lost after the collapse of People Express, Braniff, Frontier and Eastern.

The policy of rationalisation has mainly been implemented by American and European airline companies. The following table lists the job losses since 1991 chronologically:

1991	**January:**	3,000 jobs lost in the Air France merger with UTA;
	March:	3,500 jobs lost in the Air Europe collapse;
	December:	16,000 losses after the Pan Am collapse, 4,600 jobs go at British Airways, 890 at Continental, 1,300 at the Polish carrier LOT, 700 at US Air and 900 at Air Canada;
1992	**February:**	1,250 ground staff go at American Airlines;
	April:	1,100 jobs lost in the Compass Airline collapse, 3,000 lost at NorthWest airlines;
	October:	1,600 jobs lost from Dan Air (UK);
	December:	1,500 jobs lost at Aerolíneas Argentinas, 1,000 at Air Mexico, 4,000 at Mexicana, 4,200 at Sabena after merger with Air France, 4,000 losses announced by Delta, 500 at American, 6,000 for the whole of 1992 at SAS, 3,000 jobs lost at Iberia in 1992 and 1,000 losses announced at Aer Lingus;
1993	**March:**	700 jobs lost at Compas Airlines;
	May:	Nationalair collapses in Canada, 1,300 jobs lost;
	Year end:	Air Canada 1,100 jobs lost, Swissair 1,000, TAP 1,500, Canadian Airlines 2,000. 2,500 jobs lost as USAir after the merger with BA.

The opening of the airways to competition has encouraged the larger domestic airlines of the United States to develop international links. American, United, Delta, NorthWest, Continental and now USAir are competing for the North American routes which were until the 1980s exclusively serviced by TWA, Pan Am and various European companies. United and NorthWest have also developed routes to Asia and Japan.

■ Deregulation and international competition

At the Chicago Conference in 1944, legal guidelines were set for the international operation of airlines. The basic aim of the Chicago Convention was to facilitate international operation by fixing bilateral air services agreements between countries and sometimes even at a regional level.

The principles were based on the five freedoms of the air concerning air transport relations:

- The first freedom concerned the right of an airline company of one state to fly over the territory of another state.
- The second freedom concerned the right of an airline company of one state to land on the territory of another state for non-commercial reasons.
- The third freedom related to the right of an airline company to carry passengers, mail and goods from its own state to another state.
- The fourth freedom concerned the right of an airline company of one state to embark passengers, mail and goods in another state and carry them to its own state.
- The fifth freedom related to commercial transport between two states other than the airline companies' own country. This is a key condition for the growth of international air transport competition and liberalisation policies based on multilateralisation.

Although fifth freedom rights were agreed at the Chicago Convention, to date they have never really come into force. However, there have been certain bilateral agreements such as the Bermuda Agreement between the UK and the USA introducing fifth freedom rights.

Liberalisation of air transport is largely dependent on market access for private carriers and on cabotage rights.

Cabotage is the right of an airline company of one country to embark passengers, mail and goods in another country and carry them to another

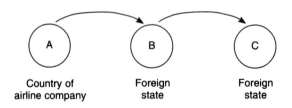

Figure 5.4   *The fifth freedom of the air*

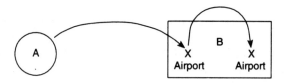

Figure 5.5 *Cabotage*

point in the same country for a fee or for a leasing contract. Cabotage introduces competition between domestic and international carriers and is one of the most debated points in the whole issue of air transport liberalisation.

Two international organisations play regulatory roles in the international air transport market: the ICAO and IATA.

- *The International Civil Aviation Organisation* The ICAO (International Civil Aviation Organisation) is a United Nations organisation involved in air transport security, operational and safety requirements and technical regulation. However, it has limited control of the economics of air transport.
- *The International Air Transport Association* The IATA (International Air Transport Association) is a non-governmental organisation and its membership is a requirement of airline companies. It complements the role of the ICAO and is concerned with the economics and finance of air transport (tariffs, operating conditions, facilities and the operation of a clearing house for inter-airline debts). It also arbitrates in inter-airline and airline–travel agency conflicts. IATA's main function has always been to set tariffs and trade agreements, although this role has been much reduced since deregulation.

Deregulation of the airline industry first appeared in the United States at the end of the 1970s and has had far-reaching consequences on the policies and strategies of all airline companies. Since then, the transformation of the industry can be attributed to three main factors:

1. Deregulation of the domestic market in the United States has been the catalyst for a general lowering of domestic and international prices.
2. The strategies of airline companies towards tourism radically changed after the competition introduced by the charter companies in the 1980s. Companies like Laker, Wardair and Capitol, although they failed, have transformed the industry.

3. General discounts on scheduled airlines have been introduced. Tour operators can now sell seats at very competitive prices to cover tourism demand, thus generating a new clientele for the airlines (this amounts to selling charter seats on scheduled airlines at an advantageous price).

These trends have transformed the structure of the air transport market by reinforcing a process of deregulation first in the United States, then in Europe and gradually in the other regions of the world.

■ The 'Open Skies' policy and the United States

The definition of 'Open Skies' adopted by the North American Department of Transportation to date concerns principally the establishment of links with European partners and aims to spread deregulation to all routes to Europe and more particularly within Europe.

The definition of 'Open Skies' has eleven main clauses:

1. *Free access to all routes*   This is the keystone of all the liberalisation and deregulation clauses. It allows airline companies to operate freely between different airports with the only limitations involving issues of security, financial guarantees and the availability of slots at the airports. Airline companies can pursue strategies that will introduce new services to satisfy demand. This is particularly important for reacting to increases in tourism demand (i.e. the opening of new hotels or holiday villages) and seasonality.

2. *No restriction on capacity and frequency on any route*   This clause allows airline companies to establish 'hubs' without restrictions. An airport becomes a hub when it is used by an airline company as a base to group and distribute traffic to other destinations in its network. The success of this strategy rests on the freedom to greatly increase certain frequencies so that both transit and direct-route passengers can be accommodated. Since deregulation of the market in the United States, hubs have been established by the main US airline companies for domestic as well as international routes leaving the US, notably in Dallas, Atlanta, Chicago, New York, Miami and Los Angeles. The extension of the Open Skies policy will considerably develop this strategy. Delta is seeking to establish itself in Frankfurt, TWA in Paris and NorthWest in Amsterdam.

3. *No restriction on operation in all international markets*   This reinforces the strategy based on creating hubs by allowing airlines to service intermediate points and to use an unlimited number of

smaller-calibre aircrafts to and from international gateways. This clause particularly favours airline companies with large fleets who can establish themselves quickly in new markets.

4. *Flexibility of tariffs* Companies are able to fix their own tariffs and this is one of the most important conditions for liberalisation of air transport. The best performing airline can service new routes and increase their market share. However, 'dumping' must be prohibited to guarantee the long-term interest of the customer. Flexibility of tariffs has been mainly implemented by North American companies and on the North Atlantic routes.

5. *Liberalisation of charter rules and elimination of restrictions on charters* Non-scheduled air transport has played a very important role in the development of tourism in some regions of the world such as the Mediterranean basin. It allows companies to address traffic problems during peak periods and to maintain pressure on keeping air fares competitive. Hence, Open Skies equally concerns charter companies who must also have the same access to the market.

6. *Liberalisation of air cargo rules* This agreement distinguished between 'all cargo' and 'mixed cargo' so that companies can select freely the type of aircraft best suited to demand on each route. This has become an important issue as many airlines have developed substantial cargo businesses. With the exception of companies in the United States, few companies specialise exclusively in the transport of cargo.

7. *No restrictions on the conversion of revenue to hard currency and its repatriation* This clause concerns agreements between countries with different economic systems, particularly where exchange-rate restrictions are operated. Airline companies need to be able to convert and move currency freely so that they can restructure, operate and market their networks efficiently.

8. *Agreement on code-sharing* This agreement has been implemented by many companies who want to reorganise their networks in partnership with other companies on an international scale. Thus, since the Open Skies agreement between the USA and the Netherlands, KLM and NorthWest have established a code-sharing system which has doubled the number of connecting flights they can offer. NorthWest can now advertise flights from Albuquerque to Karachi and gain a good position in the computer reservation network. Between both networks, twenty daily KLM and NorthWest flights form the core of the alliance. This joint management of routes has resulted in substantial savings (US$1.5 billion for each company in 1994).

Some code-sharing agreements exist outside the Open Skies policy but these are limited to sharing routes and do not involve streamlining products or the joint management of receipts and expenditure such as the Lufthansa/United agreement and the BA/USAir agreement. Agreements which do not involve joint management of the networks often result in imbalances between the partners.

9. *Airline companies to be able to ensure their own ground services abroad* This clause is central to the whole issue of market access and is now accepted in a great many countries. However, monopolies by domestic companies still exist in some countries (notably in developing countries and in Central and Eastern Europe).

10. *No regulation on commercial agreements concerning air transport operation* This freedom is, to a large extent, already in operation. In 1994, there were more than 177 alliances between 223 airline company members of IATA. These agreements have multiplied since the introduction of the Open Skies policy. This clause is outside US anti-trust laws as it allows commercial relations between competing companies. Thus, meetings between the management of KLM and NorthWest to discuss commercial links are legal within the Open Skies agreement.

11. *Non-discriminatory access and use of Computer Reservation Systems* This is one of the most important clauses to guarantee the success of the Open Skies policy and to ensure that airline companies of the participating countries achieve their sales potential. Today's marketing policies are dependent on access to computerised distribution networks.

Faced with a restructured air transport market, European companies and companies from other regions in the world do not have the means to enter the domestic market of the United States. The policy of certain European airlines has been to buy into already established North American airlines, for instance, KLM with NorthWest, British Airways with USAir and Lufthansa with Continental.

Up to 1994, only the Netherlands has accepted the United States' Open Skies policy, and, for the moment, this agreement does not concern other countries in the European Union.

■ Air transport liberalisation in EU countries

European deregulation moved one step nearer completion on 22 and 23 May 1992 when the Transport Ministers of the twelve EU countries agreed to drop restrictions on air-fare tariffs within the EU. Until then, airline companies in the EU had been required to have their fares approved by a supervisory authority. They can now set their own prices.

These measures should eliminate protectionist barriers within the EU. However, a compromise had to be reached between the more liberal countries, who wanted the measures implemented immediately, and those, such as France, Spain and Italy, who favoured a long transition period of six years. Agreement was reached that the measures were to come into effect on 1 January 1993 except for cabotage rights which will take effect on 1 April 1997.

Deregulation of air transport in Europe covers three main areas:

1. From 1993, airline companies could set tariffs freely. However, these can be opposed by the civil authorities of the countries concerned, particularly if they do not relate to the real cost of flying a particular route. This regulation is to avoid the air-fare wars which followed deregulation in the USA. Furthermore, certain European governments, like the United Kingdom's, also want to avoid extreme variations in prices.
2. The second area relates to the standardisation of operating conditions for all airline companies in Europe. From 1993, all carriers in the EU could trade from any country within the EU if they conform to three conditions:

   - at least 51 per cent of the company's capital should be owned by citizens of member countries of the European Union;
   - a minimum capital investment of 100,000 ecus;
   - the aircraft should be registered in the country that issued its certificate of airworthiness.

   The objective behind setting these condition is to prevent companies from non-EU countries to set up operation in the EU.
3. The third area concerns *cabotage rights* (the right to operate domestic flights in other EU countries and to operate flights originating from other EU countries). This right will take effect in 1997.

   The cabotage right is a fundamental step in European deregulation as it places European airline companies in a similar competitive environment to that of the United States.

Once cabotage rights are in place, the Comité des Sages recommends, in a 1994 report commissioned by the European Commission,[2] the creation of a 'single airspace for Europe' and the establishment of a separate utility responsible for monitoring a single air traffic management system. This would end the current system of European airspace and national air controls.

It also recommends that 'member states and the EU should ensure the competitiveness of the European aeronautical industry by providing the same level of support available to the US aeronautical industry'. It calls for a transitional period in which member states could have a 'one time, last time' opportunity to put carriers on a normal commercial footing. Other conditions for state aid include:

- The submission of a restructuring plan leading to economic and commercial viability within a specified time frame, along with significant interest from the private sector;
- A recommendation for restructuring plans to be scrutinised by independent professionals working with the European Commission;
- An undertaking on the part of governments to refrain from interference in commercial decision-making of carriers, and a ban on airlines using public money to buy or take over another air carrier or extend its own capacity beyond normal development.

■ Strategies adopted by airline companies

The changed economic situation resulting from deregulation has led airline companies to reconsider their strategies. Most companies have developed a double strategy: on the one hand they aim at providing for the low-volume but high-revenue business travel market, on the other they are competing with road, railway and sea transport companies and with non-scheduled airlines to service the mass transport market, which is mainly used by tourists. To this end, airline companies have developed new low-tariff strategies.[3]

Four kinds of strategies are pursued:

- Mergers, acquisitions and market concentration
- Partnership agreements
- Diversification
- Privatisation

☐ *Mergers, acquisitions and market concentration*

Since the end of the 1980s, the number of mergers and acquisitions in the airline industry has increased considerably, and those owning the newest fleets usually instigated by companies with the smallest debts and the best control of their production costs.

One result of deregulation in the United States was the disappearance of financially weak airlines such as Pan Am and Eastern, even though they controlled a large segment of the market. Less than ten years after deregulation, the three largest companies control led 70 per cent of the domestic market. To comply with bankruptcy laws, companies in financial difficulties were obliged to sell their assets, particularly their routes, but also their hubs and their aircraft. These were acquired by the financially strong companies, notably Delta, United or American.

The air transport market in the United States should be shared by the ten largest companies in the period between 1995 and the year 2000, and the three main North American companies will have consolidated their leading position. The North American domestic market is the largest in the world and the cartel will soon lead to an increase in tariffs which will affect not only prices nationally but also internationally.

In Europe, market concentration has developed between European countries, particularly involving Eastern Europe, but also intercontinentally, especially with the United States and Latin American companies. This is pursued by the financially strong airlines like British Airways, by countries benefiting from governmental support (Iberia) and those backed by nationalised banks (Air France).

In 1992, Air France bought shares in Sabena, the Belgian carrier, and in CSA (ex-Czechoslovakia) to develop an integrated network between Eastern and Western Europe. However, Air France had to sell back its share in CSA in March 1994 at the request of the Czech government. Iberia bought into several South American companies like Viasa of Venezuela and Aerolíneas Argentinas of Argentina, with the objective of establishing a dominant position on the Europe–Latin American routes.

But it is British Airways that has followed the most dynamic market concentration policy by buying a 44 per cent share of USAir, although, in conformance with US law, they have only 21 per cent of the voting rights. USAir is the sixth largest airline in the United States and controls 40 per cent of the domestic routes on the East Coast, between New York, Boston and Washington. In 1992, USAir carried 55 million passengers, had a fleet of 439 aircraft and employed 45,281 people. British Airways carried 23 million passengers, had a fleet of 230 aircraft and employed 48,000 people. The merger cost British Airways US$750 million. USAir was financially weak and declared losses of US$173 million in 1991. Its debt in 1992 was evaluated at over US$2 billion. In contrast, since privatisation, British Airways has been very profitable and declared pre-tax profits of £285 million (US$427.5 million) in 1992.

Before the alliance between United and Lufthansa, the British Airways–USAir alliance was the largest conglomerate in the world and carried 78 million passengers a year on 669 aircraft to 339 destinations in 71 countries. Lord King, the now retired chairman of British Airways, described the partnership as a truly global air transport group. It has ensured its presence in the Asian market by buying 25 per cent of Qantas, the Australian carrier.

British Airways is also pursuing a strategy of concentration in Europe. In 1992, it acquired Dan Air, bought 49 per cent of Deutsche BA, 31 per cent of Air Russia and 49.9 per cent of TAT. The agreement with TAT stipulates that by 1997, BA will be allowed to increase its participation to 100 per cent. British Airways has successfully set up operations in France thanks to the European Commission which compelled Air France to sell its 35 per cent stake in TAT when it acquired UTA and Air Inter. It also acquired Dan Air outright, adding 39 aircraft to its fleet and gaining valuable and regular slots at London's Gatwick Airport.

In other regions of the world, particularly Asia, partnership rather than concentration is favoured. Asian companies benefit from an expanding market which allows them to implement strategies of internal development. Furthermore, their competitiveness can be attributed to using a relatively new fleet (the average age of their aircraft was 8.4 years in 1992), to excellent customer service (particularly Singapore Airlines, Thai International and Cathay Pacific) and to efficient security systems and low labour costs. These factors have allowed Asian companies to continue their own development despite the changing environment which has led to concentration in the United States and Europe.

Indeed, they successfully control their costs and have a comparative advantage over European and American airlines in insurance costs, labour costs and productivity. Their insurance premiums are low because the aircraft owned by Asian airline companies are relatively new and the quality of maintenance and of the training of personnel is very high. As a result of their financial strength, they participate fully in the current movement of air transport concentration.

However, this policy of acquisition comes up against the problems of non-tariff barriers which give access to the market. For example, until 1994, TAT had not been able to obtain authorisation to open routes departing from Orly airport on which Air France and Air Inter compete. It also comes up against financial problems created by the large losses suffered by USAir in the North American market.

☐ *Partnership agreements*

The objective of a partnership is to create competitive advantages for the partners by complementing each other's services and by achieving economy of scale, particularly in maintenance and marketing costs, while still keeping their independence.

Asian and European airlines particularly favour the partnership strategy, although, since 1993, American companies are also looking for alliances. Most agreements are struck in Europe in a pattern set by British Airways. Agreements can take different forms including equity participation by partners in each other's companies.

In order to compete internationally, European, Asian and American companies are looking to consolidate their networks by entering into commercial agreements. This has become known as the rise of the Airline Mega-Consortia. Table 5.11 shows the main alliances, mergers and partnerships that are currently in existence.

The alliance grouping together United and Lufthansa, formed in October 1993, is the largest consortium in the world. Lufthansa was be privatised in 1994 and United was keen to acquire shares. To quote Sir Colin Marshall, chairman of BA, '. . . without equity participation you can never be sure of a lasting alliance'.

The partner airlines also bring existing alliances into the consortium. United's allies include Thai Airways, Iberia, Emirates, Transbrazil, Air Canada, ALM Antillean, Aloha, Ansett, British Midland, China Southern and Cyprus Airways. Lufthansa has several separate alliances such as code sharing agreements with Adria Airways, Varig, Luxair and Austrian Airlines, a marketing alliance with Finnair and freight alliances with Japan Airlines and Korean Airlines.

Thus, airlines can be involved in several alliances, sometimes with different objectives. For instance, an airline may have a ground arrangement alliance with one company but a marketing and sales alliance with another. With the large consortia still being developed, it is unclear if previous agreements will survive. For instance, before the United alliance, Air France and Lufthansa were already cooperating on staff training and technical matters. However, Air France is the major partner in the Air France alliance (the Latin Group alliance) which groups together Sabena, Continental, Air Canada.

American Airlines is still looking for a major European partner to bring into its Eagle alliance. It already has a good footing in South Africa. Delta has teamed up with Swissair, Singapore Airlines and Varig (Brazil).

The Iberian Alliance includes Iberia, Aerolíneas Argentinas, TAP and Viasa. The strategic aim of this alliance is to dominate the Europe–South America routes.

The agreements can relate to several areas:

- *Merging of commercial activities* Swissair, SAS and Austrian Airlines have a commercial agreement which in effect merges their sales, reservation and passenger services.

Table 5.11 *Global alliances, mergers and partnerships*

Alliances, mergers and partnerships	Main airlines in alliance
The British Airways Alliance	British Airways US Air Qantas TAT Deutche BA Air Russia
The United–Lufthansa Alliance	United Airlines Lufthansa Thai Airways Emirates
The Air France Alliance	Air France Sabena Continental Air Canada
The Eagle Alliance	American Airlines South African Airlines Airlines of Britain Gulf Air Lot Canadian Airlines
The Delta Alliance	Delta Swissair Singapore Airlines Varig (Brazil)
The Iberian Alliance	Iberia Aerolíneas Argentinas TAP (Portugal) Viasa (Venezuela)

Source: Adapted from *Airline Business*.

- *The organisation of hubs* KLM has extended preferential arrangements and in some case takes equity participation in airlines that supply its long-haul network at its Amsterdam hub; these are known as feeder airlines. Agreements have been reached with NorthWest Airlines, Air Littoral and Air UK.
- *Joint management agreements for setting up ground handling at airports* An example of this type of agreement is the construction

Box 5.2   *A failed alliance – Alcazar*

Realising that survival could only be ensured by merging, the medium-sized European airlines attempted to set up the Alcazar alliance to rival British Airways and Lufthansa as well as the big American carriers. Economies of scales would have brought an estimated US$1.35 billion in savings for the loss-making European carriers. Amsterdam was to be the main hub and Swissair would have assumed the presidency of the alliance.

However, despite strenuous efforts for a successful accord, the merger talks failed because the partners could not agree on an American partner to operate the crucial North Atlantic trade. KLM already had a 20 per cent stake in NorthWest in which it had invested US$450 million and it was reluctant to break this alliance. Swissair pointed out that Delta Airlines, in which it owned a 5 per cent stake, was more financially secure and would be a safer partner. Agreement could not be reached and the alliance fell apart leading some analysts to say that an alliance with a North Atlantic carrier is far more important than between European carriers.

Table 5.12   *Alcazar (failed alliance)*

Scandinavian Airlines	$5.9 bn*
KLM	$4.6 bn
NorthWest Airlines	$8.1 bn
Swissair	$4.4 bn
Austrian Airlines	$1bn
Airlines of Britain	$700 mn
Martinair	$550 mn
Total sales	US$25.2 bn
Total passengers	86 mn

* Sales in 1992
Source: *Airline Business.*

SAS is still looking for a partner and there are rumours that it may still merge with KLM. Austrian Airlines is rumoured to be considering agreements with Delta and Swissair. Swissair, stronger financially than the other companies, is under less pressure to find a partner.

project funded by Japan Airlines, Lufthansa and Air France for a new terminal at New York's Kennedy airport.

- *Commercial representation agreements*   The objective of these is to capture market share.
- *Joint investment and operating expenditure agreements*   These include block purchase of aircraft to achieve economy of scale, joint

use of maintenance workshops, negotiated insurance contracts and shared services at stopovers around the world.

● *Agreements resulting in the set-up of holding groups*   Holding groups are responsible for strategic planning, marketing, sales and accounting.

● *Merging of reservation services to include code-sharing*   This very important agreement enables joint commercialisation between several countries, for instance British Airways and USAir, and KLM and NorthWest.

☐ *Diversification strategies*

The strategic objective of following a policy of diversification is to reduce the vulnerability of the air transport carrier to the vagaries of international tourism and business. Therefore, the policy of the airline companies is to have a presence in all industries producing and commercialising air transport, particularly in the international tourism sector where they pursue three main strategies:

1. The first strategy is to contribute to the development of international tourism. For example, KLM has increased the number of flights to long-haul destinations by its subsidiary companies Transvia (in which its owns 80 per cent of equity) and Martinair (20 per cent of equity). However, it is not directly involved in tourism activities, with the exception of the wholly owned Golden Tulip hotel chain, which services the business travel market. This policy has also been adopted by Alitalia, Swissair and its subsidiary company Balair who prefer to be active partners in tourism enterprises rather than competing with their own tourism companies.

2. Another strategy is vertical integration in the tourism sector. Some airline companies develop their own travel agencies, tour operators and hotel chains, to compete directly in the tourism sector. Air France owns the hotel chain Méridien, which has more than fifty high-capacity hotels located at the main stopover destinations of the company. Furthermore, Air France is well-established in the tour operation industry with TFI (Tourisme France International) (which it owns outright and which it has set up abroad) and with Sotair, in France. Air France owns 67 per cent of Sotair whose brands Jet Tours and Jumbo are regularly among the top five tour operators in France. This strategy is also pursued by SAS which groups all its tourism activities under the trademark SAS Tourism (in particular its tour operator Vingresol).

Several other airlines have diversified into tour operation. The incoming market is another important area for the airlines. Italiatour is an associate company of Alitalia and has been trading in the UK since 1988. It is one of the largest operators to Italy, totalling close to 100,000 passengers a year. Jetabout is owned by Qantas and offers packages to Australia, the South Pacific and North America. Caravela Tours is a subsidiary company of TAP Air Portugal and has been operating in the UK since 1982, specialising in Portugal, Madeira and the Azores. Their main advantage is that they can offer a variety of scheduled flights which are perceived to be of a higher quality and less likely to be delayed. The margins for these packages are high since often unsold scheduled seats are filled on routes the airlines have to fly anyway.

3. An example of the third strategy of diversification is the one adopted by British Airways. Its subsidiary company, British Airways Holidays, does not own any company in the tourism sector. It has a policy of entering into partnerships with tourism companies already established in markets around the world.

The strategy of integration is also followed by large tourism and financial groups who want to incorporate air transport in their tourism products. In these cases, the airline companies become part of the overall strategy of these groups. In France, the financial group Crédit Lyonnais has created integrated tourism products with the company AOM and the two leading companies hiring pleasure boats, Stardust Marine and ATM. The tour operator Nouvelles Frontières integrated the company Corsair into its tour-operating activities, particularly in order to develop new destinations like Polynesia. In Britain, the tour operator Thomsons owns its own airline, Britannia, which is Britain's second largest airline company with 39 aeroplanes and the world's largest charter airline. It also owns its own travel agency, Lunn Poly, which is also the largest travel agency in Britain (in 1990, 510 agencies).

Diversification strategies are not only confined to the tourism sector. Indeed, Air France also has subsidiaries in the land transport industry (Société Auxiliaire de Transports Terrestres), in the property sector (Société immobilière aéroportuaire) and the service sector (Promexport, Sofreavia services, Servair).

☐ *Privatisation strategies*

The objective behind the privatisation strategies adopted by airline companies is to implement market concentration plans and diversification programmes and to open up to international competition. The policy of many governments is to reduce the involvement of the public sector in the national economy. As a result, national airlines are being privatised with the aim of making them more competitive.

In fact, a 1994 report on the future of the European airline industry commissioned by the European Commission calls for further liberalisation and 'ultimate privatisation' as a solution to the industry's problems.

☐ The context and methods of privatisation

The national airline industry is of strategic importance to its country and traditionally experiences a great deal of government intervention. This explains why most privatisation programmes already completed or still in progress are usually partial, with the public sector retaining more than 50 per cent of equity in the company. In situations where there has been total privatisation, generally 50 per cent of the equity must come from citizens of the country concerned. Even in the United States, where all airline companies are private, foreign investors are only allowed a maximum of 25 per cent of the voting rights even if they own more than 25 per cent of the capital in the company.[4]

For privatisation to be successful certain economic and profitability conditions must be evaluated and actions taken. It is this evaluation and also the economic and political objectives of the country which will determine if the privatisation should be complete or partial. One major condition which is accelerating privatisation around the world is the policy of deregulation and liberalisation which is strongly supported by the United States who want to see their Open Skies policy extended to all markets in the world.

Each privatisation programme is subject to different legal and financial circumstances. This is a result of the individual characteristics and history of each airline and the legal and political traditions and the level of development of the financial markets involved with the privatisation.

Three methods of privatising companies are used in the airline industry:

- *Privatisation of the main company* This is the best method for privatising companies that are highly centralised. Normally, privatisation of subsidiary companies will follow as they are strictly controlled by the main company. For example, the privatisation of Air France would bring about the privatisation of the whole group.
- *Privatising subsidiary companies independently from the main company* This type of privatisation is the easiest to implement. It can also lead to the privatisation of the whole group, when the main

company has become a holding company transferring its assets to its subsidiaries. The privatisation of these subsidiary companies will gradually drain the finances of the main company. This method of privatisation has the advantage of gradually privatising the whole group, thus enabling it to adapt step by step to the new legal and economic environment.

● *Privatising the main company and its subsidiaries* This third method assumes the privatisation of all the companies in the group including those in which the main company has only a minority stake. However, this method of privatisation is very difficult to implement. Indeed, there are complex financial and legal aspects concerning multiple equity participation between subsidiary companies and the main company.

On some occasions, privatising one company or group of companies may lead to the privatisation of the whole industrial sector. In the United Kingdom, the privatisation of British Airways paved the way for a reorganisation of the whole air transport industry in Britain. British Airways has since acquired its main rivals, British Caledonian and Dan-Air, and diversified its activities to the airport and aerospace industries.

☐ Airline privatisation in Europe

The majority of European airline companies in the EU and in Central and Eastern Europe are following a policy of total or partial privatisation.

The first airlines to be privatised were British Airways in the United Kingdom and KLM in the Netherlands, who together now represent 31.5 per cent of the passenger-kilometre traffic of the whole of the AEA (Association of European Airlines). In fact, 58.5 per cent of passenger-kilometre traffic involve wholly and partially privatised companies or companies currently in the process of being privatised. These include Alitalia, Sabena and Lufthansa.

Since 1988, the private sector has grown from less than 10 per cent to 58.8 per cent.

☐ The privatisation of KLM

KLM was the first European airline to be privatised in a programme which started in 1986. At the time, KLM was a limited company quoted on the Dutch stock exchange and was in an ideal situation for privatisation. The equity participation of the company was shared with a majority private sector capital and a smaller but significant participation by the government. Being quoted on the stock exchange gave an accurate indication of the stock market value of the company.

KLM was privatised in four simultaneous operations:

- The purchase by the company of a large part of the shares owned by the government, which now owns only 39 per cent of KLM's registered capital;
- The immediate sale of these shares to a banking syndicate, appointed to put them on the market;
- The issue of 12 million new shares to increase the registered capital of the company. These shares were immediately sold to the banking syndicate along with the 3 million shares bought from the government;
- The sale of all the shares through a banking union.

☐ The privatisation of British Airways

British Airways is the largest airline company in Europe and one of the largest in the world after its acquisition of USAir in 1992.

The privatisation of British Airways in February 1987 is the largest privatisation programme ever of an airline company. All the government shares in the company, which amounted to £900 million, were transferred to the private sector.

It took seven years for the process of privatisation to be completed. This period was necessary to turn around the economic and, more importantly, the financial situation of British Airways and to promote a new corporate image. In fact, in 1981, the financial situation of the company was very worrying. After the second petrol crisis in 1979, profits declared by the British Airways Group fell by £90 million for the 1978–79 financial year, by £20 million during 1979–80 and the group declared a loss of £141 million in the 1980–81 financial year.

For privatisation to succeed, the financial problems of the company had to be resolved. British Airway shares had to be attractive to private investors. Lord King was appointed chairman of British Airways in February 1987 with the specific brief of turning BA into a profitable company. His first action was to introduce measures to increase productivity. The workforce was reduced by 15,400 employees, from 51,000 on 31 March 1981 to 35,600 in November 1983. From 1983, the remaining staff were offered a bonus system linked to the company's profits. The success of these policies raised staff productivity by 40 per cent between the financial years 1981–82 and 1985–86.

At the same time, a programme of modernisation and rationalisation of the fleet was implemented, in order to reduce costs.

British Airways successfully changed its corporate image by introducing training courses for its staff, ranging from customer service improvement courses for ground staff to lectures on the importance of understanding client needs, and this is an ongoing programme. In 1992, the largest business class lounge in the world was opened at Heathrow Airport.

These measures significantly improved British Airways' financial situation and its debt was reduced by 50 per cent. As a result, the privatisation of British Airways was successfully achieved. The transfer of shares to the private sector was organised by a public offer of shares on the British financial market as well as on foreign markets (the United States, Canada, Switzerland and Japan).

The share price (720 million shares at 125 pence each) was set by the government, which was influenced by the state of the financial market at the time. Thus, the price set was lower than the 130 pence per share suggested by financial experts.

There were certain conditions as to how the shares were put on the market:

- 10 per cent were reserved for the 40,000 employees and retired BA staff at a 10 per cent discount;
- 20 per cent were allocated to foreign investors in the United States, Canada, Switzerland and Japan with the possibility of reducing this proportion to 16 per cent if the offer was oversubscribed by individual British investors;
- 42 per cent were reserved for British institutional investors;
- 28 per cent were offered to the public.

This distribution of shares provided a nucleus of institutional shareholders and involvement in the company by the general public and British Airways employees as well as international interest.

The public offer of shares was a tremendous success and there were 7.8 billion requests by individual investors for a total number of 720.2 million shares on offer. Of British Airways employees, 94 per cent bought a total of 73 million shares. The number of shares for sale on the international market was reduced to 17 per cent of the total while 47 per cent were finally allocated to individual investors and 36 per cent to institutional investors.

The British Airways privatisation is a good example of a successful airline privatisation programme. Since then, by internal growth and the acquisition of British Caledonian and Dan Air in the United Kingdom, Deutsche BA, TAT and Air Russia in Europe and USAir in the United States, British Airways has succeeded in becoming the largest airline in the world.

☐ Other privatisation programmes in Europe

Table 5.13 shows public sector ownership of several airline companies in Europe, most of which are considering privatisation.

Most of the current privatisation programmes in Europe are being hindered by the financial problems suffered by airline companies since 1990.

☐ Privatisation programmes in other regions of the world

Between 1992 and 1994, there were eighteen airline privatisation programmes in other regions of the world: ten in Latin America, three in Africa and the Middle East and five in the Asia–Pacific region.

Latin America

- *Aerolíneas Argentinas*   The Argentine government owns just 5 per cent of the company in which Iberia has a majority stake.
- *Aeromexico*   The Mexican government retains just 20 per cent of the company's capital. Aeromexico is controlled by private capital (the Prevoisin Group with 60 per cent) and by its employees (20 per cent).

Table 5.13   *Public sector ownership of selected airline companies in Europe, 1992*

Company	Public sector capital	Country
Alitalia	84.9%	Italy
Air Malta	96.4%	Malta
Austrian Airlines	51.9%	Austria
Iberia	100.0%	Spain
Lufthansa	35.0%*	Germany
CSA	100.0%	The Czech Republic and Slovakia
Olympic Airways	100.0%	Greece
Sabena	88.0%	Belgium
TAP Air Portugal	100.0%	Portugal
THY Turkish Airlines	98.7%	Turkey

Note: * 1994 figures.
Source: Adapted from *Airline Business* (1992 and 1994).

- *Aeroperu* 70 per cent of the company is being sold to the private sector.
- *BWIA International* 20–30 per cent of the British West Indies Airways will be sold to the private sector.
- *LAB* The Bolivian government plans to sell 70 per cent of the company.
- *LanChile* The government owns 65 per cent of the capital through the Corfo company. However, SAS have acquired 35 per cent of the company.
- *Pluna (Uruguay)* 70 per cent of the company is being sold to the private sector.
- *Varig (Brazil)* The government has a 40 per cent share in the company and a programme is in place for the sale of part of the company to the employees.
- *Vasp (Brazil)* The government owns 30 per cent and the local government of the state of São Paulo controls 30 per cent of the capital.
- *Viasa (Venezuela)* Acquisition of 45 per cent by Iberia and 15 per cent by the Banco Provincial and the Sociedad Financiera Provincial. The state owns 40 per cent of the capital.

Africa and the Middle East

Most airlines in Africa and the Middle East are wholly owned by their governments and there are few privatisation projects under way.

- *Air Africa* A study has been commissioned to research the possibility of a partial privatisation of the airline. The member states own 78.99 per cent of the capital of the country and the Air France Group 15.75 per cent.
- *Kenya Airways* A partial privatisation project has been planned with 49 per cent of the company to be sold to the private sector once refinancing and reconstruction programmes have been set up.
- *Nigeria Airways* A partial privatisation programme is planned with the sale of 49 per cent of the company.
- *Royal Jordanian* A privatisation programme is being planned.
- *SAA* A privatisation programme will be started if the South African financial market is strong enough.

Asia–Pacific

Some of the largest airline privatisation programmes have been in the Asia–Pacific region. Japan Airlines was totally privatised in 1987 and

Singapore Airlines was partially privatised with the government retaining 54.13 per cent of the company shares. There are several other planned privatisation programmes in the region:

- *Airlanka*   A privatisation programme is being implemented.
- *China Airlines*   There is a plan to sell shares in the airline to national and foreign investors.
- *Pakistan International Airlines*   A partial privatisation project is being planned.
- *Qantas*   49 per cent of the Australian airline has been sold with British Airways acquiring 25 per cent of the shares.
- *Thai Airways International*   15 per cent of the company is being sold on the financial markets.

Privatisation of airline companies is an integral strategy in the development of air transport. The effects of deregulation on the air transport industry has been to multiply the number of privatisation programmes around the world as national airline companies develop concentration and merger strategies incompatible with the traditional public service role previously assigned to them. Usually, privatisation is the best strategy to allow airlines to react successfully to the changing market.

■ The role played by air transport in international tourism development

Air transport plays a central role in the distribution of international tourist arrivals. In 1990, it accounted for more than 40 per cent of all international arrivals in the world. This large volume can be attributed to mass low-priced air transport, using high-capacity aircraft. Between 1980 and 1990, passenger movements by air increased by more than 50 per cent while international tourist flows increased by 49 per cent. The growth in air transport and of international tourism flows is one of the basic characteristics of the current development of world tourism. This twofold expansion has, however, been accompanied by great structural upheavals.

Comparative international analysis of the air transport and tourism sector

The development of the international air transport market is characterised by a strong geographical concentration of air transport and international tourist flows, brought about by the stabilisation of charter traffic and the growing attraction of the Asia–Pacific region.

The sharp concentration of air transport and international tourist flows becomes particularly highlighted when the breakdown of international airline traffic is analysed according to route.

The demand for international air services is concentrated around three main poles: North America, Europe, and Japan and the new industrial countries of Asia. In 1990, air traffic in and between these three poles accounted for over 75 per cent of world passenger traffic.

To a large extent, this is due to international tourist flows. In 1990, North America, Europe and East and South-East Asia – according to WTO statistics – produced over 80 per cent of the world's international tourists.

Air routes between Europe and Africa are the sixth busiest in the world and traffic is considerably higher than between North and Central America and on South Pacific, Central and South Atlantic routes.

On the other hand, intra-Africa air traffic is very low, with only 3,946 million RPK in 1990 and an annual growth between now and the year 2000 expected to be 5.8 per cent below the world average. Air transport structures in Africa must urgently be adapted to meet demand, particularly from the tourism sector. In effect, the growth of demand for international air transport is closely linked with that of international tourism. According to WTO estimates, in 1990 there was a total of 426 million international tourist arrivals. Arrivals by air account for over 40 per cent of this total (in 1989, they accounted for 41 per cent).

Table 5.14 *Regional breakdown of scheduled traffic, 1981–90*

Percentage of total number of tonne-km performed by airlines with headquarters in each region	All services		International services		Domestic services	
	1990	1981	1990	1981	1990	1981
North America[1]	38.5	37.5	22.9	19.7	58.2	55.6
Europe	31.9	34.6	35.5	38.9	27.3	30.3
Asia and Pacific	19.8	16.5	28.2	24.8	9.2	8.0
Latin America and the Caribbean	4.7	5.4	5.6	6.7	3.5	4.0
Middle East	2.9	3.1	4.5	5.3	0.9	0.9
Africa	2.2	2.9	3.3	4.6	0.9	1.2
All contracting states	100	100	100	100	100	100

[1] Canada and the United States only.
Source: ICAO.

Overall development is broadly influenced by international tourist flows. In the 1980s, developing countries increased their share of world arrivals and accounted for 21.9 per cent in 1989 with 88.3 million arrivals. Consequently, the current growth of world tourism may be regarded as a structural factor which particularly favours air transport.

Between 1971 and 1990, North American airlines increased their share of world international traffic from 19.7 to 22.9 per cent, and Asian and Pacific companies from 24.8 to 28.2 per cent. On the other hand, the share of European companies fell from 38.9 to 35.5 per cent, and of African companies from 4.6 to 3.3 per cent.

Problems of equipment and infrastructure associated with international tourism development

Aircraft, equipment and infrastructure have to be constantly updated to cope with the growth of the international tourism industry. As a result, many problems arise:

- *Adapting the fleet to the strong demand for tourism during the high season*   Adding jumbo jets to the fleet does not solve the difficulties caused by too rigid a supply and a very elastic demand. One solution to this problem is to hire and use aircraft from companies in other countries, even in other regions of the world. This is, however, a very expensive option and can raise several problems. For instance, the welcome and the in-flight service are not always consistent with what the tourist expects from the company it has bought the services from. A hypothetical example is that of a German airline hiring an aircraft from a French or Spanish company which provides a non-German-speaking cabin crew for the flight.
- *Ground and station equipment and hospitality services*   Many Third World countries cannot accept night flights because they lack ground and station equipment or staff.
- *Aircraft maintenance and insufficient infrastructure*   Certain airline companies and certain airports, particularly in the Third World, are not able to provide adequate guarantees of security to satisfy insurance companies and, consequently, they are not insured. In these circumstances, they are not used by tourism organisations and therefore do not contribute to international tourism development.
- *Air fare tariffs*   The fares charged by airline companies directly influence international tourism flows. International tourism develop-

ment is hampered because airlines in some areas in the world (Africa, for instance) suffer from high operating costs resulting from their low productivity. In contrast, South East Asian airline companies have very high productivity and succeed in keeping their prices low.

While some countries and regions apply protectionist policies which keep the prices high, others have an Open Skies policy to encourage competition and keep prices low. Several countries allow a certain amount of competition but still regulate the industry to ensure that prices remain relatively high. This is normally to prevent the arrival of too many tourists, particularly if their presence is resented by the local population.

Available and efficient transport structures are key conditions for the development of international tourism. Air transport, even if not the predominant mode of transport, is vital to countries far from generating markets, the medium- and long-haul destinations. Restrictive regulation of the market has in many cases impeded tourism development. Certainly, by favouring monopoly or near-monopoly situations and by limiting competition, it has resulted in high tariffs. Unfortunately, this situation still exists in several regions of the world.

The deregulation of the air transport industry has created considerable upheaval, first in the United States and on routes to North America, then on all international routes. By focusing the process of deregulation on free access to the market, the industry has become very competitive with many new companies entering the market. As a result, prices have substantially fallen and many countries now have the opportunity of becoming important tourism destinations, even those which are geographically far from the major generating markets. However, the way air transport adapts to the requirements of international tourism largely depends on the strategic objectives of the airline companies. Alliances and mergers are creating new forms of concentration which create additional constraints to the development of certain tourism destinations. Accordingly, it is important to find ways of encouraging collaboration and cooperation between the tourism sector and the air transport sector. In particular, issues associated with the commercialisation and the computerised distribution of tourism products and flights must be studied in detail. For instance, will the development of global distribution systems (GDS) bring opportunities for the tourism sector or will hotel and tourism companies become dependent on the strategic aims of the airline companies?

These concerns determine the sales and marketing strategies of companies selling tourism products.

References

1. Caucal, R. 'Vers une Nouvelle Approche des Relations Entre le Tourisme International et Compagnies Aériennes'. Thesis, Caen, June 1983.

2. Comité des Sages, European Commission Report on the Privatisation of the European Airline Industry, 1994.

3. Vellas, F. *Le Transport Aérien*, Paris, Economica, 1993.

4. Rapp, L. and Vellas, F. *Airline Privatisation in Europe*, ITA Report and Studies, 1993.

Further reading

Baily, E. Graham, D. and Kaplan, D. *Deregulating the Airlines*. Cambridge, Mass. MIT Press, 1985.

Banfe, C. F. *Airline Management*. Englewood Cliffs, Prentice-Hall, 1992.

Chew, J. 'Transport and Tourism in the Year 2000', *Tourism Management*, 8(2), pp. 83–5, 1987.

Doganis, R., *Flying on Course*. London: Routledge, 1981.

Gialloreto, L. *Strategic Airline Management – The War Begins*. London: Pitman, 1988.

Heath, *Airline Economics*. Lexington, MA: Lexington Books, 1982.

Shaw, S. *Airline Marketing and Management*. London: Pitman, 1990.

■ *Chapter 6* ■

Selling and Marketing the Tourism Product

The tourism product market: definition of the tourism package; the
classification of tourism packages; economic characteristics of tourism
products
Tour operators: definition; tour operators in the world;
Packaging the tourism product: market research; negotiating contracts with
different suppliers of tourism services; designing the product; negotiating
the package; finalising international contracts
Selling and marketing the product: the brochure; marketing by travel
agencies; advertising and promotion
Global distribution systems: definitions; the main GDSs; the problems of GDS
regulation; strategies to improve the use of GDSs in developing countries

In order to achieve commercial success, tourism product designers and
distributors offer products specifically adapted to the needs of the
consumer. These are sold at competitive prices and should be perceived
to have a good quality–price ratio. The tour operator packaging and
selling tourism products should enjoy a high reputation and an image of
quality. Success depends on an expert knowledge of the market, skilful
packaging of the products and an ability to commercialise them.

■ The tourism product market

The tourism product market is composed of goods and services designed to
satisfy the demand for holidays and business travel. Tour operators
develop packages that are either sold directly though their own distribution
outlets or through travel agencies (retailers) on a commission basis.

□ *Definition of tourism package*

Travel packages are organised trips following predetermined and detailed
programmes involving several tourism services. The packages are sold in
advance at a fixed price.

- *Preliminary organisation* Tourism products are developed and established well before client demand is actually expressed. The tour operator will choose the destination, the means of transport, the accommodation and the level of escorting and guidance included in the package before offering the product to the public. Tours can be fully escorted with guides and tour managers present throughout the holiday or limited to company representatives meeting clients on arrival and assisting with departure at the end.
- *Services provided* At the most basic level, the service provided may just consist of the holiday stay. More complete products offer several other services. These include return transport, escorting, transfers, accommodation, provision of meals, entertainment and insurance. Certain companies offering holidays with a particular focus (for example, cultural tourism and health tourism) also provide specific services.
- *Fixed prices* The price of the product is set in advance and usually payment is settled before the journey begins. For certain products (holiday clubs, mixed formulas in which only parts of the tourism components are provided) credit payment is becoming increasingly frequent.

□ *The classification of tourism packages*

There are two types of tourism packages: the 'all-inclusive' holiday and the 'mixed-formula'.

□ The 'all-inclusive' package

This is the traditional package in which the operator provides all the services. Products in this category include full-board holidays, organised tours and cruises.

- *Full-board holidays* 'Full-board' holidays involve return travel arrangements and transfers, accommodation and all meals. This type of holiday has mainly been offered by hotels at resorts, although recently 'holiday clubs' such as Club Méditerranée are providing similar services as well as including entertainment and sports facilities.

  There are several variations on this type of holiday. Products are being developed offering half-board (breakfast and dinner included), breakfast only and the increasingly popular self-catering holidays in apartment hotels.

- *Organised tours* Organised tours usually combine accommodation with excursions. They can be on a full-board, half-board or breakfast-only basis. Certain tours are fully escorted by tour managers while others may just include travel and entrance fees. Transportation during the tours is either by coach, by plane or, more rarely, by train.
- *Cruises* Cruises are all-inclusive packages. The development of this type of tourism product is compensating for the decline in the number of sea-travelling passengers. There are fewer than 200 cruise ships in the world (in 1994) sailing mainly in the Caribbean and in the Mediterranean. They can cruise the whole year round as the tourist season in the two major zones falls at different times.

☐ The 'mixed formula'

These are packages which offer transport to and from the destination with other services. 'Fly–drives' combine flights and hire-car at the destination. 'Flight + hotel' packages include flights to the destination and hotel vouchers which can be used at a number of tourist resorts and sites. Many innovative products are being developed offering travel and accommodation with specialised services for special interest groups: sport holidays (skiing, golf, motorcycling, fishing, etc.); holidays based around cultural themes (art, history, archaeology, etc.); holidays including health treatments at health and spa resorts; adventure travel and holidays 'off the beaten track'; incentive and conference travel, etc.

☐ *Economic characteristics of tourism products*

Tourism products have three main economic features: inelasticity, complementarity and heterogeneity.

☐ Inelasticity

Tourism products are *inelastic* because they do not adapt well to changes in short- and long-term demand. In contrast to tangible goods, services such as hotel nights and airline seats cannot be stocked. These products are said to be *perishable*. Short-term increases and falls in demand for a product will have little influence on its price. It is the long-term fluctuations which determine the composition of the product and its selling price. Tourism products are dependent on existing superstructures

Box 6.1   *Cruising: a new package holiday for the 1990s*

The cruising holiday, once exclusively for the wealthy, is set to become the package holiday of the 1990s. World passenger volume has been on a steady upward trend since 1980 when it stood at under 1.5 million. In 1993, it had increased to 4.5 million. Forecasts show that the growth rate is accelerating and estimates for 1996 are 6.25 million. The sector's value in 1993 was US$6 billion.

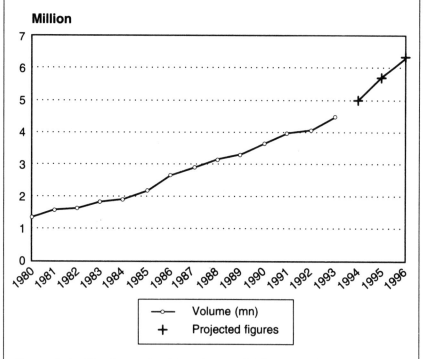

Source: Cruise Lines International Association and Solomon Brothers.

Figure 6.1   *The cruise industry: world passenger volume, 1980–96*

Three main factors are behind the changes in the industry:

- Increased capacity and larger ships
- A changing consumer profile
- New destinations

Increased capacity and larger ships

There were 120 cruise ships in service in 1985. By 1994, fleet capacity had increased 55 per cent to 175 ships. The largest cruise line company, Carnival Cruise Lines founded in the USA in 1972, operates 21 ships.

The largest cruise line companies in the world are Carnival with 31,159 berths (21 ships); Royal Caribbean, 17,727 berths (11 ships); P & O Princess, 15,188 berths (12 ships); Klosters, 14,474 berths (17 ships); Costa, 8,609 berths (8 ships); Chandris, 6,684 berths (6 ships) and Cunard, 5,376 berths (7 ships). P & 0, the third largest cruise line company, is spending US$1 billion between 1994 and 1997 to add three new ships to its fleet. Royal Caribbean, the second largest company, is also expanding its fleet.

A changing consumer profile

The cruising sector owes its sustained growth during the recession of the early 1990s to its traditional clientele: the over 50s. Indeed, this age group, less affected by the economic downturn, continued enjoying this type of holiday. However, the market is changing. With new capacity coming into the market, margins are under threat. Because of high running costs, profitability depends on occupancy and price levels. Discounting to encourage early booking is now becoming a norm to secure occupancy. As a result, the volume of passengers has increased dramatically. For instance, British passenger numbers trebled between 1986 and 1995 to 264,000. New entrants in the industry are directing their products to specific target groups. The Walt Disney Corporation is introducing cruises aimed at the family market. Airtours, the second largest tour operator in the UK, following the example of Carnival in the USA, is offering cruises at budget prices, thus attracting a younger market. In 1994, Airtours spent US$30 million on a cruise ship and offers 7 day cruises in the Canaries for as little as £399 (including flight to and from the UK). With the average cost of its other cruises at £1,500, Airtours has introduced a whole new concept to the UK market: the budget package cruise.

New destinations

The main cruising destinations are the Caribbean and the Gulf of Mexico (particularly for the American market which is the world's largest market) as well as the Mediterranean. The growth of long-haul travel is also reflected in the number of new cruising itineraries on offer such as the Far East, Alaska and the South Pacific Islands. This greater choice of destinations is a significant factor in the growing popularity of cruising holidays.

at destinations such as hospitality facilities, transport and accommodation. The economic crisis of the 1980s resulted in a structural change in the pattern of demand for hotel accommodation. While demand for hotels in the three-star category declined, demand for one- and two-star hotels increased. Hotels in the four- and five-star categories, especially the large hotel chains, continued to enjoy high occupancy from an international clientele benefiting from a favourable exchange rate.

☐ Complementarity

The tourism product is not just one single service. It is composed of several *complementary* sub-products. Production of the overall service and the quality of the service is dependent on the components complementing each other. A shortcoming in one of the sub-products will undermine the final product. This remains one of the major difficulties in tourism production.

☐ Heterogeneity

The tourism product is said to be *heterogeneous* because it is virtually impossible to produce two identical tourism services. There will always be a difference in quality even if the nature of the proposed service remains constant. This heterogeneity allows the possibility of a certain amount of substitution within the different sub-products. However, the resulting product will never be exactly the same. Substituting one hotel for another, even if they are of the same category, will create a different experience and produce a different final product. The experience can also vary within the same hotel. Rooms sizes are rarely the same, they have different window views and different situations within the hotel (for example near noisy lifts). Variations in transport affect the final product. Aeroplanes may be more or less full, with different levels of in-flight service, older coaches may be less comfortable and trains may be cancelled or their timetables changed at the last minute.

■ Tour operators

Tour operators design and sell travel packages. They are most firmly established in the UK, the USA and Germany. This industrial sector is also rapidly developing in other European countries and in Japan. In contrast to travel agencies, tour operators are large national and sometimes international companies.

☐ *Definition*

Tour operators are commercial tourism firms specialising in the manufacture of travel packages. They are quite different from travel agents whose main activity is to sell and market tourism products. Tour operators are wholesalers and travel agencies are retailers. Most tour operators also acquire the legal status of travel agencies or associations who package and sell tourism products to their members.

☐ *Tour operators in the world*

☐ Overview of Europe's largest tour operators

Germany has the largest tour operators in Europe with five companies in the top ten European companies ranked according to their annual turnover. The German tour operator TUI has by far the largest turnover (2,590 million ecus in 1992), followed by the British operator Thomsons (1,623 million ecus). The other large German operators are NUR, ranked third (1,220 million ecus); LTU, fourth (1,206 million ecus); DER, seventh (1,056 million ecus) and ITS, ninth (893 million ecus).

Kuoni of Switzerland, the fifth largest operator (1,190 million ecus), specialises in long-haul travel and is well-implanted in other countries, particularly Britain and France. The largest Scandinavian company is NRT Nordisk from Sweden and is the eighth largest operator in Europe. France is represented by Club Méditerranée (sixth, 1,122 million ecus) and Nouvelles Frontières (eleventh).

☐ Tour operators in the United Kingdom

The United Kingdom pioneered the concept of tour operation in the nineteenth century. The UK is one of the largest producers of packages in the world with nearly 10 million sold each year. There are many companies involved in packaging tourism products and marketing them to the general public. As a result, tour operation is now a highly competitive industry.

The competitive nature of the business has prompted the larger operators in Britain to secure market share by using a variety of tactics. Consequently, many smaller operators have suffered and some have disappeared. Several have overstretched themselves by making mistakes in their forecasting, committing themselves to too much transport and accommodation capacity which they have been unable to sell. Others have been involved in discounting and price wars which have left them too weak to compete.

In 1991, the larger tour operators in Great Britain were involved in a serious scramble for market share which followed cutting the selling price of their products to the barest minimum. Three major operators emerged

from the vicious price wars which ended with the demise of the second largest operator, the International Leisure Group. This has resulted in margins being squeezed. In 1993, the average profit margin in the industry was 5 per cent. Thomson and Airtours survived on 4 per cent, while Owners Abroad's yield was just 2 per cent.

In 1994, Thomson controlled 34 per cent of the market, Owners Abroad (renamed First Choice in 1994) 12 per cent, Airtours 18 per cent and Cosmos 7 per cent. Together they sold more than 70 per cent of packages in Britain.

Price wars have been the scourge of tour operation in the UK since the 1970s and many of the largest companies have fallen in this volatile business. As a result, the structure of the industry is forever changing (see Table 6.1).

British tourists are now aware of the strategies used by tour operators to entice them to consume products. They know now that they should wait for bargains and discounts and book late, and they expect very high standards at very low prices. Normally, by March of each year, tour operators should have sold 60 per cent of products. Now, they are only selling 20 per cent. People wait longer and operators have to reprice their holidays in January. The 1992 summer season ended up with 1.7 million seats-worth of over-capacity. By mid-season 1994, there were more than 2.5 million holidays unsold despite a 15 per cent rise in sales on 1993. This resulted in a price war launched in June 1994 for 1995. The major tour operators were discounting 15 per cent off the brochure price before the brochures were even launched.

Table 6.1   *The changing profile of the tour operator market in the UK*

Rank	1972	1987	1990*	1991
1	Clarksons	Thomson	Thomson	Thomsons (3,015,269[†])
2	Thomson	Intasun, ILG	ILG Travel	Owners Abroad (1,621,404)
3	Sunair	Horizon	Redwing	Airtours (827,500)
4	Horizon	Skytours	Horizon	Yugotours[!] (340,000)
5	Cosmos	BA Holidays	Airtours	Iberotravel (284,100)
6	Global	Wings	Falcon	Best Travel (237,264)
7	Blue Cars	Airtours	Kuoni	Unijet (195,750)
8	Lunn Poly	Best Travel	Best Travel	Cosmos Air (164,000)
9	4S	Yugotours	Yugotours	Aspro Travel (107,043)
10	Lyons	Cosmos Air	Shearings	The Air Travel Group (100,313)

* 1990 rank is based on turnover, all other years based on passengers carried
[†] Number of packages sold (1991–1992)
[!] Due to the current problem in the Balkans, Yugotours is not operating
Source: Authors, taken from various sources (ABTA, Mintel).

Thomson travel group

Thomson Holidays, the largest tour operator in Britain and one of the largest in the world, is owned by the Canadian group, Thomson Corporation.

The company was launched in 1965 by the independent British operator Skytours. It was then acquired by the Canadian media group, Thomson Corporation, along with the air charter company Britannia Airways, and immediately merged with three other British tour operators (Riviera Holidays, Gaytours and Luxitours) to become Thomson Skytours.

In 1972, Thomson Skytours became Thomson Holidays after the acquisition of the travel agency group Lunn Poly. United under one banner, the three activities (tour operator, airline, travel agency) enjoyed seventeen years of continuous growth.

In 1988, Thomson Holidays signed the largest contract ever seen in the British tourism industry and acquired Horizon Holidays, based in Birmingham. Horizon was then the third largest tour operator in the United Kingdom after Thomson and the International Leisure Group (ILG) and owned three other companies: Wings (long-haul operators), OSL (villa rentals) and HCI (family holiday clubs). Horizon Holidays also owns a charter airline company, Orion. The acquisition was approved by the Monopolies Commission and Horizon was integrated into Thomson Holidays and Orion into Britannia.

By now the current structure of Thomson was already apparent with the three divisions: Thomson Tour Operation, Britannia Airways and Lunn Poly. In 1994, these three divisions are the largest companies in the United Kingdom in their respective sectors.

The acquisition of Horizon was largely motivated by the fierce competition between Thomson and its rival ILG. In 1984, Thomson controlled 19 per cent of the overseas package tour market with ILG at 10 per cent and Horizon Holidays at 7 per cent. By 1988, the gap had been significantly reduced with Thomson now controlling 29.3 per cent, ILG 24.8 per cent and Horizon 12 per cent. Thomson's decision to buy Horizon confirmed its leading position in the British tour operation industry by securing 40 per cent of the market. However, because of the strong competition in the industry, profits on each packages were often less than £1 and the cost of acquiring Horizon had been very high. In 1989, Thomson registered a large loss.

In 1990, the group was forced to introduce drastic cost-cutting measures. It also reduced the number of holidays offered: the 3.1 million packages sold in 1989 represented a drop of 31 per cent compared to 1989. Thomson's share of the market dropped to 30 per cent but the average price per customer increased by 17 per cent. As a result, Thomson registered a large profit in 1990.

Since then, the situation has further developed. ILG folded in 1990, leaving Thomson the undisputed leader in the British market, with a forecasted 7 per cent annual growth in sales for the next five years and profit margins increasing from 1 or 2 per cent to 3 or 4 per cent.

Thomson is also supported by its subsidiary companies Lunn Poly and Britannia.

Lunn Poly was acquired by Thomson in 1972. In 1983, it had just 50 agencies. By 1994, there were over 500 which take 20 per cent of summer bookings in Great Britain.

Since 1988, when it bought 275 new agencies nationwide, Lunn Poly has become the largest distribution network in the United Kingdom. Based in Leamington Spa, in the Midlands, it employs 2,800 people. It mainly sells tourism leisure products and its business travel sales are virtually non-existent. Without relaxing on its traditional product, Lunn Poly is also specialising in more targeted products such as cruises, the domestic market and flight-only travel with some success. Indeed, sales in these sectors have increased by 55 per cent, 27 per cent and 70 per cent respectively.

To remain the leading company in the market, Lunn Poly has pursued two strategies: higher profitability and higher quality. To this end, it has developed training structures for its personnel and signed an agreement with Istel, who supply the main computerised distribution system for tour operators. Istel terminals have been installed in 75 per cent of Lunn Poly's points of sale. The travel agencies can now reserve packages offered by many tour operators (including Thomson) from the Istel screen in real time.

Britannia, the airline branch of Thomson, was created in 1962. By 1993, it was carrying 7.64 million passengers and was the second largest airline in Great Britain after British Airways. Approximately 80 per cent of its passengers are Thomson clients. In fact, Britannia is careful that the occupancy should not rise above this level.

In 1988, Thomson acquired Orion, the charter airline branch of Horizon Holidays. Its two Airbus A-300 were immediately sold but the seven Boeing 737–300 were integrated into Britannia's fleet, thus increasing its capacity by 40 per cent.

However, the economic recession in Great Britain has affected the company and there was a fall in profits in 1990. Its traffic also fell from 7 million passengers in 1989 to 6.2 million in 1990. In an effort to raise its profitability, it restructured, reducing its workforce by 220.

After an experiment in the scheduled airline business, Britannia returned to charter operation, keeping just two scheduled lines, Luton–Belfast and Athens–Gatwick. In 1994, Britannia operated a fleet of 36 aircraft, mainly Boeing 737–200s.

☐ Tour operators in Germany

Germany is the main European market for package tours. It also has the greatest tour operator concentration with two main companies: TUI (Touristik Union International) and NUR (Neckermann und Reisen) producing over 50 per cent of total German sales. Unlike British tour operators who belong to firms solely dedicated to tourism or to transport, German tour operators are subsidiaries of large commercial retailers, banks, work councils, trade unions and associations of travel agencies.

The production of packages is extremely concentrated with TUI claiming 33 per cent of the market and NUR 18 per cent. TUI is a holding founded in 1968. It is composed of an association of independent tour operators and large travel agencies. It was formed to compete against the tourism branches of the major department stores who benefited from an extensive distribution network. NUR was founded in 1963 by the department store Neckermann und Reisen and then was acquired by the Karstad chain. TUI is now the most successful tour operator in the world. This is because it offers a wide choice of destinations (over 4000 resorts) and has a very extensive brochure and catalogue distribution system (over 20 million copies of 30 different brochures). More than 2.7 million people travel with TUI providing a turnover of 5 billion DM.

The structure of TUI arises from certain events that took place well before 1968, the official date of TUI's founding. In 1956, two tour operators, Scharnow (based in Hannover) and Touropa (Munich), became associated. The following year, a third tour operator, Hummel Reisen, joined the group. In 1962, the Monopolies Commission allowed them to operate joint programmes based on railway products. In 1966, this was extended to products using air transport. Consequently, Scharnow and Touropa consolidated their collaboration. A year later, in 1967, the two tour operators took equity participation in each other and integrated Hummel Reisen into their operations. That same year, Dr Tigges Fahrten, specialising in educational travel, associated with the trio. As a result, TUI was created.

Thus, TUI originated from the merging of three main tour operators: Touropa, Scharnow and Hummel Reisen.

● *Touropa* Touropa was created in 1948 by the travel agencies Dr Degener, Deutsches Reisebüro DER, Hapag-Lloyd and Amtliches Bayerisches Reisebüro (ABR). Today, these companies (apart from Degener) are still partners of TUI. Initially, Touropa offered train tours, then diversified into cruises, before selling its first products in 1964 using charter flights.

- *Scharnow*   Scharnow was created in 1953 by Wilhelm Scharnow, a travel agent from Bremen, Hanns-Albrecht Sieffert from the Walter Kahan Reisbüro (Bielefeld), Reisebüro Bangeman (Hannover) and several other travel agents. Convinced that the two Germanys would be soon reunited, the tour operator decided to establish its head office in Hannover because of its central position. Like Touropa, Scharnow first sold train journeys before offering in 1956 its first flights to Sicily, Majorca and Italy. In 1962, Scharnow developed its first charter series to Majorca, Tunisia and the Costa del Sol, carrying 6,139 passengers in the first year. The size of its market increased spectacularly to 250,000 in 1972 and 636,000 in 1973.
- *Hummel Reisen*   The company was created in 1953 by travel agencies attached to two newspapers: *Die Welt* and *Hamburger Abendblatt*. Their other partners were the travel agency Lührs (also from Hamburg) and Reisebüro Strickrodt (Hannover). Like the two previous companies, it first specialised in train journeys in which it subsequently became the specialist within TUI.
- *Dr Tigges Fahrten*   Dr Tigges Fahrten was founded in 1928 at the very beginning of organised travel by Dr Hubbert Tigges and his wife Maria. The objective of the company was to offer educational trips to Europe. In 1934, they sent a group of 37 Germans to Majorca. Tigges also specialised in pilgrimages to Rome, Lourdes and Fatima. It started programmes using air transport from 1954.

Once established, TUI acquired several other companies like:

- *Transeuropa*   Created in 1955, this tour operator was acquired in 1968 by the owner of the mail order firm Quelle, Gustav Schickedanz, who had been offering budget travel since 1962. In 1971, Quelle associated with the department store Karstadt to launch Transeuropa Reisen which became the third largest German tour operator. The next year, Transeuropa was bought by TUI in exchange for a 17 per cent participation for Quelle and Karstadt in TUI. Transeuropa was positioned as the budget travel specialist registering the highest sales in the TUI group. When Karstadt decided to acquire the mail order company Neckermann, the Monopolies Commission insisted that it separate from TUI. It then came under the control of the competing group, Horten AG.
- *Airtours International (Frankfurt)*   This company was launched in 1967 by the travel agency groups DER, ABR and Hapag-Lloyd and by Airtour Flugreisen (Düsseldorf). Backed by Lufthansa, it used scheduled fights. In 1970, TUI bought Airtours and integrated it completely in 1973.

- *Seetours International (Frankfurt)* This company was founded in 1960 by Holland American Line and its German agent, Alf Pollak. It is the largest cruising company in the German market. In 1969, it became a partner with TUI.

In 1989, TUI published its financial results for the first time: 20 million DM for a turnover of 3.2 billion DM, a 1.6 per cent fall. This amounted to a 60 per cent drop in performance. To redress the situation, TUI decided that the workforce should be streamlined. To achieve this, 172 jobs disappeared (although not through compulsory redundancy) and the commercial strategies were reviewed. In April 1990, TUI decided that it should not position itself as a general tour operator, but rather as a grouping of specialist operators. The brands Touropa, Scharnow, Transeuropa, Hummel and Dr Tigges disappeared to be replaced by brands based on actual destinations. TUI is used as the general name of the company rather than the names of the founding companies. Now, publicity and promotion can be concentrated on marketing the destinations rather then on promoting company brandnames. TUI publishes seven brochures for different winter destinations, fourteen for summer destinations and eleven specialist brochures, in total 25 brochures. To inform travel agents and the general public of the changes in the company, it organised a campaign which included visits to distributors, familiarisation trips and events designed to distribute information.

Another strategic decision was to develop its participation in the hotel industry. Through the Robinson Club (the German equivalent of Club Méditerranée) and Iberhotel, TUI already owned 45,000 beds. In 1990, a new department, headed by Christian Windfuhr (ex-vice-president of Holiday Inn in the Far East), was created, exclusively concerned with this sector.

The restructuring appears to have been successful. TUI launched a programme to foster the loyalty of their clientele and these measures have resulted in an increase in sales. In 1990, TUI had 2,000 employees for 6 million clients (groups and individuals).

☐ Tour operators in France

Despite recent rapid growth, the tour operator sector in France is smaller than in other European countries. Club Méditerranée is the one company to be strongly represented in foreign markets, the USA in particular. There are 300 tour-organising companies in France employing more than 20,000 people for approximately 1,500,000 clients. The main operators are Club Méditerranée, Nouvelles Frontières, Sotair, Fram, Look Voyages and

---

Box 6.2 *The TUI group*

- **Tour operation**
  In Germany:
  Wolters Reisen, specialist to Scandinavia (100 per cent ownership);
  Take Off, low-cost last-minute reservations (100 per cent);
  Seetours International, cruises (75 per cent);
  Air Conti, air tour programmes (55.9 per cent).
  Abroad:
  Terra Reisen International, Austria (100 per cent);
  Ambassador Tours, Spain (77 per cent);
  Touropa, Austria (50 per cent);
  Chorus, France (40 per cent);
  Arke, the Netherlands (40 per cent).

- **Hotels**
  Club Robinson (Germany): 16 clubs, two hotel-clubs and a lodge: a total
  of 9,478 beds (100 per cent);
  Iberotel (Spain): 35 hotels, 19,000 beds (100 per cent);
  Dorfhotels + Bauderdorfer (Austria): 4 villages, one village-hotel (100 per
  cent);
  Grecotel (Greece): 7 hotels, 4,964 beds (50 per cent);
  Riu (Spain): 22 hotels, 9,309 beds (49 per cent).

- **Ground operators**
  Dr Degener Reisebüro (100 per cent);
  Airtour Greece (90 per cent);
  Ultramar Express (77 per cent;)
  Pollman's Tours and Safaris Ltd (51 per cent);
  Tantur (50 per cent);
  Holidays Services (50 per cent);
  Viajes Isla Blanca (30 per cent).

Paquet for cruises. Several associations and new travel organisers have also entered the market with new travel formulas (flight + services of a representative at the airport only or adventure trekking tours).

However, faced with the competition from German and British tour operators, the top three French tour operators share just 30 per cent of the national market whereas the top two British companies have more than 60 per cent of their national market.

This is why, under the auspices of certain financial establishments (Caisse de Dépôts et Crédit Lyonnais, in particular) various important legal and financial associations have been formed, ranging from cooperation agreements (Sotair–Fram–SNCF) to complete integration (Club Aquarius and the airline companies Air Outre-Mer, Air Liberté and

Minerve in the Club Méditerranée and Wagon-lits et Tourisme in the hotel group Accor).

French tour operators are developing vertical integration policies particularly with the air transport sector (Corsair and Nouvelles Frontières, and Air Liberté and Look Voyages). Some airline companies are also integrating with other sectors, for instance, Air France acquired the operator Go Voyages in 1993 and Air Inter has launched its own tour operator.

☐ Tour operators in Switzerland, the Netherlands and Scandinavia

Tour operators in the Netherlands, Switzerland and Scandinavia have a very high penetration rate in their respective markets. As much as 40 per cent of the Swedish population buy package tours from Swedish tour operators. This strong demand for international travel is due to several factors: the high income enjoyed by the residents of these countries (Switzerland has the highest per capita income in the world); their geographical situation necessitating air transport for short sunshine holidays (Scandinavian countries) and a supply particularly well-adapted to the needs of the market (the Netherlands).

Table 6.2 *The largest tour operators in France*

Company	Turnover (in millions of French francs)	Net profit (in millions of French francs)
1. Club Méditerranée	7,597	409.00
2. Nouvelles Frontières	3,608	23.90
3. Sotair	2,030	8.30
4. Voyages Fram	2,000	47.00
5. Chorus	1,140	22.00
6. Voyages Conseil	807	−16.60
7. Kuoni France	663	3.70
8. Voyage du Monde	599	4.80
9. Mondial Tours	520	−2.40
10. Frantour Voyages	490	−
11. Asia	275	4.30
12. Transtour	258	0.28
13. Hervouët International	238	14.70
14. Planète/Akiou	234	0
15. Pacha Tours	230	0.70

Source: *Echo Touristique*, 1991.

In these countries, the package tour market is very concentrated. The top three operators in Holland (HIT Holland International, Arke Reisen and Neckermann Holland) cover over 50 per cent of the market. In Switzerland, there is an even stronger concentration with Kuoni, Hotelplan, Airtour and Imhog accounting for 70 per cent of package tour sales. In Sweden, Vigresor, Atlas, Spies and Reso supply more than 70 per cent of the packages sold in the country. The success of these tour operators is attributed to the quality of the services they provide. Kuoni now exports part of its products to markets in neighbouring countries.

☐ Tour operators in the United States and Canada

Packages holidays offered by North American tour operators are mainly to domestic destinations (70 per cent): Florida, California, Hawaii, Puerto Rico and Quebec. International travel is mostly to the Caribbean, Europe and Latin America. The largest operators in the United States are American Express, Thomas Cook, Caravan Tours and Gateway Holidays, and in Canada, Canadian Pacific and Tour Montroyal.

☐ Tour operators in Japan

The production of package tours in Japan only really developed in the late 1960s. This development is hampered by short annual leave and the low proportion of trips taken abroad. Despite this, international travel is increasing very fast with 14 million trips taken in 1993. The most important tour operators in Japan are Japan Travel Board, Taipan Creative Tours and Nippon Express.

The development of the tour operator sector in the world is tending towards a high concentration of large tour operators. Their strategy is increasingly becoming more global with cross-holding agreements and equity participation such as Otto Reisheim's company Metro acquiring Kaufhof, and Airtours' acquisition of a Scandinavian tour operator for £90 million.

■ Packaging the tourism product

Packaging tourism products involves several stages which can take several months and sometimes several years. The three main stages are:

- Market research
- Negotiation
- Commercialisation of the product

☐ *Market research*

The aim of market research is to understand and analyse the key elements associated with a particular market and its environment. Because of the specific nature of the tourism product, each market research survey should be tailor-made to the aims of the project. However, the research methodology remains constant. It analyses the environment of the project, the characteristics of supply and demand, time schedules, controls and costs.

The strategic aim of market research is to test different hypotheses so as to identify the most realistic ones. Research is based on surveying a sample of the relevant target population. The results provide both quantitative and qualitative information. The most important research tool in survey work is the questionnaire. Two types of questions are used in surveys: the closed question which is very exact and seeks to establish precise data, and the open question designed to understand customer motivation. Surveys provide a range of information on consumer behaviour towards a specific product. They reveal attitudes, reactions and prejudices (political, cultural, climatic and social) towards destination countries. This is very important in the understanding of international tourism.

Three main questions must be addressed to gather the information required from a market survey:

- Who should be questioned?
- What should be observed?
- How should it be undertaken?

The first question pertains to the size of the sample to be surveyed and the *sampling method* to be used. The most frequently used method is random sampling where the interviewer chooses respondents at random. A more controlled method is to choose a sample from the same geographical area matching the socio-professional class of the population the research is trying to reach.

The second question relates to the *nature of the information*. It is important to understand who is the potential clientele and to target it. The aim is to identify a potential group of consumers in order to adapt products to their needs and mount an efficient promotional campaign.

The third question concerns *interview technique*. The interview can be held at the home of the respondent using a structured question-naire. Certain questions are very precise requiring definite answers while others are more open, often forming part of a conversation. This method yields more complete information but is expensive. For this reason, interviews are often conducted by telephone or questionnaires are sent through the post. The data gathered by these techniques is less reliable than that of the personal interview and there is a higher 'non-response' percentage in the sample. A very productive method is the short structured questionnaire at locations where respondents are assembled and available for interview (for example, waiting rooms at train and bus stations and airports, etc.).

☐ Negotiating contracts with different suppliers of tourism services

The product manufacturer assesses the motivation and purchasing power of a potential market by undertaking market studies. Once he is satisfied that he has enough information on the target market's demand for tourism products, he must:

- design products that match the demand of the target market;
- create 'packages' by negotiating the required services with suppliers of each of the elements making up the product;
- finalise contracts with them.

☐ Designing the product

Faced with intense international competition, the manufacturer must design his products to meet the requirements of the consumer. He must have a good knowledge of the tourist-generating market and of the quality–price ratio of the products he plans to offer.

☐ Knowledge of the market

This is based on the body of information gathered by the market surveys. It relates to:

- *The clientele* – segmentation by age, by professional category, by area, by income bracket, by lifestyle and by usual holiday preference;

- *The competition* – choosing the right elements to differentiate the final product from that of the competitors; having the necessary promotion and publicity superstructure available to reach the target clientele;
- *Tourism resources at the destination area* – natural resources, cultural resources, superstructure and services, entertainment and excursions.

☐ The best quality–price ratio

The manufacturer's strategic aim is to offer products that correspond more closely to consumer demand than those of his competitors. To implement this strategy, he must consider three points:

- *Competitiveness*   This is the fundamental element of the quality–price equation. The manufacturer must successfully manage a range of products catering to different market segments. Each product should be carefully targeted at a particular market segment by offering the desired quality at the price the consumer is willing to pay, in other words the *best quality–price ratio*.
- *The product range*   Extending the product range has several benefits: it offers the consumer a wider choice of products; it contains competition by 'controlling' a large enough slice of the market to eventually dissuade competitors; it allows necessary adjustments dictated by changes in market tastes or circumstances to the company's supply, by constantly diversifying the content and the type of products it offers (innovation); it averts commercial vulnerability to political instability, fluctuations in exchange rates and competitor actions.
- *Strategy*   Extending the product range must not jeopardise the competitiveness of prices and the efficiency of management. It is therefore essential to formulate a *product-range strategy*. This must be flexible enough to adapt products to the changing tastes of consumers, to fluctuations in the exchange rate and to variations in consumer purchasing-power.

Consumer purchasing-power is particularly important in determining the quality–price ratio of a product. It is affected by exchange rates and changes in the cost of living both at the destination and in the country of origin.

The specific design of products and the quality image of the tour operator will strengthen his competitive position and play an important role in his commercial strategy.

☐ *Negotiating the package*

The manufacturer must negotiate hard with each supplier to be able to offer competitively priced quality products to the market-place. He makes arrangements with several suppliers: transport companies (airlines and road transport), suppliers of accommodation, catering and entertainment and those providing services for certain specialised products such as cultural tourism, health tourism and so on. Price elasticity in tourism can be extremely high. J. L. Petitjean, the Managing Director of Air Charter International, noted that 'for certain markets, a 15 to 20 per cent drop in price can double the market potential'.

Negotiation in these circumstances can be a very difficult process. The tour operator has a greater chance of success if he has a good image in the market-place and a large client base. He must also be financially strong to guarantee the operation of the product and to be in the position to pay his suppliers in advance.

The manufacturer will often choose destinations in low-cost countries because of their low labour costs, low taxes, government subsidies, incentives designed to attract foreign visitors or favourable exchange rates. These destinations must however fit customer tastes and have a good quality–price ratio. Several countries deliberately keep down the price of their tourism services. This is known as 'dumping'. Their objective is to attract hard currency although quite often the end benefits may be disappointing. Because of their financial muscle and the guaranteed business they can supply, the larger tour operators have particularly strong negotiating powers and can obtain very competitive prices.

Certain tour operators avoid being too dependent on suppliers by integrating some of the services they offer. For instance an airline company may set up a tour operation and a hotel chain. It can therefore offer products that correspond specifically to a market segment and launch advertising campaigns to reach it on several fronts. Many airlines in the world have adopted this strategy. British Airways offers products to different market segments, for the budget-conscious, for the long-haul traveller and 'BA Holidays' at the top end of the market and city breaks. Italiatour is an associate company of Alitalia and has been trading in the UK since 1988. It is one of the largest operators to Italy transporting close to 100,000 passengers a year. Caravela Tours is a subsidiary company of TAP Air Portugal and has been operating since 1982 specialising in Portugal, Madeira and the Azores. Their main advantage is that they can offer a variety of scheduled flights which are perceived to be of a higher quality and less likely to be delayed. The margins for these packages are high as often unsold seats are filled on routes the airlines have to fly anyway.

Several hotel chains and large tour operators also create subsidiary companies to supply them with the necessary services. Thomson, the largest tour operator in the UK, distributes its products via its retail arm, Lunn Poly, the largest chain of travel agencies in the UK, and fly their clients on their own airline, Britannia, the largest charter airline in the world with a fleet of 36 aeroplanes.

Associations may also develop hotel, transport or hospitality services. This is the case for instance of 'la Caisse Nationale des Ouvriers du Bâtiment', an association of construction workers in France who own the hotel Chem in Tunisia.

The aim of negotiation is to reach the best competitive price for a satisfactory quality–price ratio. The selling price of the tourism product includes commissions to travel agents or other distributors, marketing costs, administration costs and the risk cost of falling short of the forecasted sales volume for the product.

☐ Finalising international contracts

Once negotiations have been successfully agreed, international contracts are drawn up with the different service suppliers: agency contracts with travel agencies at the destination countries; contracts with hotels; charter agreements, etc.

These contracts allocate responsibilities to spread the commercial risk between suppliers and the operator. Generally, the tour operator is responsible for the package he has designed. He must pay for services he has ordered, notably transport and accommodation allocations that he has not used. This risk is built into catalogue prices which are calculated on an 80 to 90 per cent take-up rate. This is one of the biggest risk factors facing the tour operator. For this reason it is essential that he develops a range of very diverse products to many different destinations to compensate for any downfall due to political instability, fluctuations in the exchange rate and so on, as well as bad choices of product or errors committed in product packaging.

If the operator charters an aeroplane, the empty flights must also be costed into the final price. These usually occur on the return leg of the first flight of the tourist season, and on the outbound flight at the end of the season. Furthermore, the tour operator must set his price on the basis of a provisional usage rate which is normally less than 100 per cent, usually around 90 per cent.

As a general rule, the elements that make up the cost of a trip in Europe can be broken down as shown in Table 6.4.

Table 6.3   *Package tour costing example (London–Canary Islands, one week, half board, 3-star hotel)*

Service	High season (in pounds sterling)	Low season (in pounds sterling)
1. 7 days half-board per person	150	90
Transfers	8	8
Ground handling	4	4
Sub-total	162	102
2. Flight		
(London–Tenerife–London)	180	130
Other Costs	10	10
Sub-total	190	140
3. Commissions		
Tour operator 8%	28	19
Travel agent 10%	38	26
Total 'selling' price	418	287

Table 6.4   *Cost elements of an organised trip (%)*

Distribution (travel agent commission)		10
Tour operator margin		8
Cost of production		82
Administration/management	8–12	
Accommodation	24–42	
Transport	30–50	
Cost		100

Source: Eurostat-Dafsa, 1988.

However, competition has forced many service suppliers and particularly tour operators to reduce their margins. For example, leading tour operators in Britain have been compelled to reduce their margin to, at times, less than 1 per cent for some products.

■ Selling and marketing the product

The tour operator will either offer his products directly to the market or sell them through travel agents. Whichever method of distribution he

Table 6.5 *Tour operator profit margin* in a highly competitive situation*

	Cost (£ sterling)
Travel agency	28
Airline company	105
Administration	20
Transfer	5
Hotel	115
Tour operator profit	2

* Based on an average price of £275 for a 15-day package to Portugal.

chooses, sales will hinge on products being presented in brochures designed by the tour operator and on marketing and advertising campaigns.

☐ *The brochure*

This is the main marketing tool used to sell tourism packages. The larger tour operators, particularly in Germany, the UK and in France, print over one million copies of their brochures. These are distributed through travel agencies and their own retail outlets. Brochures are also sent directly to past clients or potential future clients that have been identified by market research.

The selling techniques used in brochures are colour photographs depicting the highlights of the holiday, promotional pricing designed to attract the consumer's attention and the quality of the layout.

However:

- The use of colour photographs increases the production cost of the brochure considerably. The conversion rate of brochure pick-up to sales is between ten to thirty brochures for one sale.
- Promotional pricing means advertising the lowest possible price for a product. This usually corresponds to the low-season tariff which applies for a very short period, that is, the cheapest price charged for the product. This is a much used technique even though the promotional price advertised is quite different from the real price of the products sold in the brochure.

The advantage of the brochure is that it represents the tangible evidence of a service that will be consumed in the future (and often quite a long time in the future). Because of the high expense of designing and producing a brochure, only the larger tour operators with strong financial power can afford the cost. Therefore the supply of tourism packages is concentrated in the hands of a few operators. Furthermore, the lead time necessary to bring a product to the market can be between six months and a year. The risks of inflation, fluctuations in exchange rates and the price of petrol make it difficult to predict prices so far ahead. Tour operators now include the price list separately from the main brochure in order to react to changes whenever necessary. However, this reduces the strategic impact of advertising promotional prices.

☐ Marketing by travel agencies

Travel agencies are tourism firms whose main activity is to sell tourism products on a commission basis to consumers. There are approximately 30,000 travel agencies in the world, concentrated mainly in the industrialised countries, particularly Europe. According to the WTO, 70 per cent of agencies are in Europe, 14 per cent in North America, 8 per cent in Asia and the Pacific, 4 per cent in Latin America and 4 per cent in Africa and the Middle East. Generally, these agencies are simply distributors of tourism products and are often very small businesses.

They cooperate nationally within large professional associations such as FUAAV (Fédération des agences de voyage) in Paris, ABTA (Association of British Travel Agents) in the UK and ASTA (American Society of Travel Agents) in the USA. International associations such as WATA (World Association of Travel Agencies) promote relations between member agencies all over the world.

The economic activity of travel agencies is based around transport sales (ticketing) and the marketing of tourism packages.

Ticketing is the main activity of most agencies. This involves booking transport space (airline, ship, train, and road transport) but also associated tourism services such as hotel or holiday home reservations, car-hire, travel insurance and leisure services (ski passes, sports lessons etc.).

Transportation sales are the bulk of the agency's business (two-thirds of American travel agencies' turnover come from airline ticket sales). To sell airline tickets, travel agencies must be accredited by IATA (International Air Transport Association) or by an airline company member of IATA. The organisation protects both consumers and airline companies against travel agency bankruptcy and also serves to regulate the industry.

☐ Advertising and promotion

Marketing and advertising campaigns are often undertaken by different organisations whose interests are complementary:

- Governmental tourism organisations from destination countries are responsible for general information and promotion of the destination;
- Tour operators and travel agencies mount marketing campaigns to sell their products.

National tourist organisations cooperate with tour operators and travel agencies who sell products to their destination. Ultimately, the destination's success in attracting tourists is linked to the operators' and agencies' ability to sell products to the market. Certain agencies cooperate very closely with private companies mounting coordinated promotional campaigns while others prefer looser arrangements.

Operators who develop products in destinations which are not promoted by a government agency bear the total cost of promoting both their products and the destination. They may eventually share some of these costs with travel agencies.

A product made up of several integrated services is promoted on different fronts by each supplier. For instance, an airline company which owns a tour operation and a hotel chain will launch a coordinated marketing and advertising programme to sell a complete tourism package. Each service provider, while belonging to the same corporate group, has an interest in the tourism product and wants to promote his particular service.

Advertising messages aim at highlighting three main points: the price of the product, the content of the product and the quality image of the tour operator.

- *The price* quoted in the advertising message is generally the cost of the product in low season.
- *The content of the product*   The advertising message emphasises the positive attributes of the product and differentiates it from the competition. Publicity campaigns focus on the added services which augment the product. These are enhanced services in transport, accommodation, catering, entertainment or services catering to particular interests (cultural, health, sports, etc.).
- *The quality image of the tour operator* is very important. A company which enjoys a 'high quality' label has a stronger negotiating position with service suppliers thus allowing it to secure more competitive prices. This in turn makes its products even more attractive to the public.

The marketing costs shouldered by tourism firms are mainly made up of:

- brochures and leaflets distributed to travel agencies, at trade fairs and travel exhibitions;
- posters;

- advertisements, newspaper features and competitions in the media;
- commercials on the radio, on television and at the cinema;
- postage of brochures to past and potential clients;
- the organisation of press conferences, sometimes with professionals and local representatives (debates and cocktail parties), in the towns of the target market;
- familiarisation trips for journalists and product distributors (travel agents).

■ Global distribution systems

The growth of global distribution systems (GDS) and computer reservation systems (CRS) in the 1980s and 1990s has been remarkable. Single-access information systems offer information on the products of the airline companies or hotel chains that own them. Travel agencies can now access information on all air carriers and related tourism services which distribute their products through a global distribution system network.

GDSs process information and bookings more efficiently than single-access systems, and are quicker and easier to use than printed timetables and tariff guides. They are now an essential tool in marketing international tourism.

Global distribution systems were first introduced and developed by the large airline companies in the United States. At the beginning of the 1970s, Carter's policy of air transport deregulation led to massive database requirements. These systems were then developed in Europe and Asia. Although the systems are regulated by anti-trust laws which ensure that all transport companies are treated equally, there are frequent claims that the airlines controlling them display information on the screen in ways that favour their own services.

World information and distribution networks play a decisive role in the international tourism sector since they bring the buyers and producers of tourism products into contact. Unlike goods, services are sold before the consumer has had a chance to appraise their various qualities and before he has travelled to the receiving country. Global distribution systems are therefore indispensable and have a virtual monopoly in the sale of air and tourism packages.

☐ *Definitions*

GDSs have three principal characteristics, differentiating them from simple information systems. They are systems of:

- Information
- Reservation
- Sales

This third function, marketing – the most important for tourism enterprises – must be interconnected with the others to ensure the effectiveness of the system. In effect, unlike the traditional systems used by any given airline or hotel chain, a single GDS terminal provides immediate access to all the service companies which have opted to market their products through this network.

Businesses (air carriers or independent commercial companies) that control a CRS either partly or entirely are known as 'vendors'. They make their system available to third parties like travel agents who provide information to the public.

Participating carriers pay to have their services included on the CRS. However, vendors may sometimes store schedules and fares of airlines that have not paid them a fee for the system. There are three levels of interaction between the end-user and a CRS:

- the first level of participation is referred to as '*on call*'. This involves telephoning for availability and booking;
- the second level is called '*on demand*'. The message is sent electronically and the response time is between 10 and 20 seconds;
- the third level is '*on availability*'. The booking is made in real time with confirmation in less than two seconds.

This third level is the one most frequently used.

☐ *The main GDSs*

The main tourism distribution networks are highly concentrated and to a great extent dominated by American and European airlines. The five main system vendors are:

- **Galileo international** – an association of the American network Covia–Apollo developed by United Airlines, and the European network Galileo, established in Great Britain by British Airways, Alitalia, Swissair, KLM and Olympic Airways;
- **Sabre** – (created by American Airlines) was the largest network in the world before the Apollo–Galileo merger;
- **Worldspan** – established by Delta, TWA and NorthWest, and is associated with the Abacus network which was created by a group of Asian airlines;

- **Amadeus** – set up in response to the large American networks by the European airlines Air France, Lufthansa, Iberia and SAS;
- **Abacus** – created by the Asian carriers.

GDSs are mainly concentrated in North America, Europe and the Asia–Pacific region. Latin America and more particularly Africa have not however developed any systems and are poorly equipped in terms of terminals. They are still using the traditional SITA system, which does not offer the same possibilities.

☐ *The problems of GDS regualtion*

There are many obstacles to and disciplinary measures governing access to GDS networks. These include:

- *unfair rights of access*, mainly in terms of the breakdown of costs between system vendors, carriers and suppliers of tourism services;
- *the monopolistic market aspects* of worldwide information systems which make it almost impossible to develop new complementary systems in developing countries;
- *restrictions on displaying* the information and fares of certain suppliers of services.

The main problem lies in the discriminatory treatment of carriers, service suppliers and enterprises in countries which do not have GDSs. Discrimination can be particularly apparent in relations with travel agencies, particularly where display of the requested information is concerned. All the methods used by host systems to determine the order of displaying commercial information should be based on objective criteria meeting consumer requirements, such as the cheapest fares, the shortest and fastest routes, the number of stops and the characteristics of each product supplied. When GDS displays disregard these priorities and are biased in favour of certain carriers or suppliers of tourism services, other enterprises are put at a serious disadvantage. In effect, in 90 per cent of cases, travel agencies only use the first page of the information they have requested from the host system. Consequently, the priorities given to the display of certain information contained in the first page can trigger major distortions, particularly for airlines and travel agencies in developing countries, as is the case in Africa.

The principles of GDS regulation were formulated by the ICAO. They relate to information on itineraries involving one or several international sectors which can be accessed directly by travel agencies. They do not, however, concern air transport companies using GDSs internally or at their own retail outlets. Passengers who contact a carrier direct expect to be offered products that benefit the company.

The ICAO principles relate to:

- Participation of carriers
- Relationship with travel agencies
- Storage and display of information
- The integrity of the data
- Processing strategic information
- Personal data protection and free access to information
- Operating in foreign markets
- The rules of reciprocity

These various principles should ensure greater equality among the various GDS member suppliers of services and at the same time enhance protection of consumer rights.

Strategies to improve the use of GDSs in developing countries

In order to improve the participation of developing countries in global information and reservation systems, measures related to both the international and national organisation of these systems must be adopted. In effect, conditions of access do not necessarily pose the greatest problems for travel agencies and for suppliers of tourism services in developing countries. On the other hand, major difficulties stem from the use of possibilities offered by GDS computerised systems. Many agencies in developing countries do not have the 'back office system', that is, the complementary data-processing tools and the technical knowledge which would allow them to use data-processing more effectively and advantageously.

In these conditions, there are two priority measures which will enhance the access of developing countries to global information and reservation networks:

1. *Making the systems neutral* Either by adopting international codes based on the ICAO model (one of the stated aims of IATA, which is developing a code for airlines), or by respecting the national codes developed in the United States and in Europe, applied to all global networks established by the GDSs. At the time of writing, only the US code, which came into force in September 1992, has been completed.

The main provisions and regulations in this code should provide broadly neutral systems. According the US code, GDSs should:
- provide complete and unbiased information about all the services supplied by member companies;
- not be biased in favour of GDS owners; give all companies access to reservations, including those which use internal reservation systems.

In EU countries, the regulations issued in 1993 contain similar provisions reinforcing the principle of neutrality. In the absence of a real international regulatory system, however, this neutrality cannot be guaranteed, as proved by the actions which have been periodically brought by companies complaining of discrimination (for example, the Sabre–Amadeus lawsuit over access to Air Inter's reservation system).

2. *Improving the use of networks*   This can mainly be achieved by improving the professional qualifications of GDS users in companies. An interesting example is provided by the Star programme set up by the EU to aid the European regions which are lagging behind in the use of computerised networks. This programme, which only affects a limited number of regions generally situated on the periphery of the Union, has two principal aims: providing assistance in fitting the regions out with basic computerised equipment and promoting methods of use for small and medium-sized enterprises through specific training programmes (courses and seminars). The purpose of these actions is to enhance operational use of the resources provided by the new computerised systems to be established in small and medium-sized enterprises. In developing countries, such actions would serve to resolve the problems caused by the inadequate use of the possibilities offered by GDSs.

Thus, measures to improve access to global information and distribution networks should be complemented by measures to improve their use by tourism operators in developing countries.

Because of these measures, GDSs could play a vital role in promoting the growth of the tourism sector in developing countries and meeting the basic aims listed by the IATA:
- worldwide compatibility avoiding all types of conflicts;
- sufficient flexibility to integrate technological changes and innovations in tourism products;
- the guarantee of access on the basis of non-discrimination and affordable costs.

The development of international tourism relies on effective commercialisation of tourism products. Tourism is an amalgam of services which can only really be experienced at the moment of their consumption and which, unlike manufactured products, cannot be systematically reproduced in an identical way. Successful selling of tourism products requires establishing a relationship of trust between the client and the salesman. The reputation of tour operators, hotels and airline companies is therefore very important. Furthermore, in an increasingly competitive market, it is often access to information which ensures the success of marketing. Therefore, active participation in computerised reservation networks is extremely important. Unfortunately, the conditions of participation to these networks are not equal for all countries. In particular, African and South Asian countries are not generally endowed with sufficient hospitality structures to be well-represented on the GDS networks. Limited access to information on the tourism products they offer restricts their representation on the international market which means that these countries are falling further behind in their power to attract international tourists.

This chapter has highlighted the importance of access to information in a competitive market. The following chapter explains how limited access to finance for tourism investment further increases international inequalities.

Further reading

Ashworth, G. J. and Goodhall, B. C. *Marketing in the Tourism Industry*. London: Routeledge, 1990.

Bello, D. C. and Etzel, M. J. 'The Role of Novelty in the Pleasure Travel Experience', *Journal of Travel Research*, 24(1),pp. 20–6, 1985.

Booms, B. H. and Bitner, M. J. 'New Management Tools for the Successful Tourism Manager', *Annals of Tourism Research*, 7(3), pp. 337–52, 1980.

Buck, R. C. 'The Ubiquitous Tourist Brochure: Explorations in its Intended and Unintended Use', *Annals of Tourism Research*, 4(4), pp. 195–207, 1977.

Cooper, C., Fletcher, J., Gilbert, D. and Wanhill, S. *Tourism Principles and Practice*. London: Pitman, 1993.

Dernoi, L. A. 'Farm Tourism in Europe', *Tourism Management*, 1983

Heath, E. and Wall, G. *Marketing Tourism Destinations*. New York: Wiley, 1992.

Holloway, J. C. and Plant, R. V. *Marketing for Tourism*. London: Pitman, 1993.

Kotler, P. *Marketing Management: Analysis, Planning, Implementation and Control*. 6th edn, New Jersey: Prentice-Hall International, 1988.

Middleton, V. T. C. *Marketing in Travel and Tourism*. Oxford: Heinemann, 1988.

Morrison, A. M. *Hospitality and Travel Marketing*. New York: Delmar, 1989.

Wahab, S., Crampton, L. J. and Rothfield, L. M. *Tourism Marketing*. London: Tourism International Press, 1976.

Witt, S. and Moutinho, L. *Tourism Marketing and Management Handbook*. Hemel Hempstead: Prentice Hall, 1994.

WTO. *Concept and Production Innovations of the Tourism Product*. Madrid, 1983.

■ *Chapter 7* ■

Finance and Investment in International Tourism

Financial ratios and investment in tourism: method of developing an
  expenditure and profitability forecast
Investment appraisal: return on investment; payback; discounted cashflow or
  net present value
Sources of finance: equity finance; loans; leasing: leaseback
International financing and investment aid: the characteristics of investment
  grants; the different types of grants; sources of international financing;
  financing of European projects

Investments in the tourism industry are *extremely capital-intensive* because
of the high cost of superstructure and equipment. Capital is tied up for
long periods and returns on investment are very slow. The particular
structure of investments in the tourism industry, similar to industries
requiring heavy investment, needs to be taken into account in the strategic
management of tourism firms.

At this point, it is apposite to differentiate between the *providers* of
tourism superstructure such as the hotel and transport sectors and the
packagers and sellers of tourism products such as tour operators and travel
agents. The hotel and transport sectors require initial heavy investment to
provide the physical elements of the tourism product (for example, the
hotel and its fittings, the aircraft or the coach). Their investment will only
be recouped over a period of several years. Tour operators (and to a lesser
extent travel agencies) require large amounts of available untied capital as
collateral to pay for the services that they commit themselves to before the
season. Capital is tied up for a much shorter period and is often used for
currency exchange-rate speculation. Indeed, in highly competitive markets
where profit margins are small, such as in the UK, exchanging currency at
the right time can determine whether the season will be profitable or not.

Because the tourism product results from a combination of different
sectors, tourism firms in one sector often have a major interest in the
financing of tourism superstructures and services in related sectors. For
instance, tour operators may finance the development of hotel complexes
in resorts where they bring their clients to ensure that they have the

capacity they need. Airline companies may guarantee the financial security of tour operators who use their services extensively. However, financial backing generally focuses on marketing campaigns.

Many tourism firms are *labour-intensive*. It is difficult to adapt the production of their services to fluctuations in demand. Moreover, operating costs are virtually the same whether the product is being consumed or not.

These financial and technical constraints mean that particular care must be taken in the finance and management of tourism firms. Investment analysis forecasts prescribe the amount of funding necessary, the terms of finance, management accounting and profitability requirements.

Capital investment in fixed assets is very high compared to turnover and profitability forecasts play a determining role in investment decisions in the capital-intensive sector of the industry.

The hotel industry is particularly representative of the difficulty faced by investors in the tourism industry. There are two main problems in the financing of tourism infrastructure and services:

- choosing the investment decision method and the investment criterion;
- and choosing the sources and terms of financing for the investment.

■ Financial ratios and investment in tourism

To illustrate the method used in investment decisions, we use the example of a hotel project which presents the typical problems encountered in superstructure investment: the large amount of capital required, the slow capital turnover, the rigid operating environment and the low profitability.

The method is based on the development of an accurate operating cost forecast, a provisional investment budget and a profitability forecast. Before proceeding, it is necessary to collect all the basic information concerning the envisaged investment, and make receipt and expenditure forecasts.

☐ *Method for developing an expenditure and profitability forecast*

A forecast operating account (similar to a profit and loss account) must be developed to determine the potential profitability of the hotel. This is the first step in the decision to invest and would be used as an internal document for decision-making. The account is presented Table 7.1 overleaf.

Table 7.1   *Forecast operating account*

	Amount
Operating revenue (sales) Cost of sales	
Gross profit Other expenses	
Operating profit Interest cost and other charges	
Profit before tax Tax	
Profit after tax	

☐ The gross profit

The gross profit (GP) is the operating revenue minus the cost price of goods and services sold.

$$\boxed{\text{operating revenue}} \; - \; \boxed{\begin{array}{c}\text{cost price of}\\\text{goods and}\\\text{services sold}\end{array}} \; = \; \boxed{\text{gross profit}} \qquad (7.1)$$

- *The operating revenue* This is obtained from forecasts of hotel receipts, receipts from restaurants and bars and activities associated with the hotel. These estimates are obtained from forecast occupancy and utilisation and from the ruling prices in the industry (as adapted to the particular hotel).
  - *Forecast occupancy* is usually obtained by interviewing potential clients and from surveys at the proposed location of the hotel. From these studies, the percentage daily room occupancy over a year is estimated, as is the number of meals served and the bar service (drinks and snacks).
  - *Ruling prices* are those that are being charged for similar services in the industry and serve as a yardstick to estimate total revenue. They consist of the average price charged for rooms occupied by one or two people, the price of meals, breakfasts, drinks and associated services.

- *The cost of sales*   This is the cost of goods and equipment necessary to run the hotel, restaurant, bar and associated services (discotheque, swimming pool, etc.). The cost price is dependent on the terms that have been negotiated with suppliers (for example, centralised buying by hotel chains, cooperatives, etc.). It also includes labour costs of operating staff, occupancy costs and commissions. These are salaries, social security contributions, bonuses and so on (but not the cost of the administrative staff). The level of the labour costs depends on the type of hotel. For example, a modern two-star 45-room hotel with a standard restaurant employs eight to ten full-time staff.

  Occupancy costs are the costs associated with the facilities used by the guests of the hotel (for example, water, energy, heating, bathroom accessories, laundry). Commissions are bonuses paid to firms or individuals for bring business to the hotel (for example, commissions paid to tour guides to entice them to use the hotel restaurant for group events such as banquets, meals or cocktail parties).

☐ The operating profit

The operating profit is the gross profit minus other expenses.

$$
\boxed{\text{gross profit}} \;-\; \boxed{\text{other expenses}} \;=\; \boxed{\text{operating profit}} \qquad (7.2)
$$

Other expenses are expenses that are not directly attributable to the daily cost of running the hotel and are therefore less affected by occupancy levels. These would include the cost of administrative staff (for example, the director and the accountant), administration costs (postage, telephone, office supplies and paperwork), advertising costs or contributions (in the case of members of hotel chains), transport costs (for example, shuttle bus to and from the airport), insurance, maintenance and repairs (although this would of course increase with higher occupancy) and depreciation.

☐ Profit before tax

Already the operating profit gives an indication of the potential profitability of operating the hotel; however, the decision to invest must take into account the cost of borrowing money. To arrive at the profit before tax, the cost of borrowing (i.e., interest and loan repayments) must be deducted from the operating profit.

$$\boxed{\begin{array}{c}\text{operating}\\\text{profit}\end{array}} - \boxed{\begin{array}{c}\text{cost of}\\\text{borrowing}\end{array}} = \boxed{\begin{array}{c}\text{profit before}\\\text{tax}\end{array}} \qquad (7.3)$$

☐ Profit after tax

The final area to consider is taxation. This varies from country to country (even between different regions within countries). However, many countries are now granting a number of tax concessions to attract investors for tourism projects. To arrive at the net result or the profit after tax, tax is deducted from the profit before tax.

$$\boxed{\begin{array}{c}\text{profit}\\\text{before tax}\end{array}} - \boxed{\text{tax}} = \boxed{\begin{array}{c}\text{profit after tax or the}\\\text{net result}\end{array}} \qquad (7.4)$$

The forecast net result determines the forecast profitability of the investment and addresses the following questions:

● How is the maximum required investment evaluated?
● What is the maximum loan required to achieve the forecast profitability?

■ Investment appraisal

Once the potential profitability of the project has been assessed, a decision must be taken on the type of investment method most suitable to appraise the project. There are several methods of investment appraisal. Here, we examine three of these methods: return on investment, payback and discounted cashflow.

☐ *Return on investment*

This method looks at the rate of return on the investment over the entire life of the project. The net cashflow or gross operating result (GOR) before depreciation and financial charges is a function of the total investment (Iv):

$$\boxed{\begin{array}{c}\text{profit}\\\text{after tax}\end{array}} + \boxed{\begin{array}{c}\text{financial}\\\text{charges}\end{array}} + \boxed{\text{depreciation}} = \boxed{\begin{array}{c}\text{gross}\\\text{operating}\\\text{result}\end{array}} \qquad (7.5)$$

Let us look at a project which is based on the following hypothesis: assuming assets will retain their value in real terms (such as the building of the hotel), depreciation of no more than 4.5 per cent of the investment, maximum financial charges amounting to 5 per cent of the investment, and projected profit after tax representing 4.5 per cent of the investment, the gross operating result would be:

$$GOR = (4.5\% + 5\% + 4.5\%)Iv$$

or $14\%(Iv)$

Therefore, the level of investment which can be supported by that income is:

$$IV = \frac{GOR \times 100}{14} \tag{7.6}$$

The forecast operating account gives a preliminary indication of the likely interest by investors in the project and its potential viability. However, this method of appraising the investment does not take into account cashflow during the life of the project or, indeed, the length of the project.

☐ Payback

This method focuses on the length of time taken to pay back investors and is based on the cashflow from the project. It assumes that at the end of the project life, assets will be worthless, and therefore it looks for regular returns which are high enough to operate the business and to pay back investors. This type of investment appraisal is most suitable in situations where assets depreciate relatively quickly such as in the transport industry. However, this method is rigid as it does not take into account the timing of cashflows, or of cashflows after the payback horizon.

☐ Discounted cashflow or the net present value

This method of investment appraisal considers that the value of a sum invested is worth more at the time of investment than at the end of the life of the project. Therefore, the appraisal must be made on the discounted value of the cashflow or the net present value of the cashflows at the time of the investment.

For example, let us consider an investment of US$1,000,000 in a project over a period of five years at an annual cost of capital of 10 per cent with annual profits of US$200,000. The formula to work out the value of the initial investment at the end of the project is:

$$P = P \times (1 + i)^n$$

P is the invested sum
i is the interest rate per period as a decimal
n is the number of years (or periods) on the investment

Therefore:

$$US\$1,000,000 = 1,000,000(1 + 0.10)^5$$
$$= US1,610,510$$

This is known as the compounded cashflow. The amount of money which needs to be initially invested in order to achieve this sum at the end of five years is known as the Present Value (in this case US$1,000,000).

To work out if the investment is worthwhile, the year-on-year profits are multiplied by the present value of the investment each year: the discount factor. The discount factor is the present value of 1 unit of the amount received at the relevant number of years.

The formula to calculate the discount factor is:

$$\frac{1}{(1 + i)^n} \qquad (7.7)$$

Therefore at a 10 per cent interest rate the year-on-year discount factors for different years are:

$$1 \text{ unit in year } 1 = \frac{1}{(1 + 0.1)^1} = 0.909 \qquad (7.8)$$

$$\text{year } 2 = \frac{1}{(1 + 0.1)^2} = 0.826$$

$$\text{year } 3 = 0.751$$

$$\text{year } 4 = 0.683 \text{ etc.}$$

If cashflows generated over the life of the project in our example are taken away from the initial investment, the following table is obtained:

Year	$000		$000
0	−1,000,000 × 1.000	=	−1,000,000
1	200,000 × 0.909	=	181,800
2	200,000 × 0.826	=	165,200
3	200,000 × 0.751	=	150,200
4	200,000 × 0.683	=	136,600
5	200,000 × 0.564	=	112, 800
			−253,400

At net present value rates, the investment over five years should be rejected. In fact, the investment will only be profitable after eight years:

Year	$000		$000
			−253,400
6	200,000 × 0.513	=	102,600
7	200,00 × 0.467	=	93,400
8	200,000 × 0.424	=	84,800
			27,400

In this case, the investment decision must consider if it is worth tying up the capital for this length of time or if a better return could be obtained elsewhere.

The discounted cashflow method is a more sophisticated method of investment appraisal and is particularly appropriate for larger investments. Its main drawback is that it assumes a single discount rate for the life of the project which often is not the case.

These methods, however, do not constitute automatic means of decision-making. There are several other considerations which depend on:

- *The type of management envisaged*   Will the hotel be managed by the owner or will a manager be appointed? If so, what is the expected level of managerial expertise?
- *The means of financing the operation*   Particularly, who will supply the furnishings? The owner of the property? A non-trading real estate company? Or a public venture company?
- *Forecast charges and anticipated profits*   In particular, could forecast labour costs be controlled, taking into account inflation in salaries?

■ Sources of finance

There are several methods of financing tourism investment. The most important are:

- Equity finance (owners' investment, mainly shares)
- Long-term borrowing (loans)
- Leasing
- Leaseback

Many countries, particularly those of the Mediterranean, benefit from government grants to finance investment projects. These include government loans, government loan guarantees, subsidies and preferential interest rates on loans, and tax benefits.

□ *Equity finance*

The objective of the shareholding system of financing is to obtain capital from the owners of the business and include outside investors by issuing shares with the aim of increasing the company's funds. All companies will have equity capital and this type of financing is particularly important for those that are growing rapidly but cannot raise sufficient loans for their requirements. However, only very large firms are allowed to issue shares to the general public.

□ *Loans*

Borrowing capital, particularly from banks, is currently the commonest method of financing investments. In the tourism sector, loans for equipment which are often eligible for public subsidies are extended by specialised organisations, often chosen by the government.

□ *Leasing*

Leasing involves a specialised company not connected with the business which finances part or all of the investment of the tourism project. The tourism firm signs a contract with a leasing company which agrees to supply equipment for a negotiated price. The equipment is rented for a set period after which the tourism firm has the opportunity of buying the equipment at a predefined price lower than its initial cost. This method of financing first appeared in the United States in the 1950s.

In addition to equipment, many tourism businesses apply the principle to the buildings they occupy and take them on a long-term lease rather than owning them outright (freehold).

☐ Leasing plant and equipment

The equipment may be heavy (aeroplanes, coaches) or light (kitchen equipment, furniture). This kind of investment can replace traditional financing by loans or complement it.

A major advantage of the leasing system is that it allows a profitable firm with limited resources to use them in the most efficient way. Funds for equipment are obtained from leasing companies. There are, however, certain conditions to this type of funding. The rental is fixed for a certain period during which time neither party is allowed to terminate the contract, unless a specific situation arises. This period will generally be less than the estimated working life of the equipment. At the end of the obligatory rental period, the tourism firm has four options:

- to return and replace;
- to return the equipment to the leasing company and not replace it;
- to buy the equipment at a price previously agreed in the contract;
- to renew the rental contract (taking into account the wear and depreciation of the equipment).

Besides the financial advantage that brings down the cost of loans, plant- and equipment-leasing is tax-deductible. However, it should be noted that the cost of leasing can be more than the cost of traditional loans, although this may be offset by savings on maintenance costs.

☐ Leasing buildings

Leasing premises allows the tourism firm to operate from a base on a secure rental basis. This system is particularly beneficial to small tourism enterprises which cannot afford the total cost of buying premises. However, sometimes the low returns that tourism investments normally provide are insufficient for small enterprises to meet the yearly repayments required by leasing companies.

☐ *Leaseback*

In certain cases, a hotelier who owns his hotel can resort to a leaseback procedure which consists of selling the property to a specialised company which will lease it back to him. This releases previously invested funds to the hotelier.

■ International financing and investment aid

International financing of tourism investments comes either in the form of transfers or private loans directly concerning tourism activities, or loans from international organisations to finance the infrastructure needed for the development of international tourism. Loans from the international organisations are granted by the World Bank Group to developing countries. This association includes the World Bank, the International Development Association (IDA) and the International Finance Society (IFS). The common objective of these institutions is to improve the standards of living of developing countries by making financial resources provided by industrialised countries available. In the past, the World Bank Group has assisted in financing major hotel projects. Today, these organisations are mainly concerned with infrastructure, in particular in the transport sector.

Financial assistance is granted in the form of long-term loans (World Bank), low-interest loans (IDA) and equity participation (IFS). However, banks have many priorities and quite often there is insufficient investment in tourism projects. As a result, the economic tourism potential of many countries is under-exploited and a particularly appropriate way of developing is wasted (in small insolated countries, for instance).

In fact, the amount of financial aid granted for tourism investments from the public sector is determined by the importance of tourism in the economy for a large number of countries and by the specificity of the tourism sector compared to other productive sectors. Government grants come in various forms, from promotional campaigns to bolster the image of the country to granting tax exemptions on the operation of tourism activities. Whilst tourism is always considered to be within the private sector, its expansion has prompted an increasing coordination between governments and professionals in the tourism sector, particularly in the areas of finance and investment. Generally, projects must yield sufficient revenue to attract investors. As a result, governments have to undertake the financing of infrastructure which is often very costly.

☐ *The characteristics of investment grants*

There are three types of financial incentives granted by the state to investors:

- *Reduction in the cost of investing* The objective of these incentive measures is to reduce the cost of investing in tourism projects. They include direct capital subsidies, loans at preferential interest rates, tax exemption on construction material and the sale or leasing of land below the market price.
- *Reduction in the cost of operating* These measures aim to reduce the cost of operating their business to tourism firms. These generally include tax exemptions, return of duty on equipment, grants for training and so on.
- *Investment guarantees* The aim of these guarantees is to reassure potential investors, particularly abroad. In such cases, governments guarantee the repatriation of capital and profits and, on occasion, even guarantee loans. In many countries, measures are frequently introduced to encourage tourism firms to reinvest their profits in the host country.

Incentives, although often very advantageous, are not always enough to attract investors. Indeed, tourism flows can be diverted for political, economic and non- economic reasons. Thus, the risk involved in investing in tourism is higher than in many other sectors. Consequently, the image of a country plays a crucial role. Therefore, one of the characteristics of public aid is for governments to establish an appropriate legal and economic environment to attract the investment necessary for the development of tourism.

☐ *The different types of grants*

The different types of investment grants available for tourism projects are subsidies, preferential loans, loan guarantees and interest rebates, and fiscal measures.

☐ Subsidies

Subsidies are sums of money awarded to the contractor of the tourism project by the government (usually as a lump sum), which do not have to be repaid. The main advantage of subsidies is to reduce the cost of investments and, often, the size of loans.

Subsidies have very swift effects and require little management. In fact, the only managerial actions are:

- to decide to grant a subsidy to a given project;
- to check that the subsidy is being used for the reason it was granted;
- to check that the project will fulfil the functions for which it was awarded the subsidy over a predetermined period, for instance three to five years.

Such financial aid can be effective. For instance, a project financed with 20 per cent equity participation and 80 per cent loan may have to pay such high interest on the loan that it loses all viability. A subsidy of 20 per cent of the total cost, bringing the size of the loan down to 60 per cent, would ensure that the project can meet the interest payments from its profits. Therefore, subsidies are important for solving cashflow problems during the set-up phase of the project and for initiating certain tourism policies. Besides, the administration of the system is inexpensive and the economic and social effects, particularly on employment, are very obvious.

The subsidy system is currently used in many countries: Greece, Austria, France, Italy and especially the United Kingdom (Northern Ireland). Subsidies are granted to many sectors of the tourism industry, for instance, to finance superstructure (in the hotel trade) and to develop natural resources (fishing, leisure and sport centres for tourists, etc.).

☐ Preferential loans

Governments may grant loans to investors in tourism projects at interest rates below the market rate. Preferential loans should be distinguished from tax relief or interest discounts, where the government contributes the difference between an interest rate fixed at a certain level and the market rate.

Managing a preferential loan implies:

- a detailed feasibility study of the proposed project to ascertain when interest and loan repayments will be made;
- controlling the regularity of the interest and loan repayments;
- ensuring that the loan is used for the reason it was awarded;
- ensuring that the project is actively run throughout the period of the loan.

Austria in particular applies this system to its hotel and tourism transport industries. These loans are granted at a 5 per cent interest rate for a maximum period of 20 years for up to 50 per cent of the total investment.

☐ Loan guarantees and interest discount subsidies

Loan guarantees

Governments or specific organisations guarantee loans granted by commercial banks for the development of tourism. For a project to qualify, studies are undertaken:

- to evaluate the project's capacity to fulfil the terms fixed by the commercial bank;
- to evaluate the failure risk of the project, in other words, the likelihood that the guarantee will be called upon.

In this system, the commercial bank is in charge of administering the loan and the public organisation will only intervene in the event of default from the borrower.

Interest discount subsidies

This consists of settling the difference between the rate fixed by the government and the rate charged by the commercial bank.

Interest discount subsidies allow more projects to be financed with a fixed sum rather than with a system of loans. However, the effects on the financing of the investment are only significant if the discount is substantial during the first years of the project. Greece and Portugal particularly favour this form of aid.

☐ Fiscal measures

Fiscal incentives specific to the tourism sector are an important form of public aid. However, they are usually only available once the business is generating profits and not at the launch stage of the project. For instance, the provision for depreciation which reduces taxes on profits only has an effect on the investment once it starts making profits.

Different fiscal measures are applied in different countries. In Italy, there are several financial and fiscal incentive schemes designed to attract foreign investments, for instance, a lower VAT rate on the purchase of imported goods. In Spain, important fiscal advantages are granted to investors by the state and by local government in areas of 'national tourism interest'.

☐ *Sources of international financing*

International financing of tourism investments is provided by public sources, such as international organisations, and private sources, such as the international debenture markets and clearing.

International organisations which provide financial aid are the European Union in Europe and the World Bank and its subsidiaries in developing countries.

☐ Financing by the World Bank

The World Bank (also called the International Bank for Reconstruction and Development – IBRD) does not usually intervene directly in the tourism sector. However, significant possibilities exist for indirect intervention where the IBRD co-finances projects with classic export credits (buyers and suppliers). This type of co-financing selects the most competitive suppliers by inviting them to tender.[1]

As financing is assured from several sources including the IBRD, the quality–price ratio is carefully assessed. Projects sponsored by the World Bank are divided into sections with some sections financed directly and others eligible for export credits guaranteed by public insurers.

Certain projects cannot be divided into sections either because of their nature or because of the level of the investment required. In these cases, the Bank consults with the credit insurers in the countries of potential suppliers to encourage them to extend guarantees. Subsequently, invitations to tender are launched and the most competitive suppliers are selected. If the suppliers selected are from a country where credit insurers have given their commitment, the Bank co-finances (at a fixed percentage rate) with the guaranteed commercial banks.

These are the only financial packages which allow equipment exporters in the tourism industry access to international financing from the World Bank.

☐ The international debenture markets

This type of financing is only feasible for large tourism development projects undertaken with financially important buyers. It consists of acquiring (both short- and long-term) resources by offering international debenture bonds to the general public. The particularity of these bonds lies in their international nature which means they benefit from a favourable fiscal system. Indeed, tax in this case is not taken at source.

The resources are raised by the banks and are made available to foreign buyers so that they can pay their suppliers. This procedure requires two contracts:

- a commercial contract between the buyer and his suppliers providing for cash payment by using the funds raised;
- a financial agreement between the bank or banks and the foreign lenders setting out the repayment terms.

The banks are responsible for repaying the subscribers whatever the circumstances of the final debtor. Repayments are either made at regular dates agreed in the commercial contract or in one go at the expiry of the contract. This second possibility is generally financially more advantageous because the buyer's repayments can be temporarily invested. In any case, if the bank loan is at risk from the debtor defaulting, it is covered in the same way as a traditional buyer's credits.

These bonds can be drawn in either national or foreign currencies (the United States dollar is the most frequently used currency).

□ The possibilities of financing by clearing

There are many forms of clearing. They are important sources of tourism investment financing based on loans using potential tourist receipts as collateral. Tourism flows generated by the investment ensure its finance. This is the case for bilateral agreements between countries of different economic development for financing new tourism investments in different ways.

Barter

A tourism enterprise from an industrialised country and a local partner sign a two-stage contract:

- the tourism enterprise from the industrialised country commits itself to buying local products and selling them on. In this way it raises foreign currency;
- it will then supply its own production and use the foreign currency as payment.

However, although this is a secure method of guarding against payment default, it is rarely used because tourist products are not easy to barter.

Countertrade

This involves the signing of two contracts:

- a standard export contract for which 'traditional' guarantees and financing are required;
- a commitment by the enterprise from the industrialised country to import a certain amount of local products over a specific period. To abide by this commitment, the enterprise must sign import subcontracts at the appropriate time.

In this case, there is a risk of default because currency obtained in the country that is importing (through purchases made) is not usually used to pay for exports.

Buy-back

The exporter agrees to buy back all or a proportion of goods that have been manufactured using the material or service he has exported (for instance, a commitment to marketing and selling sojourns at a hotel where the exporter has provided the equipment).

Clearing agreements

States experiencing financial difficulties can still maintain tourism business by applying for clearing agreements. These agreements are signed by two states with centralised foreign trades who want to balance and record their exchanges including tourism. If a credit balance is shown at the end of the year, it is normally carried forward, thus opening a buying potential for the creditor country. Consequently, opportunities for firms from industrialised countries become available even if they have not signed clearing agreements. These consist of exporting from a country which generally shows a debit balance towards a creditor country.

☐ Financing of European projects

☐ Financing of European Union projects by the EFRD

The EFRD (European Fund for Regional Development) is the main organisation which finances European Union tourism projects. The EFRD,

Box 7.1 *An example of investment procedures and incentives: Western Samoa*

In 1990, tourism accounted for 17 per cent of Western Samoa's GNP and the island received nearly 50,000 tourists. In line with its long-term development objectives of attaining a greater degree of self-sufficiency and self-reliance and balancing regional development, in 1990 the government passed the Enterprise Incentives and Export Promotion Act, which provide a range of incentives for industry, including tourism. Once a tourism project has been approved by the Department of Trade, Industry and Commerce, domestic and export enterprises become eligible for a number of different types of incentives:

FISCAL INCENTIVES

Tax Holiday

This concession provides for exemption or relief from income tax during a five-year income tax period, or a ten-year extended period, with normal taxation starting thereafter.

Carry-Forward to Losses

Provision to carry forward operational losses experienced during approved income tax period for tax deduction after the income tax period.

No Tax on Dividend

Dividends paid out of profit of an approved domestic enterprise during the granted income tax holiday period and two years thereafter are not liable to taxation.

Write-off of Capital Cost

If an extended income tax period has been granted, provision to allow write-off of capital costs, excluding cost of free whole land, against taxable income over a period determined by the Enterprise Incentives Board.

Import/Excise Duty Exemption

Exemption or relief of customs/excise duty on specified articles, during the five-year customs/excise duty period, or up to ten-year extended customs/excise duty period. The customs/excise duty may also be refunded if the specified articles are purchased in Western Samoa.

Company Tax

Company tax is 39 per cent for resident companies and 48 per cent for non-resident companies.

Box 7.1 Continued

Personal Income Tax

This is on a sliding scale starting from a minimum rate of 10 per cent to a maximum of 45 per cent.

The Western Samoan government is also considering an extension of the tax holiday period to ten years for accommodation with a minimum level capital cost; granting of lump-sum depreciation or capital items used for modernising existing plants and equipment; investment relief; tax deduction for overseas promotion and additional customs duty concessions.

OTHER INCENTIVES

The Western Samoan government also grants other incentives to encourage the tourism industry: **Provision of Land** (long-term leases on liberal terms and conditions are generally available for developing a number of sites); **Training facilities** (courses and training programmes sponsored in Samoa and scholarships for Samoans to attend quality training colleges abroad); **Marketing and Promotion** (the Western Samoa Visitor Bureau in concert with the national carrier, Polynesian Airlines, publishes marketing materials and sponsors international travel fairs. It generally represents the country in generating markets); **Repatriation of Profits** (freedom is provided to repatriate both capital and profits as long as the original investment has come to Western Samoa through the recognised banking system or in another approved way); **Work Permits** (these are generally granted to expatriates if the necessary skills are locally unavailable. They last six months and are renewable upon request by the local firm).

AVAILABILITY OF FINANCE

Loan capital from commercial banks on soft terms with long repayment periods and low interest rates is not usually available for development projects. However, the Development Bank of Western Samoa (DBWS) generally grants loan capital on easier terms than the commercial banks and has in recent years positively reviewed all loan applications for tourism projects. Interest charged on such loans varies from 8 to 14 per cent with a maximum repayment period of 15 years and a small grace of 3 to 12 months depending on the construction period.

The government is hoping to persuade the commercial banks to grant development loans with longer periods of repayment and concessionary interest-rates to approved tourism projects that are entitled to tax holiday status. It is also trying to reinforce its own approach to international lending institutions such as the ADB, EIB, IFC and the IDA for soft loan facilities to finance private tourism development projects either directly or through the DBWS. Future funding for hotel projects of major size will be expected to come from abroad and the government actively encourages such foreign investment in the country.

ADB = African development Bank
EIB = European Investment Bank
IFC = International Finance Corporation
IDA = International Development Association

Source: *Tourism Investment Guide*, Fiji, 1992.[2]

created in 1975, was conceived as an institution to grant financial aid for the support of national tourism policies in the least developed regions of the Community (mainly Greece, Portugal, Sicily, Sardinia, Madeira and the Azores). There are three types of scheme:

● Co-financing of national public aid for industrial and service projects
● Co-financing of infrastructure – Joint tourism projects, such as the air transport infrastructure of the Greek Islands, and improvement of airport security.
● Co-financing of 'endogenous' development. This includes assisting companies with market studies and promotional campaigns. This scheme makes grants available to support the tourism promotional budget of tourism enterprises.

There are various situations where the EFRD will finance more than 50 per cent of the investment:

● Grants for community or national programmes. Programmes are either a defined theme, a geographical area or an activity sector which have been designated to receive grants, including grants from the EFDR;
● Aid for one-off projects
● Other aid

The projects that are most likely to be financed are those that reduce seasonality, exploit the historical, natural, environmental and cultural heritage and develop rural tourism.

☐ Financing by the European Investment Bank

The European Investment Bank (EIBs) intervenes as an interest discount subsidy organisation which lends resources that it has raised on international markets at preferential rates.

In 1989, the EIB financed tourism projects to the value of 239 million ecus. Projects that have received finance from the EIB include the Channel

Tunnel, Disneyland, Paris, and airport expansions in Frankfurt, Munich, Hamburg in Germany and Stansted airport in the UK.[3]

It also offers specific types of finance to developing countries:

- The financing of projects
- The acquisition of disposable funds in currency (this is equivalent to credit aid to the balance of payments)
- Extending the borrowing capacity of countries that have limited potential for borrowing on the international financial markets.

Finally, the intervention of the EIB can contribute to improving the credit-worthiness of local debtors.

☐ Financing by the European Development Fund (EDF)

The EDF is considered to be the non-political arm of the European Union's interventions in developing countries. These interventions follow the Lomé Conventions which are committed to tourism development. Projects which involve regional cooperation are equally encouraged.

The type of actions supported by the European Union include training of tourism professionals, promotional actions and the development of new tourism products (for instance, developing organised tours to break the monoculture of beach resort tourism).

The recipients of these grants are usually the countries themselves, or other governmental agencies and approved local commercial enterprises. The funds are allocated to three types of grants:

- Non-refundable subsidies
- Loans with special terms (40-year repayment period including a 10-year period of grace, interest rates of 1 per cent or less)
- Equity participation in local companies

Generally, suppliers are invited to tender, although certain operations are negotiated by contract (technical assistance, for instance). Firms in the EU compete with those of the ACP (Africa, Caribbean and Pacific).

☐ An example of projects funded by the European Union – the United Kingdom

The United Kingdom applies for a variety of grants from different European bodies, depending on the type of project it is undertaking.

The European Investment Bank, which is concerned with developing further European integration, funds mainly infrastructure projects such as the Channel Tunnel (2.4 billion ecus), a new bridge over the River Severn and water supply projects.

Regions where the average income is less than 75 per cent of the European average can apply for 'Community Support Funds' from the ERDF. In Britain, parts of the Midlands, the North (such as Tyne and Wear), Scotland and Wales qualify for these grants. Tourism projects supported by the fund include the redevelopment of the industrialised river banks housing large shipyards which have become derelict. The Tyne and Wear Development Corporation region attracted £450 million from the private sector to build hotels, office blocks, residential homes and a Water Park and as a result created 10,000 jobs. To attract this private investment, it needed the support of European funds to initiate the development.

In Wales, the ERDF, in partnership with government development initiatives, supported the Swansea Maritime Quarter located on an attractive coastline as well as projects in West Wales to create new economic activity and rural development in farm tourism operations.

Schemes at local level can also qualify for EU funding. The local authority Waltham Forest in north-east London has received £820,000 in European grants, of which £360,000 was used to fund the Human Resource Initiative Programme to integrate people with learning difficulties into the workforce of the hospitality industry.[4]

The financing of tourism investment represents an enormous constraint for many countries. Indeed, tourism is both a heavy industry and a labour-intensive industry and the management of its tourism production is particularly difficult. Furthermore, investors are difficult to attract because profitability in the industry is low, payrolls are large and the market is increasingly competitive. Consequently, the public sector must intervene to help find the capital required to develop the tourism sector. For this reason, many countries pursue local, national and international policies to provide the infrastructure necessary for tourism development. However, many problems still exist. For instance, preferential financial conditions such low interest rates are granted to certain types of enterprises but not to others, which distorts overall tourism development. Furthermore, in certain regions these financial advantages are often not large enough to provoke a significant economic impact. In fact, the economic impact is limited to direct employment concerned with receiving, assisting and serving tourists. Direct and especially the indirect effects on internal production are weak because tourism production in these countries is reliant on imported material.

Thus, to evaluate the consequences of the investments made and the amount of extra financial means that must be mobilised, the economic impact of tourism must be analysed in depth.

References

1. WTO, *Directory: Multilateral Sources of Financing for Tourism Development*, Madrid, 1993.

2. *Tourism Investment Guide*, published by the Tourism Council of the South Pacific, Suva, Fiji, 1992.

3. Study on European Funding for the Tourism Industry, internal publication, Surrey Research Group, Surrey University, England; 1994.

4. Ibid.

Further reading

Davis, H. D. and Simmons, J. A. 'World Bank Experience with Tourism Projects', *Tourism Management*, 3(4), pp. 212–17, 1982.

Dyson, J. R. *Accounting for Non-Accounting Students*. London, Pitman, 1991.

Kotas, R. *Management Accounting for Hotels and Restaurants*. Surrey University Press, 1991.

Owen, G. *Accounting for Hospitality, Tourism and Leisure*. London, Pitman, 1994.

United Nations Conference on Trade and Development (UNCTAD) *The Outcome of the Uruguay Round: an initial assessment – supporting papers to the trade and development report*, 1994.

UNCTAD, *Trade and Development Report*, 1994.

■ *Chapter 8* ■

The Economic Impact of Tourism

International tourism and employment: the characteristics of employment in the different branches of tourism; trends in employment

Employment and human resources: training in the tourism industry

Tourism and economic development: macroeconomic policies of tourism development; the objectives of tourism policies; the resources necessary for the implementation of tourism policies; the tourism multiplier

The ecological and socio-cultural effects of international tourism: the ecological effects; the socio-cultural effects

Tourism and international trade: trends in international trade and international tourism; imports in tourism consumption

The balance of payments: balance of payments and tourism; methods of integrating tourism transactions in the balance of payments; the economic importance of tourism in the balance of payments

Evaluating the economic impact of tourism provides information necessary for the formulation of tourism development policies. These policies determine the type of infrastructure and superstructure a country needs to invest in to encourage the most appropriate kind of tourism production. However, because of problems of definition (for instance, whether the impact of day-visitors should be included) and because of the relative inaccuracy of tourism statistics, it is difficult to measure the economic impact of tourism accurately.

Nevertheless, the analysis of the economic effects of tourism is vital to the analysis of global economics. Tourism is the most productive industrial sector in the world and accounts for 12 per cent of its GNP. It is also the sector that creates the most employment, with over 100 million employees.

The influence of tourism extends to several fields of economic activity:

- Employment
- Human resources
- Development
- Foreign trade
- The balance of payments

■ International tourism and employment

The growth of tourism in both industrialised and developing countries has created many jobs (mainly semi-skilled and unskilled). Because of the numerous industries directly linked to tourism (hospitality, transport, accommodation, entertainment, travel agencies and related services, administration, finance, health etc.), it is very difficult to evaluate all its effects on employment. Furthermore, tourism is also indirectly supplied by several other industries: construction, agriculture, manufacturing and processing.

The impact of tourism on employment can be considerable for many small countries, which then become dependent on the industry and the receipts that it brings. In some countries in the Caribbean, 50 per cent of the working population is employed in the tourism sector or in a related industry.

In contrast, in the largest tourism countries which are also industrialised countries with high populations, the tourism industry employs only 5 per cent of the working population. It should be noted, however, that more employment is created by the tourism sector than by any other growing industry. This is particularly true in the developing countries where employment created in export industries is far inferior to employment created by tourism.

The effects of tourism on employment must be analysed not only from the quantitative angle but also from the qualitative angle by appraising job skills.

☐ *The characteristics of employment in the different branches of tourism*

Employment in tourism, which is a service industry, is dependent on the particular needs of tourists. The ILO (International Labour Office) has identified a number of general characteristics of employment in the hotel industry.[1]

- *A low level of technical expertise*   Many jobs in the hotel and catering industry do not require technical knowledge: kitchen porters, kitchen assistants, luggage attendants and porters, lift attendants, security guards, odd-job men, cleaners and laundry assistants. This is negative for the image of the industry, particularly in countries where pay for these types of jobs is very low because of high unemployment and the availability of manpower.

- *A high labour mobility*   Even if the work is not of a seasonal nature, there are often peaks and troughs of activity and the tendency is to call on additional staff (extras) for a few days or even for just an evening. As budgets are squeezed, the number of temporary or part-time staff increases.
- *Unsociable work periods and unsociable hours*   The unsociable hours that people in the industry are required to work (weekends, evenings and holidays) and the fact that they must take their own holidays outside the tourist season further adds to the difficulty in recruiting personnel, especially young staff.
- *The length of the working day*   Operating a hotel requires the organisation of teams of workers at well-defined periods during the day and at night. And, because of the enforced 'break' in the afternoon, periods on duty are very long. Work patterns in multinational hotel chains are increasingly similar to those in other economic sectors but, for people who work in small hotels or in independent restaurants, there is often no shift system and they have to work throughout the whole period, which can become a strain on family life.[2]
- *Physical fatigue*   The majority of jobs in the kitchen and associated with cooking are very tiring and physically uncomfortable. The atmosphere is sweaty, there are heavy loads to carry, most of the work is done standing, and there is intense activity during peak periods which causes nervous tension.
- *Psychological constraints*   Staff who are in contact with clients must be patient, in control and good-humoured. They must remain calm, polite and smiling even when customers are complaining (often unjustly) and criticising. Furthermore, some positions have a particular dress code which emphasises a certain level of neatness and elegance. These employees are often required to have good elocution, the knowledge of several foreign languages and a certain level of tact.

Despite technological advances, the skills level necessary for many jobs in the tourism industry is low, as confirmed by the ILO studies in the hotel industry.

The number of jobs created is very high, particularly in developing countries. However, in the hotel industry, the ratio of bed to employees is increasing, particularly in industrialised countries. The ILO calculates an average of:

$$\frac{\text{Number of hotel employees}}{\text{Number of beds}} = 0.50 \quad \text{or}$$

$$\frac{\text{Number of jobs}}{\text{Number of rooms}} = 1$$

Only hotels at the top end of the market achieve this ratio. The ratio at lower-category hotels has decreased substantially over the years (less than 0.3 in two-star hotels). However, in developing countries, employment in the hotel industry remains very high because labour is cheap and hotels are often built as separate units (holiday villages) which require more technical installations (generators, air-conditioning, swimming pools, golf, tennis). The ratio is therefore much higher, generally over 1.5 (Kenya and Tanzania, 1.6; Egypt and the Seychelles, 1.8).

Employment statistics show that the proportion of women employed in the industry is generally more than 50 per cent. The proportion of foreigners employed in tourism is also very high in Northern European countries (25 per cent in Germany, 35 per cent in France and Switzerland). These percentages can be very high in developing countries, for instance in Cameroon, where 32 per cent of hotel and catering employees are from elsewhere.

☐ *Trends in employment*

Trends in employment in the different branches of the tourism industry should include all employment created: direct employment, indirect employment and ancillary employment. However, because it is difficult to compile this statistical information for all the sectors concerned with tourism activity, the studies are limited to employment created in the hotel industry, the catering industry and the retail and service industries which are directly linked to tourism.

In certain countries and regions of the world (for instance, most of the Mediterranean Islands and the Caribbean) employment attributable to the tourism industry is as high as 30–35 per cent of total employment. The hotel and catering industry creates the largest number of jobs (at times as much as 75 per cent of the total) although job creation in other sectors (like transport) is developing rapidly. According to the ILO, there are 100 million people employed in the tourism sector, half of which are employed in the hotel and catering industries. Internationally, there is no particular pattern for the number of people employed in this sector. Countries as diverse as the United States, the CIS and Japan employ a large number of people in their hotel and catering industry, whereas other countries, even those with a large tourism industry such as France and Switzerland, employ relatively few people.

■ Tourism and human resources

□ *Training in the tourism industry*

The objective of organising professional training projects is to balance employment and training, whether it is the number of employees that have to be trained or the level of skills that have to be developed. The need for professional training in the tourism industry is particularly acute in developing countries where many new tourism destinations are being created. Training programmes are also necessary in industrialised countries which need to adapt constantly to technological advances and because of the recent 'professionalisation' of tourism.

In developing countries, professional training policies are usually supported by bilateral technical agreements, particularly between English-speaking countries (for instance, UK–South-East Asian countries), French-speaking countries and Spanish-speaking countries (Switzerland or France–African countries, Spain–Latin American countries) or with international organisations like the ILO, the EU and the WTO. The WTO and the EU play a leading role in the following areas:

- planning and organisation of professional training in the hotel trade;
- the economic aspects of training;
- evaluation of skill needs by sector;
- tourism management;
- regulating working conditions following international conventions and recommendations.

Depending on the specific needs of each country, training projects aim at introducing apprenticeship systems, basic and on-the-job training and even installing new management systems. To this end, permanent training centres have been established.

In industrialised countries, the emphasis is on further training although the importance of basic training is still recognised. The introduction of new technology usually affects both employment and training. In the short and medium term, staff must be trained to use new technology. The purchase of new equipment inevitably changes the nature of the work. To a varying degree, every department in the hotel or in the restaurant is affected. The introduction of electronic databases and information systems involves mainly front- and back-office activities and new cooking equipment will modify the nature of food preparation. For the moment, restaurant service and housekeeping have little involvement with new technology.

Table 8.1 Employment in the tourism industry

		1989			1991			1992		
		Total	Men %	Women %	Total	Men %	Women %	Total	Men %	Women %
Austria	HC	123,047	38.0	62.0	131,240	39.4	60.6	136,543	40.1	59.9
Belgium	H	13,032	47.7	52.3	14,666	46.1	53.9			
	R	59,891	47.9	52.1	59,485	48.8	51.2			
	HR	93,376	46.7	53.3	74,151	48.3	51.7			
	V	4,099	34.8	65.2	4,086	33.3	66.7			
	A	10,607	49.7	50.3	10,541	46.3	53.7			
	O	5,747	35.2	64.8	5,727	34.3	65.7			
Finland	HR	73,000	20.5	78.1	69,000	23.2	76.8	63,000	23.8	76.2
Germany	HR	692,700	43.2	56.8	774,800	41.0	59.0			
Norway	HR	58,000			57,000			59,000		
Sweden	HR	94,500	37.6	62.4	98,000	36.7	63.3	91,000	39.6	60.4
Turkey	HR	134,034			145,530			153,168		
	V	9,910	63.6	36.4	11,000	65.4	34.6	17,150		
	A	1,635	66.2	33.8	1,985			1,990	63.4	35.2
	O	1,868			2,420			3,874		

UK	H	288,200	37.4	62.5	296,000	39.3	60.7	289,200	40.7	59.3
	R	287,500	38.7	61.3	291,900	41.0	59.0	295,500	41.6	58.4
	HR				1,442,700	40.0	60.0	1,442,500	40.7	59.3
	O	828,400	39.4	60.6	854,800	39.9	60.1	857,800	40.4	59.6
Canada	H	168,000	39.3	60.1						
	R	573,000	43.1	56.9						
	HR	768,000	41.7	58.2						
	V	27,000	25.9	74.1						

H: staff employed in the hotel trade.
R: staff employed in catering.
HR: staff employed in hotel catering.
V: staff employed in travel agencies.
A: staff employed in national tourism administrations.
O: staff employed in other sectors of the industry.
Source: OECD.

Because tourism is a service industry, it influences employment significantly. For many countries, it is fundamental to their development policy.

Box 8.1 *Training in Romania*

Romania has formulated, with the help of the European Union PHARE programme, a policy of restructuring tourism training. This policy is based on the organisation of new courses and the modernisation of the National Tourism Training Institute.

Faced with the need to renovate Romania's tourism sector, new tourism curricula have been implemented. The experience of EU countries has shown that modernising the tourism sector leads to sharp increases in productivity resulting in a considerable reduction in unskilled labour. Therefore, it is important in the medium term that the training programmes involve all levels of personnel in the tourism industry.

In addition, specialised training programmes have to be developed at a local level to train employees in tourism and hospitality. In 1994, the PHARE programme organised a number of courses to update the knowledge of Romanian tourism and hospitality teachers and to train managers in the industry to help them adapt to market economics. The management course consisted of 5 modules (general management, financial management, marketing, hospitality management and tourism management).

■ Tourism and economic development

For most countries, production, consumption and employment resulting from international tourism are important contributions to their economic development.

However, development is not just associated with increases in production. Social, human and environmental aspects must also be taken into account. The growth of international tourism and its effects are often criticised and sometimes the industry is rejected when it reaches the tolerance threshold of the local population.

For this reason, it is damaging to follow tourism policies with the sole objective of increasing foreign reserves. Unfortunately, this situation is all too often the case. International and domestic tourism in every country should be based on an overall policy which links tourism development plans with social and economic development plans. Thus, it is vital to:

- determine the objectives and the resources of macroeconomic tourism development policies;

- evaluate the multiplier effects of these policies on production and consumption;
- and assess the limits of the policies with respect to the protection of the natural and social environment.

Macroeconomic policies of tourism development

The economic impact of tourism involves the majority of the productive sectors in the economy and most countries are implementing macro-economic policies of tourism development. However, because of the number of sectors involved, tourism policies are often not treated individually and are integrated into policies of other sectors: balance of payments policies, industrial policies, monetary policies and land planning policies.

This attitude underestimates the contribution of tourism in economic development and wastes an important potential growth area. For this reason, macroeconomic policies are increasingly essential, particularly after the global economic crisis of the 1980s and 1990s, which revealed the frailty of foreign trade and the economic growth of both industrialised and developing countries. International tourism should be exploited as an economic phenomenon which can contribute to a rapid and sustained recovery of the world's economy. For this to occur, macroeconomic tourism development policies should be developed at a national level with common objectives and with the necessary resources to implement such policies.

The objectives of tourism policies

Tourism policies have both economic and non-economic objectives.

The non-economic objectives concern the freedom of movement (including capital) and of communication between citizens from different countries. Policies also have a cultural objective in promoting and, in some cases, reviving the natural, artistic and architectural heritage of countries.

The economic objectives are both qualitative and quantitative. Tourism policies aim at encouraging certain types of consumption in order to increase production in specific industrial sectors or in specific geographical areas. These policies have a controlling effect on economic growth, foreign trade and employment.

If $\triangle D_i$ is the increase in tourism demand:

GD = global national demand
GO = global national supply
TP = total production
X = exports
M = imports
N = employment
P = price

Scenario 1

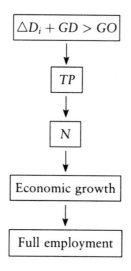

Scenario 2

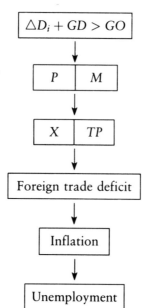

It should be noted, however, that international tourism brings a double risk: inflation and foreign trade deficit.

The reality is often a mixture of both these scenarios. Nevertheless, the dominant scenario will depend on the characteristics of each country.

If the country is industrialised and has an economy producing below capacity, scenario 1 is dominant and a growth in international tourism demand will be positive for the country.

If the country is a developing country with an economy suffering from a lack of productive sectors and insufficient infrastructure and super-structure, scenario 2 will be dominant and a growth in international tourism demand will have negative repercussions on the country.

Therefore, the vital role of international tourism policies is to rectify the negative aspects of tourism and to encourage the positive consequences.

For this to be possible, there must be resources to implement the policies.

The resources necessary for the implementation of tourism policies

With the growing importance of international tourism and its far-reaching consequences, tourism policies are increasingly of an interventionist nature, both in industrialised countries and in developing countries. They rely on the same resources as do global economic policies and planning. These resources can also be specific to tourism.

The global economic policies of a country rely on many resources to encourage the development of its tourism activities. These can be grouped into three categories: financial and fiscal resources, economic resources and social resources.

- *Financial and fiscal resources*   These involve credit, interest-rate and taxation policies. Their objective is to create a favourable environment for savings, investments and the creation of new tourism activities which will benefit the whole economy. A lowering of taxation, combined with a drop in interest rates, encourages tourism as this stimulates a growth in tourism investments, thus creating a competitive supply which ultimately results in a growth in demand.
- *Economic resources*   These concern budgetary and monetary policies. They have a significant effect on domestic prices and on exchange rates. A too rapid expansion of the budget and of the money supply will have negative effects on the national economy and will increase

Table 8.2   *Ratio of receipts in the travel 'account' of different countries compared with their GNP (%)*

	1988	1989	1990	1991
Austria	8.0	8.5	8.5	8.4
Belgium–Luxembourg	2.3	2.0	1.9	1.8
Denmark	2.2	2.2	2.6	2.7
Finland	0.9	0.9	0.9	1.0
France	1.4	1.7	1.7	1.8
Germany	0.7	0.7	0.7	0.7
Greece	4.5	3.7	3.9	3.7
Iceland	1.8	2.0	2.2	2.1
Ireland	3.0	3.1	3.4	3.5
Italy	1.5	1.4	1.8	1.6
The Netherlands	1.3	1.4	1.3	1.5
Norway	1.7	1.5	1.5	1.6
Portugal	5.8	6.0	6.0	5.4
Spain	4.8	4.3	3.8	3.6
Sweden	1.3	1.3	1.3	1.1
Switzerland	3.9	4.0	3.8	3.1
Turkey	3.3	3.2	3.0	2.5
United Kingdom	1.3	1.4	1.4	1.3
Europe	1.8	1.8	1.9	1.8
Canada	1.1	1.1	1.2	1.2
United States	0.6	0.7	0.8	0.9
North America	0.7	0.8	0.8	0.9
Australia	1.3	1.1	1.2	1.4
New Zealand	2.3	2.3	2.3	2.4
Japan	0.1	0.1	0.1	0.1
Australasia–Japan	0.2	0.2	0.3	0.2
OECD	1.0	1.1	1.2	1.1

Notes:
Totals for 1970 to 1991 are revised figures.
Totals for 1992 are preliminary estimates.
Figures on receipts exclude international transports.
Source: OECD.

inflation and the foreign trade deficit. In these conditions, the measures taken in the budget to stimulate tourism demand are virtually ineffective. Therefore, monetary and budgetary macroeconomic policies are not enough to encourage tourism demand. However, a lowering of the exchange rate as a result of devaluation can have a stimulating effect on international tourism demand.

- *Resources associated with social policies* These resources directly influence tourism development and relate to regulation concerning the length of the working day, holidays and professional training. In France, for instance, the introduction of a fifth week of statutory holiday has had a significant impact on tourism, particularly winter tourism.

A comparison of the ratio of receipts in the 'travel' account with the GNP of different countries reveals that there are considerable differences between countries in the importance of their respective tourism sectors. For instance, although the United States is the country which has the greatest tourism receipts, these represent just 0.8 per cent of its GNP, whereas tourism receipts represent 8.5 per cent of Austria's GNP.

☐ *The tourism multiplier*

The multiplier measures the effects of extra expenditure on an economy.

☐ **The concept of the multiplier effect**

This multiplier concept is based on a Keynesian analysis. It tracks money spent by tourists as it filters through the economy. The revenue decreases in a geometric progression at each round as a result of *leakages*. The leakages which take revenue out of the system at each round are due to savings, taxation, expenditure abroad or on imported products.

A distinction should be made between *the multiplier* which measures the relationship between new investment and the increase in production and income and *the acceleration* which measures the relationship between an additional consumption which induces additional investment and the increase in production and income.

The formula for calculating the multiplier is:

$$\triangle R = K \triangle I$$

with: $\triangle I$ = increase in investment

$\triangle C$ = increase in consumption

$\triangle R$ = increase in income

and

$$\frac{\triangle C}{\triangle R} = \text{the marginal propensity to consume} \qquad (8.1)$$

K is the increase coefficient that is applied to the initial spend. It is the income multiplier which is inversely proportional to the marginal propensity to consume.

$$K = \frac{1}{1 - \frac{\triangle C}{\triangle R}} \qquad (8.2)$$

It should be noted, however, that the multiplier effect can be impeded by inelasticity in supply or by the high number of imports which also tends to increase with the rise in income and inflation.

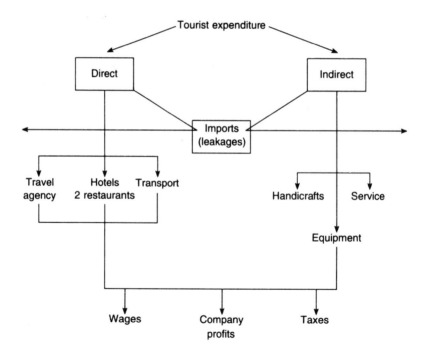

Figure 8.1   *The tourism multiplier*

☐ Tourism expenditure and the multiplier

In international tourism, the extra expenditure which is the cornerstone of the multiplier system can take several forms. It can either be expenditure related to international tourism investments or expenditure by tourists, foreign firms and foreign organisations.

Expenditure can be divided into direct expenditure, indirect expenditure or induced expenditure.

- *Direct tourism expenditure* This category consists of expenditure by tourists on goods and services in hotels, restaurants, shops and other tourism services. It also includes expenditure on goods exported because of tourism or investments related to tourism in the region.
- *Indirect tourism expenditure* This corresponds to transactions between businesses caused by direct tourism expenditure. For instance, it includes purchases made by hotels from local suppliers and goods bought by suppliers from the wholesaler.
- *Induced tourism expenditure* This consists of increased consumption expenditure resulting from the increase of income provided by direct tourism expenditure. For example, hotel staff use their salaries to buy goods and services.

☐ Different kinds of multipliers used in international tourism

There are four kinds of multipliers which are normally used in international tourism: the sales multiplier, the production multiplier, the income multiplier and the employment multiplier.

- *The sales multiplier* This measures the additional direct, indirect and induced turnover generated by additional tourism expenditure.
- *The production multiplier* This measures the extra production as well as taking into account increases in stock levels at hotels, restaurants and shops as a result of increased commercial activity.
- *The income multiplier* This measures the receipts (income) generated as a result of extra tourism expenditure. The income multiplier can be expressed either as a ratio, representing direct and indirect income created by unit of direct income, or, more frequently, by expressing the total direct and indirect income generated by the increase in final demand.

- *The employment multiplier* This measures the effect of extra economic activity on employment. This multiplier can be expressed in two ways, either as the number of direct and indirect jobs created by each unit of extra tourism expenditure, or just as the direct employment created for each unit of tourism expenditure.

☐ The use of the multiplier

The multiplier is a tool used to analyse the economic effects of increases in tourism expenditure and its influence on other sectors of the economy. The value of the multiplier depends on the particular features of tourism in the area studied and the characteristics of the local economy. In particular, the economic composition of an area is the key factor which will determine the

Table 8.3 *Tourism receipt multiplier*

Country or region	Value of normal coefficients of tourism receipt multipliers
Ireland[1]	1.776–1.906 (2.674 to 2.87)[1]
United Kingdom[1]	1.683–1.784 (3.163 to 3.354)[1]
Dominican Republic	1.195
Bermuda	1.099
East Caribbean	1.073
Antigua	0.880
Missouri (state)[1]	0.879
Bahamas	0.782
Walworth County, Wisconsin[1]	0.777 (1.52)[1]
Cayman Islands	0.650
Grand County, Colorado[1]	05.98 (1.34 to 2.50)[1]
Door County, Wisconsin	0.550
Sullivan County, Pennsylvania	0.443
South West Wyoming[2]	0.380 (0.528)[1]
Gwynedd, North Wales	0.370
St Andrew's, Scotland	0.337
South West England	0.330
Greater Tayside	0.321
East Anglian coast	0.320
Isle of Skye	0.250 (0.410)[1]

[1] These multipliers have been expressed as ratios. The normal value was calculated from data provided in the original texts.

[2] For South West Wyoming, these figures are sectorial receipt multipliers.

Source: WTO.

size of the multiplier. The greater the range of economic activities in the area, the greater the chance of a high number of exchanges between them and therefore the greater the size of the multiplier. But a high number of imports brought into the area will reduce the value of the multiplier. This is often the case in developing countries where economic assets are modest.

The WTO has calculated values of the tourism sales multiplier related to production and the tourism income multiplier for a number of regions (see Table 8.3).

☐ The limitations of the tourism multiplier

There are several difficulties associated with the calculation of the international tourism multiplier.

- *Insufficient data* There are many tourism products and a great number of economic sectors involved. As a result, the calculation of the multiplier requires a vast bank of detailed data which is difficult to compile. Without sufficient statistical information, the calculation is not accurate enough to be used in planning tourism development.
- *Variations in the marginal propensity to consume* The marginal propensity to consume can change, even over a short period. These trends are difficult to forecast. Yet it is essential to have an accurate assessment of the propensity to consume, without which the results would not be correct.

  It is also important to assess the effect of the multiplier on inflation. The effect on prices mainly concerns inflation brought in by foreign tourists with high spending power, which disrupts the equilibrium of the market, particularly in developing countries. Inflation originating from the tourism sector spreads throughout other economic sectors and contributes to widening the social and structural gaps in destinations. This is especially damaging to developing countries but also to industrialised countries, for example in Southern Europe: Italy, Spain and the South of France.
- *The inelasticity of the supply* Most multiplier studies assume that supply is elastic in all the sectors of production, or, in other words, that firms can increase their production as tourism demand increases.

  However, increasing supply in some sectors is often not possible. Tourism businesses, particularly in developing countries, are confronted with a number of problems:
  - lack of available resources in factors of production, capital and skilled labour force in the national economy;

- shortage of foreign currency which affects the importing of equipment and goods necessary for the development of local production;
- the inefficiency of certain sectors with insufficient productivity. In the agriculture and fishery sector an increase in demand brings price rises which lead to the risk and even the necessity of importing more competitive products which will usurp the place of national products.

- *The static feature of the production function*   This is another example of the inelasticity of the supply. The multiplier concept is rigid because it presents the past but cannot really conclusively predict the future. For instance, it cannot take into account the level of future savings in the system. It has to assume that goods will be bought in the same proportions, of which, of course, there is no guarantee.

- *The time factor*   The static nature of the multiplier model does not take into account the length of time necessary for the multiplier effect to influence the economy. To assess the importance of the multiplier effect on the economy, it is essential to know how quickly the induced transactions are carried out. This depends on many structural and social factors, such as adaptability, capacity to train, initiative, changes in administrative practices in both private and public sector. Leakages are greater in countries where production is not diversified as they are obliged to import consumer goods and manufactured goods as well as capital and staff.

As a result, the multiplier in international tourism planning should be used with caution. It has been particularly criticised when used in certain economic and tourism development plans in developing countries. Indeed, it is difficult, even impossible, to estimate the impact of international tourism on development when the production capacity of the country is very weak and it is technologically backward. On the other hand, in industrialised countries the tourism multiplier is important.

The ecological and socio-cultural effects of international tourism

The economic, socio-cultural and ecological effects of international tourism are the effects on prices, notably inflation, the social consequences on the population in destination countries and damage to natural resources (pollution in particular).

□ *The ecological effects*

These are damage to the natural environment, notably by the urbanisation of natural sites, the development of access infrastructures (roads, motorways) and the contamination of rivers and beaches. However, international tourism also finances land development programmes which help to combine visits by tourists with the preservation and even improvement of tourism sites and attractions. The challenge is to preserve the environment of the site while still allowing a certain number of tourists. A 1994 UNESCO survey showed that tourism represents the main occupation for local populations living at historic sites. Seventy natural sites were surveyed, representing more than 40 million tourists annually. The results showed that tourism plays a more important part in local economies than agriculture.[3]

The survey also showed that there is no real problem of co-habitation between tourism and the local population when tourism revenues are high.[4]

However, many sites considered tourism a threat to wildlife and vegetation and many sites considered that their infrastructure was insufficient to control the damage caused by tourism. Tourism development policies concerning the environment are becoming increasingly important and the WTO is launching many environmental programmes.

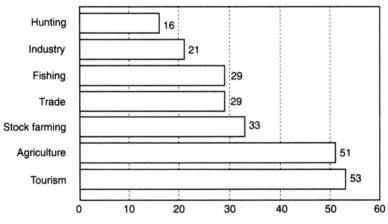

Local population (living on site) earn a living from these industries.
(Number of sites: multiple responses possible)

Figure 8.2 *The main occupations of local population on 70 World Heritage sites*
Source: UNESCO/UNEP.

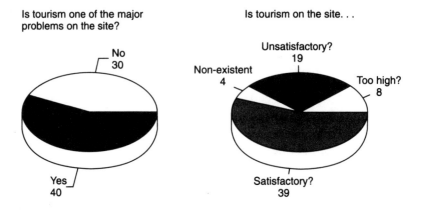

Figure 8.3   *The impact of tourism on World Heritage sites*

Box 8.2a   *The 'Ten Commandments' of protecting World Heritage sites*

The international workshop Managing Tourism in Natural World Heritage Sites organised by UNEP and UNESCO in Dakar, Senegal, November 1993, developed the following Ten Commandments for protecting World Heritage sites.

1. Tourism development should consider and respect the ecological and socio-cultural values of the site and should be consistent with the World Heritage concept.
2. A management plan, considering the regional context and tourism component, should be established and regularly updated.
3. Environmental assessments, including cumulative impacts, should be carried out on recreational and commercial facilities and activities before approvals are granted.
4. Monitoring programmes based on appropriate and updated indicators should take place and their outcome should be taken into account in the planning and decision-making process.
5. Local populations, in and around the site, should be involved in order that they take pride in their heritage and benefit from tourism.
6. Co-operation with the different stakeholders involved in tourism development should be sought to ensure co-ordination for the promotion of the site.
7. All site staff should be aware of World Heritage values and well trained in visitor management.
8. Relevant information and educational programmes should be put in place to ensure that visitors and local people understand and respect the site.

9. A substantial portion of the income generated through entrance fees should be directly allocated to the site for its improvement and management.
10. Each site should participate in the promotion of the World Heritage concept through all appropriate means.'

Source: WTO News, no. 3, May/June 1994, p. 19.

Box 8.2b *The World Heritage List*

UNESCO's World Heritage List arose from the 1972 World Heritage Convention, which affirmed the existence of a heritage common to the whole of humanity, and which is responsible for its protection and conservation. Today, 95 Member States have 411 sites on the List, the best known of which include Venice in Italy and Abu Simbel in Egypt. However, it also includes 90 natural sites and 16 so-called 'mixed sites', combining an exceptional natural and cultural heritage, such as Tassili plateau in southern Algeria with its rock paintings.

These natural sites vary considerably, ranging from the Simen Park in Ethiopia, which receives virtually no tourists, to the Great Smoky Mountains Park in the USA which is visited by almost nine million people annually. The biggest natural site on the List is the 35-million-hectare Great Barrier Reef in Australia, while the smallest is the Mai Reserve in the Seychelles which covers just 18 hectares.

Like it or not, the natural sites included on the World Heritage List are at the centre of these problems and contradictions – because they form the most select club of nature parks, *'the Nobel Prize Winners of natural reserves'*, according to Jim Thorsell of the International Union for the Conservation of Nature (IUCN). They include some of the finest scenery in the world and the best-stocked games reserves containing some of the rarest species. They are therefore a rich seam for tourist exploitation. They are all the more attractive because they have, by definition, managed to preserve nature in the raw. So they are at the exact apex of the radical turn that tourism is starting to take. *'Being part of the world heritage has become a selling point'*, says Professor Trevor Atherton of the Bond University in Queensland, Australia. *'In countries like New Zealand (where more than 30 per cent of the land is now listed) or Australia, the promotion of tourism is increasingly based on the prestige of heritage sites.'* Kakadu Park polled its visitors and found that 80 per cent of them knew it was on the World Heritage List. For 40 per cent of them that was one, or the sole, reason for their visit. The prestige of the list is so great that it may be time to think about finding a way to claw back a small fraction of this windfall, to enable it to keep up its work of protecting the environment and to help the worst-funded sites in the Third World.

Source: UNESCO Sources No. 55, Nicholas Michaux, p. 8.

☐ *The socio-cultural effects*

The socio-cultural effects resulting from certain forms of international tourism can upset the social and cultural equilibrium of the visited countries. It can disrupt cultural traditions (for example, religious festivals disturbed by tourist groups or, worse, reenacted for the sake of the tourists and thus demeaning the ceremony). However, there can also be positive effects which reinforce local culture and contribute to reviving ancient traditions. Tourism in the United States has revived ancient crafts such as jewellery- and ceramic-making by Indians in Arizona and New Mexico in the region of Santa Fe and Taos.

An example of international cooperation is the joint tourism policy of the United States and Mexico which focuses on promoting tourism products around the Camino Real linking Santa Fe to Veracruz.

Box 8.3   *The Camino Real: a historic trail*

The Camino Real Project

In 1989–1990, the Camino Real Project launched a series of historical and archaeological investigations to ascertain the location (in New Mexico, Texas and Chihuahua, Mexico) of the ancient *Camino Real de Tierra Adentro*.

The New Mexico State Highway and Transportation Department has now designated a *Camino Real Auto Route*, choosing roads which most closely follow this ancient path. Thirty-three highway markers, with brief explanatory texts and distinguished by a Camino Real logo, have been put in various places. They invite modern travellers to share an experience of the past. The route follows four-lane highways, narrower roads and, in two cases, suggests alternative routes onto sections of unpaved roads. These last should only be attempted by the adventurous and never travelled without first checking on local conditions.

El Camino Real de Tierra Adentro

First blazed by Juan de Oñate in 1598, this Camino Real (there were many others) is one of the oldest and most important highways in North America. For three centuries it linked New Mexico with the Hispanic world to the south. Conquistadors, missionaries, settlers and traders etched a path which stretched over 1,800 miles from Mexico City to Santa Fe, New Mexico. With the coming of the railroad in the 1880s, the Camino Real was abandoned to the desert and disappeared from maps and memory. For centuries it was, however, the South West's main conduit for technological, political and social change. The crops, livestock, manufactured goods, ideas and social institutions which it carried would help to create the American West. Rescuing this vital highway from oblivion commemorates the Native

American, Hispanic and Anglo American contributions to national identity of the USA.

Ecotourism

The concept of Ecotourism is encouraged. The few physical traces of the ancient road which remain are all on private land. Ecotourism places responsibility on visitors to leave all sites undisturbed. In encouraging travel through small communities and to lesser known sites visitors contribute to the appreciation and preservation to pause, to look, to photograph, in an imaginative effort to erase the modern scenes before their eyes and replace them with vignettes from long ago; to conjure up images of ponderous carts with creaking wooden wheels laden with goods from Mexico; the hurrying march of Kearny's troops on the conquest of California; the carriages and stage coaches of the 19th century; the great bands of sheep being herded to southern markets and the battles of Indian warfare.

Source: Camino Real Project, Gabrielle Palmer, Director, 1993.

■ Tourism and international trade

Like the exchanges of commodities, international tourism exchanges are part of foreign trade policies. Services connected with international tourism have the same or even greater impact on international payments as exports and imports. For example, when a foreign tourist buys a meal in a restaurant, it is equivalent to the export of alimentary products plus the added value of catering services, including depreciation costs of equipment and superstructures.

International tourism is quite often the generator of international trade flows. For many countries, the construction of tourism superstructures and some requirements of tourism consumption necessitate importing goods and services that cannot be provided by the country.

On the other hand, countries which have acquired a reputation for expertise in tourism export (directly and indirectly) tourism equipment, goods and services.

Trends in international trade and international tourism

A comparison of trends in international trade and trends in international tourism reveals a rapid growth in both volume and value since 1950. The share of receipts generated by international tourism is 6 per cent of total

Table 8.4 *Importance of trade in tourism*

		World				Developing countries			
		1980	1989	1990	1991	1980	1989	1990	1991
Gross National Product (GNP)	US$ billion	10,219	19,294	20,899	21,582	1,584	2,745	2,829	2,872
Total exports	US$ billion	1,864	3,013	3,013	3,482	403	699	779	827
Services exports	US$ billion	745	1,331	1,598	1,694	87	155	170	176
International tourisn receipts	US$ billion	102	211	255	261	26	55	64	63
International fare receipts	US$ billion	18	40	48	54	4	6	8	7
Total international tourism receipts	US$ billion	120	251	303	315	30	61	72	70
Total international tourism receipts as:									
% of GNP	%	1.2	1.3	1.4	1.5	1.9	2.2	2.5	2.4
% of total exports	%	6.4	8.3	8.9	.0	7.4	8.7	9.2	8.5
% of services exports	%	16.1	18.9	19.0	18.6	34.5	39.4	42.4	39.8
International tourism receipts as:									
% of services exports	%	13.7	15.9	16.0	15.4	29.9	35.5	37.6	35.8
International fare receipts as:									
% of services exports	%	2.4	3.0	3.0	3.2	4.6	3.9	4.7	4.0

Annual growth rate

		89/90	90/89	91/90	91/80	89/80	90/89	91/90	91/80
Gross National Products (GNP	%	7.3	8.3	3.3	7.0	6.3	3.1	1.5	5.6
Total exports	%	5.5	12.6	2.7	5.8	6.3	11.4	6.2	6.8
Services exports	%	6.7	20.1	6.0	7.8	6.6	9.7	3.5	6.6
International tourism receipts	%	8.4	20.9	2.4	8.9	8.7	16.4	-1.6	8.4
International fare receipts	%	9.3	20.0	12.5	10.5	4.6	33.3	-12.5	5.2
Total international tourism receipts	%	8.5	20.7	4.0	9.2	8.2	18.0	-2.8	8.0

Sources: WTO for international receipts; IMF for international fare receipts and services; World Bank GNP; United Nations for total exports.

LIVERPOOL HOPE UNIVERSITY COLLEGE

world exports, although this percentage can be quite different from one country or sector to another. The distribution of international tourism exports and receipts is very similar to the distribution of total world exports and receipts, with a very high concentration in the North American and Western European regions. On the other hand, the share of developing countries is small, particularly for the export of services. In 1991, the developing countries' share was 23 per cent of total world trade and for services only, 10 per cent.

☐ *Imports in tourism consumption*

Imports include services and consumer goods destined to satisfy both tourism demand and the sectors of national production supplying tourism businesses.

It is vital to calculate the proportion of imports in tourism consumption and to understand the net contribution of international tourism to a country in order to develop tourism and economic policies. However, this is very hard to calculate accurately because of statistical and methodological difficulties. For instance, should expenditure associated with servicing debts incurred by tourism firms be included in the calculation? Similarly, should income from investment in tourism activities abroad be taken into account? Despite these difficulties, several countries do calculate the percentage of imports in their international tourism receipts.

According to the WTO, the proportion of imports as a result of international tourism is particularly high in small countries. In the Caribbean, it is over 50 per cent for Antigua, Aruba and the Bahamas. In contrast, for large industrial countries, the proportion of imports is very low, for instance just 5 per cent for Mexico.

It should be stressed that for many developing countries, the proportion of imports is very high. This is a consequence of the inefficiency of their productive sectors which cannot produce the goods and services needed by international tourism. As a result, the effect of international tourism on the balance of payments is reduced, which is why it is important for them to substitute national products for imports whenever possible.

The proportion of imports varies for each type of activity and for each country. Statistics published by the WTO indicate that for certain countries, particularly small countries like Aruba, imported products provide 85 per cent of the receipts generated by meals and drinks. Therefore, the net contribution of international tourism is very small and is generated mainly from the utilisation of the superstructures. Any decline in international tourism arrivals can have serious repercussions on the economy of these countries.

Table 8.5   *Imports in tourism consumption*

Country	Year	In percentage of international tourism receipts	Remarks
Antigua	1978	60.5	Direct and indirect effects.
Aruba	1979	58.2	Direct and indirect effects.
	1980	58.6	Direct and indirect effects.
Bahamas	1974	72.6	Includes effects induced by household expenditure.
Benin	1975	35.0	
Bermuda	1975	66.3	Includes effects induced by household expenditure.
Guatemala		25.0	Of tourism consumption in catering establishments.
		23.0	Of tourism consumption in first-class hotels.
Indonesia	1979	44.4	
Israel	1981	15.0	Estimate of tourism expenditure on accommodation, food, car rental, local transport, entertainment.
Virgin Islands	1979	35.9	
Jamaica	1982	37.0	On tourism receipts.
Kenya	1976	10.0	
Malawi	1980	15.9	Exclusively imports for tourism consumption.
Morocco	1980	16.1	Forecast of the tourism programme.
Mexico		5.0	
Nigeria	1980	39.1	On total tourism consumption.
New Zealand	1978	8.0 to 46.0	In the construction of 100- to 200-room hotels.
Uganda	1982–90	38.0 to 46.0	Forecast. Hotel accommodation.
St Lucia	1978	45.0	Direct import content.
Sri Lanka	1977	22.0	
Togo		40.0	Accommodation.
		55.0	Food.
		60.0	Purchases in tax-free shops.
		25.0	Transport and tourism trips.
		20.0	Money and stamps.
		50.0	Other tourism activities.
Tunisia		13.7	On international tourism receipts.
		14.6	Accommodation.
		20.0	Travel agencies.
		2.0	Food and drinks.
		22.1	Car hire.
		6.0	Sale of handicrafts.
		10.0	Other tourism activities.

Source: WTO.

The international exchange of services, which includes tourism services, tends to develop very quickly in a similar way to an industrial society moving into the post-industrial phase where it is more reliant on services. Countries go through important structural, economic and social upheavals. The consequences can often be traumatic (although predictable), particularly in the employment sector, which registers a fall of available manpower for many productive sectors of the economy. Faced with these difficulties, it is extremely tempting to introduce protectionist measures which restrict the exchange of both commodities and services. As a result, the development of international tourism is hampered by tariff barriers on imported goods destined for tourism consumption and the productive sectors supplying the tourism industry. Other restrictive measures which affect tourism flows include: limiting the allocation of foreign currency, prohibiting the export of the national currency, prohibiting the use of credit cards abroad, civil and legal restrictions and protectionist tariffs on air transport.

However, international tourism is most restricted by barriers which are not customs barriers. These include the imposition of trade quotas on economic activities related to tourism and ceilings on the number of people who are allowed to travel abroad.

■ The balance of payments

International tourism plays a vital role in stabilising the balance of payments of many countries. It has always been very difficult to account for tourism expenditure and receipts in the balance of payments. There has never been enough information, since many countries could not collect the necessary statistics. However, the WTO and the OECD have eased accounting procedures in international tourism, mainly by expanding the concept of tourism receipts. This has helped to develop macroeconomic policies based on sound analysis and reliable forecasts, concerning not only the influence of international tourism on the balance of payments, but also the influence of the balance of payments (through exchange-rate fluctuations) on the international flow of tourists.

□ *Balance of payments and tourism*

The balance of payments is a statistical account of all the transactions that have taken place between residents of a country and the rest of the world. The primary rule of accounting is to record as credits receipts coming from the rest of the world and as debits payments made to the rest of the world.

The balance of payments records monetary flows which generally represent the real flow of goods and services.

Tourism exchanges between a country and the rest of the world are receipts (expenditure by foreign tourists in a country) and expenditure (expenditure by nationals abroad), to which should be added the proceeds of transporting tourists internationally and the sales or proceeds of tourism equipment and engineering.

☐ *Methods of integrating tourism transactions in the balance of payments*

There are current account transactions in international tourism and capital account transactions. Tourism transactions influence the credit and debit of goods, services and transfers accounts.

☐ The goods account

All the products (consumer goods and capital goods) imported from abroad to satisfy tourism demand are on the *debit* side. It is important for a destination to reduce the debit in this account by introducing policies that favour local products over imported products. However, it should be noted that the consequences of excessive reliance on local products can dissuade tourists from visiting, by limiting their consumer choice. A consumer who cannot purchase the goods that he is used to (for instance certain foods and drinks) may choose not to travel to the destination and ultimately travel agencies will stop promoting it. Therefore, by adjusting prices a country can reduce the debit of the tourism balance and develop tourism activity.

The *credit* side includes all the products sold to tourists: food and drink, souvenirs and all other manufactured products. These sales are assessed by analysing the purchases of tourists in specialised establishments. These can also be goods which the tourist has appreciated in the visited country and which he purchases after his return home (i.e. exports).

☐ The services account

Normally, expenditure and receipts associated with tourism are classified in the 'travel' account. However, tourism expenditure is also represented in the transport, earned income and capital revenue accounts.

- *The 'travel' account* The travel account includes all expenditure by foreign tourists at the destination. On the debit side, expenditure by home tourists abroad is recorded. On the credit side, all receipts provided by foreign visitors to the home country are recorded. This does not include expenditure on international travel but does include the cost of accommodation and internal travel.

  However, the travel account should not be relied upon exclusively when assessing the influence of tourism on the trade balance. Furthermore, the balance of this account has little significance if it is not analysed in conjunction with tourism flows. If the transactions involved are few, equilibrium or even surplus on the credit side may hide the fact that international tourism is underdeveloped.

- *The transport account* Another consequence of international tourism on the balance of payments is expenditure on international transport by tourists. Normally, this is included in the transport account:
  - the destination country adds to its credit side the net costs of international transport by foreign tourists;
  - and it includes on the debit side the cost of its nationals travelling abroad.

  Therefore, the net expenditure of transport must also be added to the travel account to represent the receipts and expenditure of international tourism. This expenditure can substantially change the results. Indeed, with the development of long-haul transport, the cost of transport is often as high as the cost of the stay which is included in the travel account.

- *The earned income account* Certain transfers of money associated with earned income must be included in the balance of payments relating to tourism. Developing countries which want to attract international tourism need skilled foreign workers (specialised in different sectors of tourism, such as travel agents, hotel managers, engineers, technicians, electricians or accountants). Furthermore, they often recruit instructors from abroad to train the local labour force. The cost of recruiting abroad is paid in hard currency and can be very high, particularly in the initial phase of tourism development. It must be recorded on the debit side of the balance of payments relating to tourism (except if the cost is settled by international technical cooperation organisations – UNDP (United Nations Development Plan), ILO – or by foreign countries through bilateral agreement).

  When immigrant workers are employed in the tourism industry, notably the hotel and catering trade, they usually send a proportion of their income to their families back home. This can sometimes be very high. This currency outflow must be recorded on the debit side of the balance of payments relating to tourism.

- *The capital account* These are the costs of capital borrowed abroad (interest) or the costs of foreign capital invested in the country. The destination country must record these expenditures as debits. Certain countries attempt to limit the repatriation of capital by imposing as a condition of foreign investment that a proportion of the revenue should be reinvested in the country. However, the impact of this kind of measure is usually limited. It dissuades potential investors who divert their capital to other countries. Because the tourism sector is very competitive, it is difficult to apply strong limitations, particularly of a financial nature, if these are not being also applied in competing countries.

These different accounts (travel, transport, earned income, capital and goods accounts) confirm the importance of tourism in the balance of payments. Tourism also affects the balance of capital, and this should also be analysed to understand the economic situation of a country.

☐ International tourism and the balance of capital

The movement of capital relating to the financing of tourism infrastructure and superstructure is very important in many countries, notably in Africa, Latin America and Asia, which invite foreign capital investments. In the balance of payments, this capital is recorded as a credit as it involves currency being brought into the country. Subsequently, these receipts are used to finance expenditure (in hard currency) on infrastructure, superstructure and equipment.

However, the consequences of the movement of capital do not only appear in the annual balance but over a longer period. For example, a loan is credited immediately but is in fact a future debt burden which does not appear in the year's balance of payments. Therefore, to evaluate the impact of loans, provisional balances of payments must be established over several years. However, the development of tourism over the period must also be taken into account as it would contribute to the balance of payments by bringing in foreign currency.

There are many varied methods of integrating tourism transactions in the balance of payments and it is important to include all sectors affected by tourism expenditure and receipts to build an accurate and complete picture.

□ *The economic importance of tourism in the balance of payments*

Although it is possible to estimate international tourism receipts, estimating expenditure is far more difficult because of the number of consumers involved (expenditure by public sector organisations notably on promotion, by tourism businesses and by consumers).

The WTO has classified countries according to their international tourism situation from the tourism balance in their balance of payments. This differentiates between international tourism receipts in the tourism and travel account and payments for trips taken by residents of the country. Receipts and expenditure in the capital account, payments received from imports of goods and services destined to tourism consumption and payments resulting from investments and work abroad are excluded from the balance. The balances of the current tourism account reveal the economic situation of countries, and these can be categorised into countries with a positive balance and countries with a negative balance.[5]

Table 8.6   *Tourism balances in OECD countries (in billions of US$ – inflation included)*

	1989	1991	1992
Europe			
Receipts	102.5	130.6	145.8
Expenditure	96.7	123.2	143.4
Balance*	5.8	7.4	2.3
North America			
Receipts	41.6	54.2	59.5
Expenditure	40.8	46.6	51.1
Balance*	0.8	7.6	8.4
Australasia–Japan			
Receipts	7.7	8.9	9.1
Expenditure	27.3	28.9	31.8
Balance*	−19.7	−20.0	−22.6
OECD			
Receipts	151.8	193.8	214.4
Expenditure	164.8	198.7	226.3
Balance*	−13.0	−5.0	−11.9

* The minus signs indicate deficits. Totals having been rounded up, the balances do not always equal the difference between receipts and expenditure.
Source: OECD.

☐ Positive current tourism balances

Positive current tourism balances can either contribute to a positive balance in the balance of goods and services, reduce a negative balance or convert a negative balance into a positive balance.

Countries with positive balances can be grouped into five categories:

1. European countries which are located around the Mediterranean, mainly Spain, France, Italy and the islands of Malta and Cyprus.
2. Certain developed countries with a large tourism sector which have positive balances of similar magnitudes as those of the European countries around the Mediterranean. Austria and Switzerland are included in this group.
3. Developing countries with a buoyant tourism industry and which have a positive balance. They are located near tourism-generating countries (Tunisia, Mexico) or have invested in equipment and actively promote the destination (Thailand).
4. Caribbean countries with a large positive balance.
5. Developing countries with few international tourists but who nevertheless contribute significantly to the balance of payments. In these countries, receipts are usually less than $100 million.

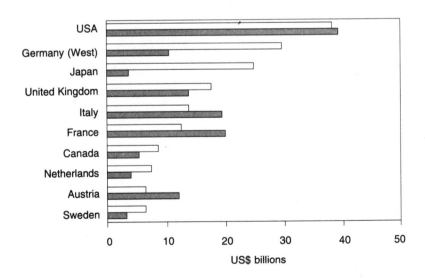

Source: OECD.

Figure 8.4 *Balance of payments for tourism, major tourism countries, 1990*

☐ Negative current tourism balances

Countries with negative current tourism balances are usually countries with a high standard of living and which have high expenditure on tourism, mainly for climatic reasons, for instance Germany, Scandinavia, Canada and the petrol-exporting states of the Gulf.

In developing countries, the most underdeveloped countries generally have negative balances as they do not have the superstructure (transport, accommodation and catering) to satisfy international tourism demand and must finance trips by businessmen, students, pilgrims, diplomats and some leisure travellers. In Africa, the countries of the western sub-region have the greatest tourism deficits, followed by Central Africa and parts of South Africa. Consequently, the main objective of their tourism policy is to institute tourism development programmes in order to attract a greater number of foreign tourists and redress the tourism balance or even turn it positive.

Tourism not only contributes to foreign currency reserves of developing countries but the tourism balance is not as prone to fluctuations in exchange rates as the trade balance.

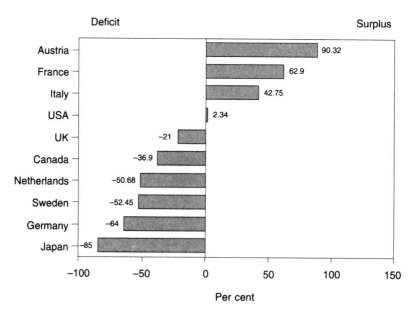

Source: Adapted from OECD figures.

Figure 8.5   *Percentage of deficit and surplus for tourism (balance of payments in major generating countries), 1990*

☐ The tourism foreign account

The contribution of tourism to the balance of payments has been very difficult to evaluate and much research has been undertaken to find methods of presenting a tourism foreign account. The most important work in this field was done by R. Baretje and the researchers of the Centre for High Tourism Studies of Aix-en-Provence in France. The tourism foreign account aims at identifying and grouping the same types of transactions involving transfers of foreign currency so that the net situation of international tourism exchanges can be assessed. This is an accounting method which consists of compiling all the financial statistics relative to international tourism, notably by auditing all the receipts and expenditure in foreign currency resulting from tourism.

The tourism foreign account not only records transactions resulting directly from exchanges with tourists but also transactions relating indirectly to tourism like transport, financial charges, salaries, training and publicity.

The main objective of the tourism foreign account is to provide planners, managers and people responsible for determining economic policy with information to plan efficient measures. Thus, the tourism foreign account contributes to the understanding of the global effect of international tourism transactions and a better understanding of the financial contribution of international tourism.

Tourism activities can have considerable impact on the economy of a country. They affect employment and human resources, economic development in the agricultural and industrial sectors and international exchanges of goods.

The economic impact of tourism is closely linked to the level of economic development in receptor countries. For instance, tourism receipts in small insular tourist receptor countries may be used to finance the imports of some goods and services consumed by tourists. In these cases, the impact is weak and may even be negative when natural resources have been damaged or destroyed by tourists. However, these situations are exceptional and the economic impact of tourism is generally positive in most countries. Thus, a major objective of policy-makers is to find ways and methods of reinforcing the positive effects of tourism and diffusing them throughout the whole economy of the country. This is the main role of organisations who provide support systems for a sustainable tourism development.

References

1. ILO *Social Problems and Employment in the Hotel and Catering Trade, Restaurants and Similar Establishments in Developing Countries*. Geneva, 1983.

2. ILO *Planning Hospitality Training*. April 1976.

3. UNESCO, *Sources No. 55*, February 1994, p. 13.

4. Ibid., p. 13.

5. OECD, *Tourism Policy and International Tourism in OECD Countries – 1991–1992*, Paris, 1994.

Further reading

Archer, B. H. 'The Value of Multipliers and their Policy Implications', *Tourism Management*, 3(4), pp. 236–41, 1982.

BTA. *Employment in Tourism*. London: British Tourist Authority, 1982.

Cooper, C., Fletcher, J., Gilbert, D. and Wanhill, S. *Tourism Principles and Practices*. London: Pitman, 1993.

Duffield, B. S. 'Tourism: The Measurement of Economic and Social Impact', *Tourism Management*, 3(4), pp. 248–55, 1982.

Duffield, B. S. and Long, J. 'The Role of Tourism in the Economy of Scotland', *Tourism Management*, 5(4), pp. 258–68, 1984.

Edington, J. M. and Edington, M. A. *Ecology, Recreation and Tourism*. Cambridge: Cambridge University Press, 1986.

Gray, H. P. *International Travel – International Trade*. Lexington: D.C. Heath & Co., 1970.

Gray, H. P. 'The Contribution of Economics to Tourism', *Annals of Tourism Research*, 9(1), pp. 105–25, 1982.

Lea, J. *Tourism and Development in the Third World*. London: Routledge, 1988.

Mathieson, A. and Wall, G. *Tourism: Economic, Physical and Social Impacts*. Harlow: Longman, 1982.

Mill, R. C. and Morrison, A. *The Tourism System*. Englewood Cliffs, NJ: Prentice-Hall, 1985.

Murphy, P. E. *Tourism: A Community Approach*. London: Methuen, 1985.

OECD. *The Impact of Tourism on the Environment*. Paris, 1981.

OECD. *Case Studies of the Impact of Tourism on the Environment*. Paris, 1981.

Pearce, D. *Tourism Development*. Harlow: Longman, 1989.

Williams, A. M. *Tourism and Economic Development*. London: Belhaven, 1988.

■ *Chapter 9* ■

Tourism Organisations and Tourism Policies

Tourism organisations: national public sector tourism organisations; national professional organisations; the World Tourism Organisation (WTO); intergovernmental organisations partially responsible for tourism; non-governmental international organisations

The General Agreement on Trade and Services and tourism policy: tourism elements in GATS; the liberalisation process – reducing tariff barriers; benefits of GATS to tourism

Promotional policies in international tourism: tourism promotion campaigns; promotional expenses abroad; the effectiveness of tourism promotion policies

Tourism policies, planning and land development: tourism development methods; tourism site development

Social tourism policies

International tourism policies and public health: international tourism and health risks; health tourism products – international tourism and improvement in health standards

The tourism policies of many countries are a component (often an essential one) of their overall economic policy. They are developed and implemented by both professionals and administrative organisations.

Despite operating in a competitive environment, the different agents of national tourism policies are called upon to cooperate by international organisations, particularly the World Tourism Organisation. They ensure the growth of international tourism by applying a set of specialised methods among which tourism promotion programmes are particularly effective and play an important role.

■ Tourism organisations

Tourism organisations aim to promote national and international tourism development and to balance the macroeconomic policies of each region and each sector involved in tourism. Nationally, these are public sector agencies and professional associations (comprising hotels, travel agencies, transport companies, etc.), and internationally, governmental and non-governmental organisations.

□ *National public sector tourism organisations*

National public sector tourism organisations are responsible for the organisation, development and operation of a country's tourism industry. They organise tourism promotion at a national level, control the activities of all tourism sectors and provide national coordination for regional tourism development.

A centralised state will either have a Ministry of Tourism, a State Department for Tourism attached to a ministry (of the economy or of foreign trade), a General Committee on Tourism or a tourism section within a ministry (for instance, the Ministry for Youth or for Sports and Leisure). The level of organisation adopted reflects the importance of tourism in the national economy. When power is controlled from the centre, tourism is the responsibility of the central administration. If power is decentralised, then tourism is the responsibility of local administrations.

The responsibility for tourism in a country which has adopted a federal system generally devolves to each federated state and to the local administration, even if the central government has a determining influence on tourism policy. In some cases, the responsibility for tourism is shared between the federated states and central government. In some countries, however, tourism policy is in the hands of non-governmental organisations, although it is recognised and controlled by the government.

The WTO has identified four key government functions controlling the development of tourism: coordination of tourism activities; legislation and regulation; planning; and finance.

National tourism organisations have the following responsibilities:[1]

- to represent the government's tourism interests on an international scale; to negotiate bilateral and multilateral agreements with the objective of increasing tourism flows between participating states; to organise joint marketing studies of tourism markets; to optimise tourism sites and well-known national resources; to encourage technical and financial cooperation; to support reciprocal relaxation of customs, police and monetary regulation and to carry out technological transfers (for instance, in hotels, winter sports resort equipment);
- to organise tourism services on a national and an international scale;
- to plan and develop tourism (formulating a tourism development plan);
- to regulate and control enterprises involved in tourism (regulations and legislation in the hotel trade, classification of hotels and restaurants, inspections and the issue of operating licences);

- to publish statistics, surveys, studies and market research (opinion polls, consumer behaviour studies);
- to promote the destination in other countries (establishing tourist offices abroad to provide information and promotion; the publication of brochures, leaflets, guides and specific tourism information);
- to promote the destination domestically (publicity campaigns in the press, on the radio and on television);
- to initiate actions to relax, simplify or eliminate customs and border police controls;
- to create structures to welcome visitors and provide tourist information (special police units have been set up in nineteen countries specifically to help domestic and international visitors);
- to provide professional training in tourism (courses, seminars and study programmes);
- to preserve, protect and utilise cultural tourism resources and those unique to the country's heritage (monuments, historic sites, cultural and artistic conservation campaigns);
- to protect the environment (setting up campaigns to protect nature, creating national parks and protecting nature reserves).

National tourism organisations must have the necessary powers and resources (human and budgetary) to carry out their responsibilities properly. Their effectiveness depends on their productivity, their organisational skills, how well they adapt to situations and on the decisions they take and implement. However, their actions are frequently hampered by insufficient resources.

Quite often, countries which claim that they consider tourism to be a priority do not provide their national tourism organisations – including their Ministries of Tourism – with sufficient material resources and staff. It is apparent that tourism still does not benefit from the advantages extended to other industrial sectors, probably because its importance is relatively recent and it lacks tradition.

Local administrations (for instance, France has several levels: regions, departments and communes) are important national tourism organisations, particularly in decentralised states. They provide their own tourism services, such as tourist information centres and tourist offices, which play an essential role in welcoming tourists and promoting tourism. Local administrations often have large budgets at their disposal to spend on tourism. Therefore their impact is determined by the resources available and the responsibilities allocated to them.

Other national administrations (central or local) have responsibilities that directly influence tourism policy. The ministries responsible for the economy, finance and planning are important in the development and implementation of policies which directly influence tourism flows: investment, loans and credits, money exchange regulation and exchange rates, and border controls. Transport policies, and therefore indirectly tourism policies, depend on the ministry responsible for transport which can impose protectionist or liberal measures on traffic (for example, the fifth freedom in airline regulation, charter traffic) and on tariffs. Ministries responsible for professional training, land development, equipment, labour, environment, agriculture, fisheries and health contribute both directly and indirectly to tourism policies.

National tourism organisations (both central and local) are crucial in the promotion of tourism policies. However, they are dependent on cooperation with other administrations, on parliaments (budget votes) and also on public opinion. For this reason, the WTO has, on several occasions, highlighted the importance of developing the public's awareness of tourism. Governments are invited to endorse the people's right to enjoy leisure and holidays, to raise their awareness of tourism, to proclaim the rights and the duties of countries and tourists in international tourism and to develop tourism flows and the economic and social activities involved in tourism.

☐ *National professional organisations*

Professionals concerned with tourism establish national professional organisations in the form of non-profit-making associations, in order to encourage the development of their professional activities and to protect the interests of their sector.

There are as many professional organisations as there are professional specialisms in domestic and international tourism (the hotel trade, travel agencies, bus and coach transport companies, tourist information centres and tourist offices, rural tourism, climatic and spa resorts, congress and conference cities, winter sports resorts, tour guides, etc.).

These professional organisations are meant to speak out on behalf of national tourism administrations. In many countries, the largest organisations are represented on advisory councils (like the Economic and Social Council and the Higher Council for Tourism) and in parliamentary assemblies. Internationally, they are grouped in non-governmental specialised professional international organisations, for instance, the World Association for Travel Agencies and tour operators (WATA); the International Association of Tour Managers (IATM) for tour guides; the European Federation of Conference Towns; the Timeshare Council and the European Timeshare Federation.

☐ *The World Tourism Organisation (WTO)*

This is the only intergovernmental organisation to hold worldwide responsibilities, encompassing all tourism activities. The Organisation plays a major role in the development of international tourism.

☐ Background

The WTO is the successor of the IUOTO (International Union of Official Tourism Organisations). The IUOTO had been an association of around 100 national tourism organisations since 1946. The WTO was created at the IUOTO Extraordinary General Assembly which took place in Mexico between 17 and 28 September 1975. The procedure adopted during the meeting ensured the continuity of international actions initiated under the old IUOTO by the new WTO.[2]

Thus the WTO is the intergovernmental organisation with responsibility for tourism and has been recognised as such by the General Assembly of the United Nations.

☐ The aims of the WTO

Article 3 of the WTO statute declares that the fundamental objective of the World Tourism Organisation is to promote and develop tourism in order to contribute to economic expansion, international understanding, peace and prosperity, as well as to promote universal respect and the observance of basic human freedom and rights without distinction of race, sex, language or religion.

To achieve these objectives, the WTO is committed to taking 'all necessary measures', with particular consideration for the interests of developing countries (art. 3§2).

Box 9.1 *Areas of activity of the WTO*

With its own resources and the consultants whose work it monitors, the WTO is able to provide assistance in the following areas:

- Inventories of existing and potential tourism resources, national tourism development master plans; formulation of policies, plans and programmes for development of domestic tourism.

- Institutional framework of national tourism administrative structures; tourism development corporations; legislation and regulation.
- Evaluation of the impact of tourism on the national economy and on the environment.
- Statistics, forecasting, statistical analysis, market research, market analysis; promotion, publicity and public relations.
- Training, feasibility studies for tourism and hotel schools, management development.
- Planning and management of the aims of national, social and cultural value for tourism uses.
- Area development, development of new tourism sites, development of particular tourism products (beaches and aquatic sports, spas, mountain resorts, ski resorts, leisure parks, wildlife reserves, national parks, cultural tourism and ecotourism).
- Tourist accommodation (planning, location, operation and improvement of hotels, holiday camps, rest homes, motels, camping sites, etc.), hotel classification systems.
- Sources and methods of finance for tourism investments. Pre-investment studies, feasibility studies of investment projects, cost/benefit analysis.
- Safety of tourists and tourist facilities.

Source: WTO.

☐ The members

The WTO has four levels of membership:

- *Ordinary members* These are countries which have ratified or accepted the constitutional statutes of the WTO: 120 countries on 1 January 1994.
- *Associate members* There are three territories that are not states (Netherlands Antilles, Gibraltar, Macao).
- *One permanent observer* The Vatican.
- *Affiliated members* There were 187 international non-governmental organisations and public and private national organisations on 1 January 1994 who are actively involved in tourism; these are airline companies, travel agencies and travel organisations, tourism institutes and research centres, hotel and restaurant chains and training centres.

These organisations join the Committee of Affiliated Members and pay a subscription fee to the WTO. They are invited to participate in the work of the different organs of the WTO and to undertake special actions that other international organisations cannot. However, in reality, this unique opportunity for cooperation between intergovernmental organisations and the most important associations, federations, enterprises and services involved in tourism does not seem to be taken up very often.

☐ The structure of the WTO

The structure of the WTO includes the General Secretariat, the General Assembly, the Executive Council, the Regional Committees, the Committee of Affiliated Members and the various commissions and specialised committees.

The General Assembly and its Regional Commissions

The General Assembly is the principal organ of the Organisation. It is composed of delegates from the associated and ordinary members (i.e., countries and affiliated members). They meet in ordinary session twice a year to adopt recommendations and agree the budget of the Organisation. Decisions are adopted by a two-thirds majority.

There are six Regional Commissions created by the General Assembly. They are charged with implementing the recommendations of the Assembly in their respective regions and encouraging intra-regional tourism. These are the WTO Commissions for Africa, the Americas, East Asia and the Pacific, South Asia, Europe and the Middle East.

The Executive Council and the Committees

The Executive Council is made up of twenty ordinary members (countries) elected by the Assembly. It meets twice a year and implements the necessary measures to enforce the resolutions taken by the General Assembly. It administers and controls the budget of the Organisation. It has four subsidiary committees: the Programming and Co-ordination Technical Committee, the Budget and Finance Committee, the Environment Committee and the Facilitation Committee. The mandate of the Facilitation Committee is to propose measures that relax administrative, customs, police and health controls and make them more flexible in order to encourage tourism movements across borders.

The General Secretariat

The General Secretariat comprises the Secretary-General and a staff of 85 international officials (in 1994) based in Madrid. The Secretary-General is charged with implementing the directives of the Assembly and of the Council. He reports on the activities of the Organisation and submits a general work programme (art. 23) in which (and from which) he has important initiatory powers. The programme reflects the Secretary General's personality and the relationship he has built up with the governments of member states. The Secretary General is the Secretariat's head of personnel. He submits the WTO's budget proposals and management accounts to the Council. He is elected on the recommendation of the Council for a four-year period by a two-thirds majority of members with voting rights at the Assembly. The General Secretary's mandate is renewable (art. 22).

The Committee of Affiliated Members

The Committee is organised into working groups (youth tourism; consumer choice and behaviour; tourism investments; tourism and employment; tourism and health; tourism and information technology).

□ The activities of the WTO

The WTO has many activities covering all fields of international tourism.

- *Studies and statistics*
  Studies: There are seven main areas of study (world tourism trends; tourism markets; tourism enterprises and equipment; tourism planning and development; economic and financial analysis; sociological impacts of tourism activity; tourism representation abroad).
  Statistics: Regional and global statistics are published regularly.
  Information: There are regular publications providing up-to-date information – for instance, the WTO News.
  Training: Workshops are organised on the techniques of financing tourism projects, training, marketing tourism products and land development.
     The WTO organises joint meetings and seminars with other international organisations, notably with the ILO (International Labour Organisation) and the UNEP (the United Nations Environment Programme).
- *Technical assistance* The WTO provides technical assistance to developing countries either directly funded by its own budgets or by delegating the project and its funding to the United Nations Development Programme (UNDP).

- *Consultations and resolutions* The World Tourism Organisation aims at encouraging *international consultation* between its different organs (including the regional commissions) by proposing specific plans or actions to member countries.

  The organs of the WTO adopt resolutions and draft recommendations to member-countries which are vital for the social development of tourism, notably, the Manila Declaration (1980) and the Acapulco Charter (1982).

Box 9.2 *The main points of the Manila Declaration 1980*

- Tourism is a basic need.
- Society has a duty to enable its citizens to participate in tourism. Holidays with pay and social tourism are objectives which will enable the least privileged to participate.
- Development of tourism from abroad should be accompanied by similar efforts to expand domestic tourism.
- Economic returns should not be the sole basis for encouraging tourism. There is a cultural and moral dimension which must be fostered and protected against economic distortions.
- Tourism should form part of youth education and training, and participation encouraged.
- Improved employment conditions in tourism should be promoted.
- Tourism resources should be managed and conserved.
- International cooperation, both technical and financial, should be encouraged.

Box 9.3 *WTO – international tourism cooperation*

1. Operational and sectorial support missions (511)

The purpose of these missions, which are mainly financed by the United Nations Development Programme (UNDP) and are usually fielded for short periods (one to two weeks), is:

- to identify technical cooperation needs in the field of tourism;
- to advise governments on the various aspects of tourism policy; and
- to formulate project proposals for funding by UNDP or other financing sources.

2. Technical cooperation projects (126)

126 projects were implemented by the WTO between 1980 and 1992 in its capacity as an Executive Agency of the UNDP. The beneficiaries may be countries, sub-regions or regions.

Achievements, 1980–92 (September)

- 511 operational and sectoral support missions
- 126 technical cooperation projects
- US$17.1 million spent on projects (1980–91)

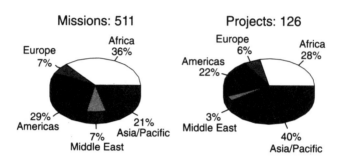

Source: WTO.

Note: Percentages are rounded up to or down to the nearest whole number and may not add up to 100%

Figure 9.1   *Breakdown of missions and projects by region (1980–September 1992)*

☐ *Intergovernmental organisations partially responsible for tourism*

☐ International organisations within the United Nations

- The *United Nations Organisation* measures were adopted at the Conference of Rome (1963) on tourism and international travel;
- The *World Health Organisation (WHO)* is interested in the protection of international tourism from health risks and the extent to which tourism contributes to raising health standards;
- The *ICAO (International Civil Aviation Organisation)* is concerned with the relationship between air transport and international tourism;
- The *IRDB (International Reconstruction and Development Bank)* and its subsidiaries finance an important part of tourism investment in developing countries;

- The *ILO* is directly involved with professional training and employment in the tourism sector;
- The *UNDP* reserves part of its budget for joint technical assistance programmes with the WTO in developing countries;
- *UNESCO* is responsible for human resources training and links between tourism and cultural development.

The contribution of these organisations to the development of tourism preceded that of the WTO which was only created in 1975. Previously, they had been more influential than the IUOTO, which only held the status of non-governmental organisation. Since the creation of the WTO and the development of its activities, these various organisations have a complementary function and cooperate with the WTO on a regular basis, even though the WTO is not part of the United Nations Organisation. These links are managed by general and *ad hoc* cooperation agreements. In this way, tourism is represented internationally, despite not being represented by a specialised organisation in the United Nations system.

☐ Regional organisations

Most regional organisations include the tourism sector among their general economic responsibilities.

The *OECD (Organisation for Economic Cooperation and Development)* studies the problems created by tourism development in member countries which have adopted market economics (in other words the main generator/receptor countries in the world). The OECD publishes an annual report on tourism policies and on the state of tourism in industrialised countries.

The majority of large regional organisations responsible for economics (the *European Union*, the *Organisation of African States*, the *African Community*, the *Association of South East Asian States*) are concerned with various aspects of the tourism sector (studies, developing common projects, recommendations to member countries). Large intergovernmental regional banks are called upon to finance tourism investments (*the European Investment Bank, the African Development Bank, the Asian Bank for Development*).

In certain regions, countries establish international institutions exclusively responsible for tourism in order to create the best conditions for the development of international or intra-regional tourism. These include *the Indian Ocean Tourism Alliance* (Comoros, Mauritius, Madagascar, Réunion and the Seychelles) and the *Tourism Council of the South Pacific*.

☐ *Non-governmental international organisations*

Non-governmental international organisations group together professional, scientific or social organisations which have already been established in different countries. Their aim is to encourage exchanges and contacts between professionals of different nationalities, to provide study groups and information departments and to send representatives to international institutions which take important tourism policy decisions. They constitute a powerful lobby at international organisations.

The main non-governmental international organisations are:

- *Travel agencies and tour operators*
  - World Association of Travel Agencies (WATA) in Geneva;
  - Universal Federation of Travel Agents Associations (UFTAA) in Monaco;
  - International Council of Travel Agents (ICTA) in London;
  - International Sightseeing and Tours Association (ISTA) in Vienna;
  - International Association of Tour Managers (IATM) in London;
  - EU Group of National Unions of Travel Agencies in Milan.
- *Transport*
  - International Air transport Association (IATA) in Montreal and Geneva;
  - European Regional Airlines Association (ERAA) in the United Kingdom;
  - Airports Association Council International (AACC) in Geneva;
  - International Union of Railways in Paris.
- *Hotel and catering*
  - Hotel Catering and Institutional Management Association (HCIMA) in London;
  - International Hotel Association in Paris (IHA);
  - Caribbean Hotel Association (CHA).

■ The General Agreement on Trade and Services and tourism policy

The General Agreement on Trade and Services (GATS) constitutes one aspect of the Uruguay round of negotiations on world trade. The principle behind GATS is the liberalisation of exchanges of services, and is adapted from the agreements on the liberalisation of exchanges of goods.

The GATS is a multilateral agreement which aims at liberalising international trade in services as a means of promoting the economic growth and development of all its members. The GATS has been established as part of the multilateral trade negotiations which, in addition to establishing new rules for services, amount to a complete overhaul of the GATT trade system.

The GATS has many implications for tourism, particularly for tourism policymakers. These were detailed in a 1994 report entitled *Tourism Services and the GATS* commissioned by the WTO, UNCTAD and the GATT.

Box 9.4 *GATS and tourism offers*

Many countries have made offers indicating possibilities for foreign suppliers to sell services cross-border and/or via a commercial presence in the following sectors:

- *Sub-sectors frequently mentioned in offers*
  Hotels and resorts: development and management
  Restaurants
  Travel agencies
  Tour operators
  Tourist guides
- *Other activities relating to:*
  Tourist transport operators
  Tourist marina operators
  Hunting
  Yachting
  Spa and thalassotherapy centres
  Local inland water tours
  Cruise ships
  Conference centres
  Tourist property management
  Tourism consultancy
  Rental of vehicles, caravans, watercraft
  Tourist shops
  Entertainment, gambling

Source: M. Handchouz, M. Kanasabe, D. Diaz. *Tourism Services and the GATS*, WTO, UNCTAD and GATT, 1994

☐ *Tourism elements in GATS*

The report defines tourism services as 'products' or outputs resulting from the activities of economic units, whether profit-making or non-profit-making, which are destined for final or intermediate tourism consumers, provided that the value of these activities can be measured in economic terms. Tourism differs from other services in that it is a final consumer orientated activity. Unlike other services tourism is not a specific type of service, but an assortment of services consumed by the visitor.

Accordingly, at international level, trade in tourism services (i.e. the provision of tourism services) occurs when a supplier of one country sells a service: (1) in his own country, to a visitor (consumer) who is resident of another country or to a supplier of another country, either through cross-border movement of the foreign supplier or via the foreign supplier's commercial presence or establishment in the first country; (2) in another country, to a supplier or resident of, or visitor to, that country, either cross-border, via an agent, through a commercial presence or by the establishment in the other country.

The key to achieving effective liberalisation in any particular sector like tourism is contained in the obligation to allow market access and national treatment.

- *Market access*   This means granting foreign service suppliers access to domestic markets. This includes allowing the provision of services cross-border or through some kind of commercial presence or through the movement of foreign service suppliers into the market.
- *National treatment*   This means that countries are obliged to treat foreign tourism service suppliers in the same way as domestic service suppliers.

☐ The liberalisation process – reducing trade barriers

The GATS agreement is a long-term undertaking in which all significant trading countries are likely to become members. Its importance will lie not so much in any liberalisation that might take place immediately as in the fact that it will enable liberalisation to occur via a continuing process of detailed negotiation between countries.

The detailed negotiations are about reducing barriers which restrict the freedom of service suppliers to operate in foreign markets, either through establishing a facility there with the necessary foreign personnel or through cross-border trade. The barriers to such trade derive from restrictions on market access and national treatment.

In terms of market access restrictions, the GATS deals with trade restrictions such as:

- maximum foreign ownership limitations;
- restrictions on the establishment of some kind of local representation – for instance, a foreign company's ability to acquire a presence in the market is blocked;
- restrictions on the ability of service suppliers to choose the type of business (e.g. company, partnership) through which they operate;
- limitations on the overall number of service suppliers allowed to operate in the market, because of a quota system or a monopoly situation.

National treatment limitations essentially relate to measures or practices which restrict competitive opportunities for foreign suppliers. These include limited use of a company's well-known logo or title, discriminatory restrictions on the mobility of foreign personnel, an obligation to involve local personnel in all projects, or nationality requirements in order to carry out specific types of work.

The Uruguay round was primarily about the clear identification and subsequent gradual reduction of such barriers. What this means in practice is that countries have begun the multilateral process of exchanging concessions relating to market access and national treatment among themselves or, in other words, the elimination of barriers to trade in services.

□ *Benefits of GATS to tourism*

The benefit of GATS to tourism is the liberalisation of international tourism exchanges of tourism services. GATS will help:

- the production of tourism services;
- the movement of people linked to these services;
- the global development of tourism.

□ The production of tourism services

There are several obstacles to business which tourism service suppliers share with other service and manufacturing businesses. The key resources of any service business are the financial, human and intellectual capital which are needed to solve business problems, exploit opportunities and compete in the market-place. What this agreement does is tackle those basic impediments to a company's ability to deploy those key resources or, in other words, to move money, information and people across borders.

This would help to ensure that suppliers of tourism services are not frustrated in their ability to take advantage of market access commitments inscribed in another party's schedule. Tourism enterprises generally need to install, maintain and interconnect with terminal and communication equipment in order to supply tourism services in another country, for example, when a travel agent in one country makes arrangements for holidays in another.

☐ The movement of people linked to tourism services

GATS will facilitate the movement of people supplying services. Tourism services are also people-intensive in the sense that the provision of such services often requires close personal contact between supplier and client. It is clear therefore that the ability to move key personnel into and out of markets can be a crucial component of business strategy for tourism enterprises with international operations.

The reality, however, is that virtually every country imposes visa and work permit restrictions, which inhibit, delay or render uncertain the movement of professional, managerial and technical personnel to where they are needed. The GATS agreement can be of use to tourism services because it provides a framework for negotiating temporary entry (meaning without intent to establish permanent residence) of service personnel into the territory of other parties.

☐ The global development of tourism

GATS will contribute to the worldwide development of tourism. It will provide *increased transparency* by way of clear and detailed information on conditions of access and operation in all services markets of GATS members.

It will also constrain – and should over time eliminate – government discrimination towards foreign service companies. A *dispute settlement mechanism* would provide rights of compensation or retaliation in cases of violation of the national treatment principle.

The increasing participation of developing countries in world services trade is provided for in the GATS through the negotiation of specific market opening commitments. The development objective relates to three main areas:

- *Strengthening the domestic services capabilities of developing countries* through access to technology on a commercial basis. In concrete terms, greater access to technology and know-how could be realised by developing countries attaching conditions to their market opening commitments, for example, minimum requirements for training and employment in foreign-owned hotels.

- *Improving the access of developing countries to distribution channels and information networks.* In the tourism sector, this refers above all to access to computerised information and reservation networks managed and owned by entities in industrialised countries.
- *Liberalising market access in sectors and modes of supply of export interest to developing countries.* For instance, this refers to the freedom to deploy abroad not only key personnel but also regular personnel in places where developing countries are supplying tourism services.[3]

■ Promotional policies in international tourism

Promotional policies to attract foreign visitors to the country are implemented by national tourism administrations called either National Tourist Offices, Organisations or Boards (referred to in this text as NTOs). However, local governments of each destination in the country and professionals in the different tourism sectors (transport professionals, travel agents, hoteliers, etc.) are increasingly called upon to join in promoting ventures and areas that may benefit them. Notably, associations or groupings with similar economic interests support and complement the promotional actions of the national tourism administration. They even at times replace them.

NTOs are allocated budgets to mount publicity campaigns designed to raise the awareness of the general public and of tourism professionals in the generating markets.

□ *Tourism promotion campaigns*

These are an integral part of marketing campaigns. The objective of promotional campaigns is to motivate three categories of potential clients to include the country in their tourism plans:

- individual tourists
- travel agencies and tour operators and organisers of social tourism
- transport businesses, in particular the airline companies

Public opinion (horizontal segmentation) as well as the opinion of professional and socio-professional categories (for instance, doctors) in a country (vertical segmentation) or a region (both vertical and horizontal segmentation) also influence tourists' decision to visit a destination.

The first stage of a promotional campaign is to conduct a market study for one or two specific products. According to WTO recommendations, a promotional campaign should always concentrate on the quality image of the country. It should be based on its symbolic characteristics, which should be presented as attractively as possible.[4]

There are several different promotional activities in a campaign: press conferences; debating evenings with professionals of the tourism industry and with the press; inviting foreign journalists to the country; documentaries and debates on the radio and on television; complimentary distribution of audio-visual material; films; slides; brochures; folklore shows and familiarisation trips for tourism professionals (e.g. travel agents).

A promotional campaign follows a well-established pattern. The appropriate market for the destination, once identified, should be targeted at the suitable moment when tourism choices and decisions are being made:

- for tour operators, promotional campaigns must be under way early enough to allow them to design and package products so that these are featured in their annual brochures (therefore, at least six months before the publication date of these brochures);
- for travel agencies, the campaign should start eight to twelve months before the tourist season;
- for tourists, at least six to eight months before the planned departure date.

A good promotional campaign satisfies the following conditions:

- it is focused;
- the organisations or people running it are known to the potential market;
- it is easy to understand;
- it addresses the particular interests of the tourist;
- it offers a product that is economically accessible;
- it is coherent (the different methods of information dissemination must communicate the same information on the destination);
- it portrays the truth.

Several market research and marketing methods (publicity films, brochures, posters) are adopted in promoting a country abroad. Promotional material for the international market is often distributed from temporary information stands at trade fairs, where they are accessible to both tourism professionals and the public.

☐ *Promotional expenditure abroad*

Promotional budgets of NTOs do not always reflect the total promotional effort. They are often complemented by promotional activities from other organisations and public and private marketing efforts at national, regional and local levels. Tour operators, transport companies (particularly airline companies) and hotel chains promote their products but also the destination country. Because of the large number of organisations now involved in promoting tourism, there are problems of coordination and coherence of content. These problems are usually solved by associations composed of representatives of the administration and of the professionals concerned. The total promotional effort must be taken into account in order to estimate the expenditure on tourism promotion abroad in real terms.

Table 9.1 *Promotional budgets of national tourism administrations in the Americas, 1993*

Country (US$000)	Promotional budget of budget	Receipts per US$1
Caribbean		
Bermuda	14,366	36
Puerto Rico	33,011	49
Central America		
Guatemala	2,705	96
North America		
Canada	18,720	297
Mexico	36,170	159
United States	12,600	4,484
South America		
Brazil	4,772	303
Chile	925	865
Paraguay	369	504

Source: WTO.

The size of the promotion budget can exceed 50 per cent of the NTO's total budget. Budgets for promoting tourism abroad finance the following functions: publicity, public relations, promotional support, fairs and exhibitions, study and information trips, seminars, work-groups, congresses, conferences, and so on.

A detailed analysis which breaks down the expenditure abroad by each function shows that, for most countries, publicity and public relations receive the largest proportion of the budget. This proportion is normally a third of the total budget but can reach up to two-thirds for certain countries.

- The aim of *publicity* is to inform the market and create effective demand (purchases) for tourism to the country. The methods of publicity used abroad by NTOs are posters, advertising in the press, documentaries, editorials, television and radio. These are supported by leaflets and brochures which are distributed to travel agencies and representative offices (National Tourist Offices abroad).

  The press is the most used method of publicity, followed by the radio and the cinema. Television is especially important in the United States.
- *Trade fairs and exhibitions* open to both the general public and tourism professionals (usually in the main tourism generator and receptor countries) play an important commercial role. They are becoming increasingly frequent around the world − for instance, in London (the World Travel Market), Paris (the Salon Mondial de Tourisme), Berlin (the ITB), Chicago and Madrid (FITUR).
- Expenditure on *promotional support* is lower than on publicity and trade fairs. It includes expenditure on printing promotional material (brochures, posters) and the cost of sending them to foreign markets. This information (which is free) is generally exempt from customs duty.
- Expenditure on *tourism offices abroad* consists of set-up and running costs. The function of tourism offices abroad is to distribute publicity brochures and provide information, implement promotional activities and cooperate with tour operators, travel agencies and transport companies.

Box 9.5 *The World Travel Market − a profile*

The World Travel Market in London is attended by senior management and trade buyers from every sector of the international industry. The importance of a business dedicated to industry professionals was reinforced by the 1993 attendance figures. 64 per cent were of managerial status and above. Two-thirds stated that their objectives were comprehensively met.

For many, the World Travel Market is the only event they attend regularly and is a vital opportunity to meet industry suppliers.

EXHIBITION ATTENDANCE

Trade visitors	43,903
Exhibiting personnel	14,459
Travel Media	1,810
World Travel Market 1993 participants	60,172

(Excludes travel and tourism students)

Whilst most exhibitions address national requirements, the World Travel Market serves the needs of the global industry.

INTERNATIONAL BUSINESS CONDUCTED

Europe (except UK)	26%
North America and Caribbean	19%
United Kingdom	17%
Asia and Australasia	17%
Middle East and Africa	14%
South and Central America	7%

OVERSEAS VISITORS

Western Europe (EU)	4,574
Western Europe (non-EU)	1,190
Eastern Europe	1,550
Middle East and Africa	1,429
North America	1,014
Far East and Australasia	608
South and Central America	328

In 1993 over 80 per cent of the business was of an international nature.

NATURE OF BUSINESS
(no. of visitors)

Travel Agency	12,726
Tour Operator	11,038
Hotel/Accommodation	6,476
Incentive/Conference Organiser	5,342
Transport: Air, Road, Rail, Shipping	4,722
Business/Group Travel	4,569
Tourist Organisation/ Association	2,467
Tourist Attractions	1,323
Technology Reservation	969

(Registration card permitted multiple choice)

VISITOR JOB FUNCTION

Chairman, President, MD, Vice President, Director	11,396
Manager	10,265
Executive	3,444
Travel Consultant, Clerk	8,082
PA, Secretary	1,209

(Excludes non-specifiers)

Source: 1993 Exhibition Report, Reed Exhibition Companies (UK).

☐ The effectiveness of tourism promotion policies

It is difficult to measure the effectiveness of international tourism promotion policies accurately. Promotion is only one element among several others (e.g., exchange rates, prices, political situation) which contributes to influencing the choice of foreign holiday taken by the tourist. Nevertheless, it is important to assess its effectiveness in order to increase wherever possible its motivating powers.

The WTO has devised promotion effectiveness indicators which are based on the relationship between expenditure on promotion abroad and receipts and arrivals of foreign tourists in the country. However, this only measures the effectiveness of promotion abroad. The budget spent abroad is divided by the number of tourist arrivals to obtain a ratio which indicates how many US dollars are needed to attract one tourist to the country. Another ratio based on dividing the amount of international tourism receipts by the amount spent on promotion gives the number of US dollars generated for the expenditure of US$1 on promotion.

Although these ratios should be used carefully, they do give useful indications of the effectiveness of promotion. The most well-known tourism countries have the highest ratio of revenue from foreign visitors to promotion expenditure. Developing countries tend to have low ratios, further evidence of the problems they face in international tourism development.

The effectiveness of promotional campaigns can be reinforced by international co-operation agreements between Tourism Ministries (or administrations responsible for tourism). The objective of these accords is either to exchange or to pool promotional means (posters, audio-visual material, joint use of representative offices) or implement joint promotional activities in generating markets.

▮ Tourism policies, planning and land development

Planning is central to tourism development. It defines short- and long-term objectives and coordinates the resources and means to implement them. These objectives have a direct influence and often even condition land development projects and infrastructure, transport and industrial projects.

Tourism planning has economic as well as non-economic aims:

- The direct economic objectives of tourism planning are to increase the national income and to create jobs. Indirectly, it seeks to increase foreign currency reserves.
- The non-economic objectives, more important in the long term, concern the protection and preservation of natural resources and aim to raise living standards by making leisure and travel available to all.

To achieve these objectives, tourism planning must coordinate ventures at an interregional level with those at a national and local level. Regional plans are developed with the support of international organisations[5] and concern programmes involving several countries in a region, for instance in West Africa and between certain countries in the Mediterranean. These interregional plans are particularly valuable to countries with few financial resources as they allow them to share the cost of building large infrastructures which can be used by all the countries in the region (an international airport, for instance). However, nationalism can sometimes impede the development of interregional planning.

Planning at a national level is more usual. It links land development plans with the objectives of tourism development and seeks to coordinate and optimise investment in tourism. Planning at a local level identifies the problems and needs of the population.

The first tourism development plans were drafted as a result of the rapid increases in tourism flows and their geographical concentration. The objective of these plans is to organise and develop leisure facilities. Tourism development is concerned with the spacial economics of a country, its regional policies and international cooperation.

Economic policies specific to the tourism sector encourage tourism development by adopting specific budgetary, monetary and fiscal measures.

- *Budgetary measures* include government financing from a budget specifically allocated to tourism (which also finances the promotion of the country abroad). This is allocated in the form of:
  - *subsidies* designed to encourage activities considered to be priority (activities in mountain areas, activities which highlight the national heritage, social accommodation);
  - *loans* to finance investments of large tourism infrastructure projects and transport and accommodation projects. Interest rates on these loans are usually very low.
- *Monetary measures* are taken to maintain the international competitiveness of a country's tourism products. Some countries are following foreign exchange-rate strategies by devaluing their currency to compensate for domestic inflation or to resist foreign competition.

- *Fiscal measures* are taxation advantages extended to tourism firms. These can be total or partial exemptions, tax reductions or tax holidays.

☐ *Tourism development methods*

There are various tourism development methods. These are adapted to the regional, sectorial and seasonal characteristics of the area. In particular, different methods are adopted in industrialised countries which have elaborate national accounting systems and developing countries which often do not have accurate enough systems for collecting statistical information. They further differ with respect to the type of sector designated for tourism development (coastal zone development, organisation of tourism itineraries and trails, programmes for developing spa zones, mountain region development, rural tourism development and social tourism). Finally, the methods used also depend on the length of time projected for the development programme. Investment in specific tourism facilities may last three to six years, whereas long-term investment (ten to twenty-five years) is usually for developing infrastructure.

Despite important differences, tourism development methods present common characteristics. All projects have three main stages:

- evaluating resources
- using financial and economic analytical techniques
- choosing priorities

☐ Evaluating resources

Tourism resources include: natural resources, cultural resources, local events such as markets, traditional fairs, conferences and congresses, festivals and sports meetings. These are listed accurately and all useful information about each resource is recorded: the location and accessibility for foreign tourists, characteristics, size, length of time and so on.

Their use in terms of international tourism depends on the quality and the quantity of superstructures, equipment and services available (hotels, campsites, second homes, restaurants, marinas, ski resorts, transport). All the superstructures must be accurately assessed in order to determine the priorities of the tourism development programme.

☐ Financial and economic analytical techniques

These are essential in tourism development plans. Econometric models are developed to determine which tourism development plan should be used and its likely economic impact on employment, production and taxation. The analytical techniques are the input–output analysis derived from the national accounting system and cost-benefit analysis.

The national accounting system – the input–output analysis

Input–output models derived from the national accounting system measure the impact of increases in tourism revenue resulting from development plans. Studies undertaken by the United Nations Conference on Trade and Development (UNCTAD) show that tourism revenue can increase four- or fivefold depending on the country and the development programme.[6] The development of tourism causes an increase in demand for many sectors of the economy. The first round involves commerce, agriculture, transport and construction. Input–output tables highlight the relationship between different sectors of the economy and determine how growth in the tourism sector leads to growth in other, if not in all, sectors of the economy.

However, leakage (the draining of portions of revenue generated by tourism out of the economy) which is mainly caused by necessary imports for the operation of tourism is very large for some developing countries.[7]

Cost–benefit analysis

The cost–benefit analysis examines not only the financial impact of tourism but also its economic, social and ecological impact. Financial analysis techniques measure the expected profitability of investment and determine its finance requirements. Investment and cost-of-equipment forecasts are used to evaluate the amount of finance necessary. However, errors in forecasting costs have to be taken into account. For this reason, several alternative plans must be developed, using different parameters.

☐ Determining priorities

Evaluating resources and performing economic and financial analyses determine the priorities and how these should be programmed in the proposed tourism development. The normal level of equipment use needs to be defined in order to ascertain its optimum potential and avoid the risks of overuse and abuse of the natural environment.

From this calculation, it is possible to:

- determine the carrying capacity of a tourism area in terms of numbers of people – this is based on the available surface area;
- determine the accommodation needs of the area, based on the type of tourism it plans to attract (luxury tourism, social tourism);
- evaluate the potential for tourism development of the land as against its urbanisation – it is here that the benefits of tourism become a particularly important factor for development;
- evaluate and determine the carrying capacity of transport, airports, train and bus stations;
- evaluate and determine the carrying capacity of area-of-leisure activities – beaches, mountainsides for alpine skiing, marked tracks for cross-country skiing.

From these calculations, a master plan for land development is drafted which accurately establishes the sites to be developed and the equipment to be installed. These priorities are established as a result of the demand forecasts and cost–advantage analyses. The objectives of tourism policy are to attract tourism flows towards sites that have been designated for investment and for heritage development and to encourage tourists to stay for the optimum length of time.

□ *Tourism site development*

Tourism site development includes the development of coastal, rural and mountain areas. In the main tourism countries, development programmes encompass the whole of the country's territory. In many developing countries, they are limited to certain sites, generally the coastal areas.

□ The development of coastal areas

There are two types of coastal land development: beach-front development and integrated resort development.

- *Beach-front development* Beach-front development consists of building tourism accommodation structures and equipment along the coastline. This type of tourism development is usually a consequence of unplanned growth which often obstructs access to the sea. More importantly it may prevent all new forms of investment. The complete saturation of the beach-front prevents inland tourism construction which needs access to the sea. To solve this problem without modifying the initial development, second and third lines of construction are built equipped with swimming pools. This type of development exists in many countries.

- *Integrated resort development* Integrated resort development consists of building accommodation structures and tourism facilities according to a development plan on a previously designated site. National and regional plans are implemented to create infrastructure and super-structure and to develop a concentration of shops and businesses, leisure and sporting facilities (marinas, swimming pools, tennis courts) and entertainment (bars, restaurants, discotheques, etc.). The construction of accommodation is based around a central point and not along the coastline. In this way, there is a better usage (and therefore occupancy) of land and the sea-front can be developed for alternative activities. However, this type of tourism development is very expensive for the local area (it requires heavy investment in infrastructure, such as roads, highways, ports, etc.) without the guarantee of success in attracting large numbers of visitors. Because of the high financial risk of this type of development, public authorities at national level are usually involved in the financing of investment (for example, in France, the development of the Languedoc-Roussillon coastline).

☐ The development of rural areas

The aim of rural development is to balance the development of agriculture and the pressures of tourism on the economy, society and ecology of the countryside. Tourism provides farmers with extra revenue which is often indispensable. Furthermore, it maintains many tertiary activities, like handicraft and cottage industries.

However, the growth of tourism also brings a rise in land prices, increased local taxation and increasing conflicts of interest. Consequently, the aim of rural tourism development is to create a better appreciation of rural zones while avoiding the degradation of the economic, social and natural environment. To this end, one of the objectives is to ensure a balance between the number of second homes and other forms of lodging, notably rural cottages and camping on farmland, which are of direct interest to the farmers.

☐ The development of mountain areas

Tourism development in mountain areas has occurred in four different stages:

- *First stage* The traditional mountain areas were climatic resorts which were originally for summer tourism. They became the first areas to acquire winter sports equipment, for instance, Chamonix in France, Courmayeur in Italy, Saint-Moritz, Davos and Interlaken in Switzerland, Badgastein in Austria.
- *Second stage* This stage resulted from the growing interest in skiing. Because the sport required longer periods of snow, either high-altitude resorts were created or existing resorts were adapted (La Molina in Spain and Pas de Casas in Andorra in the Pyrenees; Courchevel, Serre Chevalier and Saint-Gervais in the Alps).
- *Third stage* The saturation of the existing equipment and the rapid growth of winter sports tourism resulted in large high-altitude tourism development programmes based around the creation of integrated resorts such as Tignes, Avoriaz and La Plagne in France. These new resorts not only satisfied French tourism demand but also catered to foreign demand (German, Belgian, Dutch, British and American). However, the high cost of construction and maintenance of infrastructure at high altitude means that the cost of products on offer are often high. As a result, there are financial limits to the expansion of new resorts and also a need to conserve natural reserves and zones of ecological protection.
- *Fourth stage* Finally, tourism development concentrated on mid-altitude resorts based on the infrastructure of existing villages. The objective of this type of new development is to reduce the amount of the investment thus giving the opportunity of offering lower-priced winter sports holidays, closer to towns and more integrated to the local life. However, it necessitates the construction of rapid means of access to the ski areas (cable cars, roads, etc.) located at high altitude.

These four stages demonstrate the need for a general tourism development plan in mountain areas for the best exploitation of natural sites, to preserve the ecological equilibrium and to ensure real economic development in terms of increased revenues and the creation of employment.

■ Social tourism policies

The objective of social tourism policies is to allow the maximum number of people to go on holiday, either within their own country, or abroad, for the lowest possible daily cost. The advent of paid holidays, which over the years have progressively become longer for most salaried occupations, has greatly contributed to the development of social tourism.

However, the paid holiday system has not succeeded in achieving its objective of 'holidays for all'. Indeed, the cost of the stay, even if it is in relatively cheap lodgings, remains too high for many socio-professional categories, particularly in periods of economic crisis, unemployment and real-terms falls in salaries. Consequently, the objective of social tourism, which ultimately endeavours to put holidays within the reach of the entire population and not just the greatest number of people, has not yet been reached.

By its very nature and its aims, social tourism presents specific characteristics which differentiate it from traditional tourism:

- it contributes to the advancement of social progress by raising living, health and cultural standards;
- it brings people with similar circumstances together;
- it is non-profit-making and benefits from various tax exemptions.

It is further characterised by:

- the establishment of a social cost–advantage relationship which is very different to the cost–benefit relationship of profit-making tourism. It offers a social advantage for individuals, communities and social and professional categories (family, union, company);
- the involvement of social organisations: unions, pension funds, friendly societies, works councils, family allowance funds, etc.
- the little consideration for the repayment of investments in the prices charged for the tourism service;
- financial contributions in the form of subsidies, loans at very low interest rates, interest rebate and, sometimes, donations and legacies.

Social tourism is being enjoyed by increasingly diverse socio-professional categories. These can be classified by:

- *age*: the young and the retired;
- *physical ability*: people who find it difficult to leave their home and travel (the physically and mentally handicapped people);

- *income*: people who cannot afford to go on holiday and those who are subsidised by social tourism organisations to travel further than they can afford or for a longer period.

Two international organisations have greatly contributed to the development of social tourism: the IBST and the WTO.

Created in Brussels in 1963, the International Bureau for Social Tourism (IBST) groups international organisations (mostly from industrialised countries) and national organisations involved in social tourism. The Secretary-General of the IBST coordinates various actions in the fields of financing, equipment and initiatives. The IBST adopted a charter which lays down the fundamental principles of social tourism in its 1972 General Assembly in Vienna.[8] These principles were confirmed and extended by the WTO in its Manila Declaration (1980) and particularly in its Acapulco Charter (1982).

Social tourism has a much greater impact nationally than it does internationally. Indeed, international social tourism programmes are very rare. They require a much higher financial investment than national programmes because of the greater cost of travel involved. Furthermore, there is evidence that even nationally, social tourism programmes are mainly on a local or regional scale, to keep down the proportion of transport in the overall cost.

Social tourism frequently benefits from loans at very low interest rates and subsidies granted directly from public authorities. Such socially progressive policies also encourage the development of national and local tourism. Consequently, these subsidies cannot be used for international social tourism programmes.

There is a strong demand, particularly from the young and the retired, in countries which generate foreign travel, thus encouraging international tourism exchanges. The right to enjoy holidays should be extended to all citizens and should include international as well as national destinations. Therefore, to avoid social discrimination, social tourism must offer the possibility of more trips and stays abroad.

Despite the difficulty associated with organising international social tourism flows (particularly, as previously mentioned, the financial difficulties), certain initiatives, remarkable for their conception and organisation, have demonstrated what can be achieved in the field of social tourism.

▌International tourism policies and public health

Health factors play an important role in international tourism:

- because of the need to protect the health of tourists during trips;
- and because tourism is often a very effective means of improving health standards.

These two very different links between international tourism and health present a variety of problems including economic problems.

☐ *International tourism and health risks*

International tourism policies must ensure that the health of travellers is protected. When trips are taken to neighbouring countries with similar climates and of a similar epidemiological character and also endowed with similar socioeconomic and health-care structures, the health risks are either non-existent or negligible. They are comparable to the health risks encountered on a domestic trip.

However, the situation is quite different for trips abroad, often far from the home country, to areas with very different climates and epidemiological characteristics. Foreign tourists do not have the same immunities as local residents. They are all the more vulnerable as their lifestyle, particularly their diet, becomes a risk factor (for instance, when they insist on eating rare meat, because this is the way they usually enjoy it, rather than the well-done meat favoured by the local population, which is actually safer because the parasites have been destroyed). Furthermore, large tourism concentrations create new risks (pollution of drinking water or of bathing areas, for instance). The health service of the area may be non-existent or may not have enough equipment or the necessary medicine to cope with a high concentration of people.

The World Health Organisation has identified the health risks in international tourism and has proposed a number of measures to be incorporated in the international tourism policies of member states.[9]

International tourists are exposed to a number of health risks. These can be categorised as health risks while travelling and health risks at the destination.

☐ Health risks while travelling

Health risks during the trip are linked to diet, drinking water and accidents. Diet risks principally concern the conservation of alimentary products. This is particularly important in hot countries where food spoils very quickly because of the heat and becomes a breeding-ground for bacteria which can result in very serious consequences (botulism, for instance).

Drinks consumed during the trip can be a health risk, particularly contaminated or non-potable water (from drinking fountains in stations, on trains and by the roadside).

The WTO reports in its paper entitled 'Food Safety in the Tourism Sector':

During the last ten years we have been shocked by particular outbreaks of certain food-borne diseases (FBD) which have caused an unusually high number of cases or deaths for the disease in question. The following examples will illustrate this statement:

1984 In the spring of that year, British Airways was involved in a major food poisoning outbreak which affected nearly 100 passengers, aircrew and ground personnel. . . (see Box 9.5: 'Example of Solution for Eliminating Health Risks').

1987 57 Canadian tourists were affected with Ciguatera as a result of eating fish casserole in a Caribbean tourist resort, just four hours before their departure for Montreal.

1988 In Pennsylvania, USA, in September of that year 5,000 people from Pennsylvania and Delaware became ill with a viral disease caused by contaminated ice. This outbreak was a good opportunity for the Fourth US Food Protection Conference to recall that some pathogenic organisms are able to survive and grow under storage conditions of packaged ice.

1991 In Australia, at least 3,051 individuals travelling by air inside the country, developed gastroenteritis caused by Norwalk-like virus SRSV (small round structure virus). The vehicle was orange juice produced by a single company.

There is also a (lesser) risk with the means of transport used (road and rail). Prevention of road accidents requires elementary care on the part of the tourist. In air transport, the WHO, the ICAO and IATA have jointly introduced rigorous health measures. For instance, following cases of passengers and crew suffering from simultaneous food poisoning, the organisations have stipulated that pilots and co-pilots should be served different meals from other people on the flight.

☐ Health risks at the destination

There are more serious health risks at the destination, particularly in developing countries located in zones prone to climatic and epidemiologic problems. As previously mentioned, tourists have immune defences different from those of local residents and their lifestyle may make them particularly vulnerable. Furthermore, the levels of hygiene and health-care are often insufficient in these countries, which usually lack the necessary health services and medicine.

Research conducted by the WHO has listed the main health risks that tourists are exposed to:

- *Great endemic and epidemic diseases* These include malaria and bilharzia.
- *Untreated water* Untreated water does not only come from towns but also from slaughterhouses and, at times, from hospitals. It is discharged without treatment in many tourism sites and is responsible for the pollution of swimming areas (lakes, rivers, seas), springs, and underground lakes. To prevent pollution that will ultimately damage the tourism heritage of the area, it is crucial to build purification plants with a network of drainage canals. Financing this causes major problems for tourist resorts, particularly in developing countries which cannot afford the high cost of the investment.
- *Accidents* These include all types of accident risks: road, swimming, animal bites etc.
- *Lack of services and equipment* This is a particular problem for the development of tourism in many areas and includes a shortage of doctors, hospitals, ambulances and medicine.
- *Unsanitary drinks* Drinks are often produced in poor sanitary conditions or with materials that do not come up to required sanitary standards. Even if the water treatment equipment in place is satisfactory, its product is often deficient because of sporadic use and an absence of strict controls. This has led to cases of typhoid and cholera which have damaged international tourism.
- *Food* Food-borne diseases, commonly but inaccurately known as food poisoning, are defined by the World Heath Organisation as

'diseases usually either infectious or toxic in nature, caused by agents that enter the body through the ingestion of food'.[10]

The main health risk to tourists is food, notably meat and milk products. If the local food industry does not provide the necessary sanitary guarantees, then it has to be reorganised in such a way as to provide them. If this is not possible, the solution is to import alimentary products from countries which can offer these guarantees (industrialised countries). To ensure that the quality of food products is acceptable, equipment and strict sanitary controls must be introduced at different stages of production (healthy cattle, satisfactory conditions of slaughter, refrigerated transport, handling, preservation in cold storage and clean kitchens). There are very few developing countries which can offer all the necessary sanitary guarantees to cater for foreign tourists.

According to the 1991 WHO report, food-borne diseases, particularly the diarrhoeal diseases, are affecting a significant proportion of tourists, and specialists fear that these will increase. Diarrhoea is a significant health problem for children as well as for adults, particularly for travellers. Of some 450 million people who travel abroad each year for business, pleasure or other reasons, the WHO estimates that 20–50 per cent suffer from diarrhoea. In the majority of these cases, diarrhoeal diseases are caused by microbiologically contaminated foods or drinking water. Factors such as fatigue due to travelling, jet lag, disruption of eating habits, changes in climate and low level of immunity may contribute to the problem by decreasing the resistance of travellers and thus making them more susceptible to food-borne infections and intoxications.

The WHO report identified new food-borne dangers:

'Emergent' Pathogens – In recent years the 'emergence' of new microbiological hazard in foods has been only too evident. A suitable definition of their causes has been made. Seven basic reasons have been identified. They are interrelated and very rarely mutually exclusive and can be summarised as follows:

1. Changes in eating habits
2. Changes in perception and awareness of what constitute hazards, risks and hygiene
3. Demographic changes
4. Changes in primary food production
5. Changes in food processing technology
6. Changes in handling and preparation practices
7. Changes in the behaviour of micro-organisms

Examples of some 'new' pathogens are:

Vibrio vulnificus, Campylobacter jejuni, Listeria monocytogenes, Giardia lamblia, Cryptosporidium, Escherichia coli 0157, Salmonella enteritidis, not really a 'new' pathogen, but a 'renovated' virulence, domoic acid, *Plesiomonas shigelloides* (frequently associated with travellers' diarrhoea), etc.[11]

☐ Eliminating health risks

There are two ways of eliminating health risks from the food industries:

- *Solution no. 1*   The food industry must be organised in a sanitary way so that its products are adequate for tourist consumption. Several advantages result from catering to tourists: increased production, revenue in foreign currency, economic integration of tourism in the economic life of the country, a multiplier effect, an increase in the standards of food production with important consequences for locals, producers and consumers. However, organising the food industry requires investments, the costs of which must be included in the economic calculation.
- *Solution no. 2*   The food industry cannot be organised properly for economic reasons (high costs, insufficient financial means) or for social reasons (lack of skilled and trained producers, etc.). In this case, food products available locally but not fit for tourist consumption must be imported.

It is important to eliminate all potential health risks as the success of tourism is dependent on a safe and sanitary environment. There have been many examples of expensive tourist complexes being closed down after food poisoning incidents.

Importing frozen meats and milk products is certainly a drain on foreign currency reserves but it is better to accept lower returns from foreign tourism than to jeopardise the whole success of the industry by risking the health of tourists.

If, to be organised properly, meat production requires a high development level of the geographical and professional sectors, other food production is less difficult to organise:

- *fruit* – because they are naturally protected from pollution by skins and peels;

- *vegetables* – if care has been taken to water them with unpolluted water;
- *fish* – if there is fast night transport of the catch to hotels, restaurants or retail outlets.

Thus, with proper organisation, local produce can gradually be substituted for imported goods to supply tourism consumption without creating health problems.

It is the responsibility of the destination country and of tourism professionals to guarantee the sanitary quality of their alimentary products and of their catering services. Two conditions are essential to ensure effective health risk prevention:

- funds to finance the necessary actions;
- a proper management system to coordinate tourism services and health services.

These conditions can only be fulfilled within an overall development policy.

Box 9.6 *Example of solution for eliminating health risks: the case of British Airways*

In March 1984, British Airways was involved in a major food poisoning outbreak which affected nearly 1,000 passengers, aircrew and ground personnel. The operational impact was worldwide and could have resulted in the cessation of the airline's day-to-day operations. The investigation of this outbreak involved 3,103 British Airways departures from London carrying 220,553 passengers over a six-day period. The causative organism was rapidly identified as salmonella, and its introduction into the food chain was located.

The British Airways Medical Service learned some very important lessons from this very unfortunate incident:

- the Emergency Procedures Information Centre (EPIC) at Heathrow should have been opened up;
- British Airways must insist that flight crews eat specially prepared meals;
- certain 'high-risk' foods should be removed from the menu;
- management needs improved training;
- increased pre-engagement screening and medical exams;
- increased hygiene training to all catering staff; and
- increased batch sampling of all foodstuffs.

Source: WTO, *Food Safety in the Tourism Sector.*

Health tourism products – international tourism and improvements in health standards

International tourism can improve health standards in different ways: physically, mentally and socially. Travelling to foreign countries far from the usual place of residence can have a beneficial physical effect and opens the mind. It stimulates the ability to adapt to new surroundings and situations, encourages curiosity and provokes new experiences.

It provides 'compensation', a balance between working life and the need for leisure periods, and is particularly beneficial to the urban worker saturated with anxiety and stress. Group travel provides a kind of socio-therapy for people who may be lonely or socially isolated, like the aged and the retired.

The favourable climates of some tourist resorts also contribute to improving health standards. In the past, when therapeutic and pharmacological knowledge was relatively limited, patients were prescribed rest, relaxation and rehabilitation stays at thermal and climatic resorts. This was an early form of tourism. Today, there are many thermal and climatic resorts which cater for a clientele seeking treatment or prevention for a variety of ailments.

Surveys conducted since the 1970s in the industrialised countries of North America and Western Europe (the tourist-generating countries) have consistently shown that the demand for health is a primary concern. The great tourism flows toward the mountains, the sea or the countryside at weekends and during holiday periods express the profound need for 'compensation' for the stresses of urban life. In other words, they express a need for health tourism. In this modern age man has become vulnerable to new illnesses created by the industrialised society (cardio-vascular, metabolic and mental diseases). The current interest in health of many sections of the population, including the elderly, is reflected by the success of salt water and sea air cures (thalassotherapy) and of fitness programmes. Therefore, health tourism has the effect of simultaneously raising health standards and developing tourism activities.

The World Tourism Organisation was the first to study the characteristics, the different elements and the commercial conditions necessary to adapt health tourism products to the new and deeply felt needs of industrialised societies. The Committee of Affiliated Members at the WTO has created a 'Health Tourism' working group. A high-level international scientific and medical commission which was constituted identified two types of health tourism programmes: medical and non-medical.

Some programmes are based around medical treatments, in thermal, thalassotherapeutic or tourism resorts equipped with the necessary medical services. Tourists are placed under medical supervision and follow a series of preventative measures tailor-made to their needs.

The other programmes are non-medical and can be enjoyed in all tourism resorts. The objective of this type of tourism is to improve the tourist's health by making available a number of facilities and activities (walks in the open air, physical exercise, relaxation, health education, etc.). Often, these are part of an overall entertainment programme.

The WTO concluded that these two forms of health tourism fulfil the needs of a large proportion of the population and, as such, should be included in public health and tourism policies. In fact, health tourism implemented precisely the principles adopted by the WTO in the Manila Declaration (1980) and Acapulco Charter (1982).

The WTO working group recommended that as many health tourism programmes as possible should be developed all over the world. Furthermore, it highlighted several key points:

- Health tourism programmes should be based on *solid medical foundations*. Tourism success depends on the quality of the product and in this case the essence of the product is preventative medicine.
- A *specialised hospitality service* must be established:
  - to welcome tourists and inform them about the various elements of the health programme. They should be briefed on the significance of each element, their use and the results that can be achieved;
  - to manage the programme by making sure that the equipment is properly maintained and by running the services that have been scheduled;
  - to ensure that the health education message has been received and, more importantly, that it is being translated into actions which change lifestyles (better alimentary hygiene, physical exercise, relaxation, etc.);
  - to organise additional cultural activities;
  - to adapt the programme to the needs of the tourists, the length of their stay and to the season.
- *Information campaigns aimed at the general public* on the benefits of health programmes must be organised and gradually developed.
- *Promotional campaigns* in tourism markets to publicise health tourism products must be initiated and they should be aimed at either the population as a whole or at certain segments of society who might particularly require this type of tourism (urban populations, elderly people, certain socio-professional categories).

The WTO also recommended *cooperation in the media and the systematic organisation of information meetings, conferences, seminars and workshops* so that health tourism could contribute to raising the standard of living of the population. It should be affordable to all and use all forms of available accommodation, both social and commercial.

Tourism organisations such as the World Tourism Organisation play an increasingly important role in ensuring sustainable tourism development. Indeed, the growth of the tourism sector is not only dependent on the availability of finance or the solvency of the market, it is also a question of anticipating the supply and demand trends.

Hence, economic information and market trend forecasts are essential for elaborating and adapting tourism policies. The body of economic observations compiled and distributed by international tourism organisations is particularly important. By processing this information, policies for local tourism development can be incorporated into world tourism trends.

However, world economic data does not have the same impact on the policies of all countries. In fact, there are considerable differences between the tourism development policies of industrialised countries and those of developing countries.

References

1. WTO, *Role and Structure of National Tourism Administrations.* Madrid, 1979.

2. WTO, *The World Tourism Organisation in 1992.* Madrid, 1992

3. WTO, *Tourism Services and the GATS.* Report by M. Handchouz, M. Kanasabe and D. Diaz for the WTO, UNCTAD and the GATT, 1994.

4. WTO, *Measuring the Effectiveness of Promotion.* Madrid.

5. WTO, *Report on the Planning Experiences of Six WTO Regions.* Madrid, 1980.

6. Report of the Secretariat of UNCTAD, Geneva, 1 December 1971.

7. Krapf, K., 'The Role and the Importance of International Tourism'.

8. International Bureau of Social Tourism, *The Social Tourism Charter*, Vienna, 1972.

9. WTO, *Food and Safety in the Tourism Sector*, 1991; *Practical Guide for Hygiene in Tourism*. Copenhagen, 1978; *Sanitation of the Environment in European Tourism Areas*, Reports and Studies by the WHO, Copenhagen, 1979; James Bailey, *Hygiene and Sanitation in Air Transport*, Geneva, 1978.

10. WTO, *Food and Safety in the Tourism Sector.*

11. Ibid.

Further reading

Barker, M. L. 'Traditional Landscape and Mass Tourism in the Alps', *Geographical Review*, 72(4), pp. 395–415, 1982.

Braddon, C. J. H. *British Issues Paper: Approaches to Tourism Planning Abroad.* London: British Tourist Authority, 1982.

Edgell, D. L. *International Tourism Policy.* New York: Van Nostrand Reinhold, 1990.

Food Safety and Tourism Regional Conference for Africa and the Mediterranean. *Year of African Tourism.* Tunisia, 25–7 November 1991, p. 16.

Inskeep, E. *Tourism Planning.* New York: Van Nostrand Reinhold, 1990.

Johnson, P. and Thomas, B. *Perspective on Tourism Policy.* London: Mansell, 1992.

Patmore, J. A. *Recreation and Resources.* Oxford: Blackwell, 1983.

Pearce, D. *Tourism Organisations.* Harlow: Longman, 1992.

Romsa, G. 'An Overview of Tourism and Planning in the Federal Republic of Germany', *Annals of Tourism Research*, 8(3), pp. 333–56, 1981.

WTO. *Role and Structure of National Tourism Administrations*, 1979.

■ *Chapter 10* ■

International Tourism in Industrialised Countries

Tourism policies and strategies in OECD countries: international tourism policies in Austria; international tourism policies in Spain; international tourism policies in the United States; international tourism policies in France; international tourism policies in the United Kingdom
Tourism strategies and policies of the European Union: free movement and the protection of tourists; working in the European tourism industry; transport and tourism; regional development and tourism

With regards to the international tourism, industrialised countries, notably in North America and in Western Europe, have several common characteristics:

- Together, they represent a very large percentage of international tourism: 70 per cent
- They are both main generating countries and main receptor countries of international tourism
- Apart from exceptional cases (particularly Spain), international tourism is considered to be secondary to other sectors of economic activity
- The international tourism flows are between countries with similar economic and social systems although at times with large cultural differences (Japan)
- International tourism is largely within the private sector, although national administrations play an important role. The influence of the public sector is diminishing. Usually, private and public sector actions are coordinated in flexible agreements or budgetary incentives
- The main industrialised countries are members of the OECD (Organisation for Economic Cooperation and Development) and, in Europe, most countries are also members of the European Union. Both these organisations play an important role in coordinating tourism policies, determining tourism objectives and implementing methods which are in line with general economic policies

▌Tourism policies and strategies in OECD countries

OECD countries are the main tourism countries in the world both in terms of receipts from and expenditure on international tourism (Australia, Austria, Belgium, Canada, Denmark, Finland, France, Germany, Greece, Iceland, Ireland, Italy, Japan, Luxembourg, the Netherlands, New Zealand, Norway, Spain, Sweden, Switzerland and Turkey, the United Kingdom and the United States).

The OECD, unlike the EU, does not aim to formulate common economic policies for member states, but rather it investigates problems, prepares forecasts and advises on the methods that should be used for better tourism development.

The OECD countries contribute greatly to tourism development in the world. Their net tourism expenditure in developing countries was more than US$6 billion in 1991.

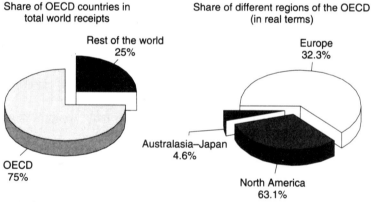

Share of OECD countries in
total world receipts

Rest of the world
25%

OECD
75%

Share of different regions of the OECD
(in real terms)

Europe
32.3%

Australasia–Japan
4.6%

North America
63.1%

Source: OECD.

Figure 10.1 *International tourism receipts*

Many OECD countries have pursued important interventionist policies, notably in the promotion of international tourism.[1] Case studies of Austria, Spain, the United States, France and the United Kingdom are developed in the following section.

☐ *International tourism policies in Austria*

The responsibility for formulating tourism development and promotion strategies in Austria is borne by the Austrian National Tourist Office

(ANTO). It ensures the promotion of all types of tourism. Its activities are non-profit-making, designed to optimise the advantages brought by tourism to the national economy. The ANTO has the following guiding principles:

- market orientation;
- the improvement of efficiency;
- the adoption of a global approach based or medium- and long-term strategies.

The ANTO collaborates closely, usually in a partnership, with all companies that are involved in tourism by providing marketing help and know-how. Its first objective as a tourism promotion organisation has been clearly defined: to motivate tourists to choose Austria as a destination. To achieve this, the ANTO has the following functions:

- to present and promote Austria and the many attractions that the country offers as a holiday destination;
- to exploit the strong points of Austria and all that contributes to creating a positive image of the destination in countries where Austria is already well-known;
- to present in a convincing manner the competitive advantages of Austria.

The activities of the ANTO cover two main areas:

- *Communication*   This involves creating and diffusing the brand image 'Austria – a holiday destination';
- *Services*   The organisation provides various services to the Austrian tourism industry.

The main fields of activity are focused on marketing abroad, market research studies, product development, communication – promotion, information and public relations, marketing policies and sales promotions.

The ANTO is funded by members of the association 'Osterreich Werbung' which consists of:

- the Federal Ministry of Economic Affairs;
- the Federal Chamber of Commerce and Exchanges;
- the nine Austrian provinces: Vienna, Lower Austria, Upper Austria, Salzburg, Tyrol, Vorarlberg, Carinthia, Styria and Burgenland.

The members of the association contribute to the budget of the ANTO in the following proportions:

Federal Ministry of Economic Affairs	60 per cent
Federal Chamber of Commerce	20 per cent
The nine provinces	20 per cent

In 1992, the ANTO's total budget amounted to 299.4 million Austrian Schillings which were broken down into fixed and variable costs.

Fixed costs: 70 per cent, consisting of:

Salaries	35.0%
Staff costs (e.g. social security contributions)	7.0%
Building, maintenance and rents	9.0%
Offices	3.4%
Travel	2.0%
Postage	7.0%
Other operational costs	6.6%

Variable costs: 30 per cent, consisting of:

Marketing activities

Publicity material	6.2%
Market research studies	0.5%
Advertising and trade fairs	9.0%
Films/photography	0.3%
Printing costs	0.6%
Public and press relations	3.2%
Sales promotions	9.0%
Reserves (advertising)	1.2%

It is, however, difficult to account exactly for the total financial contribution of all the institutions involved in Austria's tourism industry. It has been estimated that the total investment by the provinces, the regions, tourist resorts, tour operators, transport companies and foreign agents is four times higher than the sum invested by the ANTO.

Because the Austrian National Tourist Office is managed as a non-profit-making organisation, it is difficult to evaluate the cost of its successes and failures.

From a management point of view, statistics showing the number of arrivals and tourist nights are not sufficient to measure tourism trends in a given country. On the other hand, the volume of receipts in foreign currency does disclose the importance of tourism in its economy.

In 1991, the tourism sector in Austria generated the equivalent of 160 billion schillings in foreign currency, representing approximately 8 per cent of the GNP (gross national product). With a revenue of 20,000 AS per inhabitant per year, Austria is the world's leading country in terms of the volume of receipts generated by the travel and tourism sector. This represents 32 per cent of total export receipts and is the sector that provides the country with the most foreign currency.

The great success of international tourism in Austria is largely a result of the ANTO's promotional efforts and of public sector financing. The major difficulty is coordinating the different interests and priorities of the provinces. The role of the tourist offices in each province must be strengthened in order to bolster the effectiveness of promotion inside the country.

☐ *International tourism policies in Spain*

International tourism is central to Spain's economic development policy. Since 1991, the state has entrusted tourism promotion to the 'Instituto de Turismo de España' which reports to the Department of Industry, Trade and Tourism.

The responsibility is shared by two chief executives. One is in charge of tourism policy which includes:

- coordination with the Autonomous Communities;
- multinational and bilateral international cooperation;
- the commissioning of studies, reports and projects involving the tourism sector and its infrastructures.

The other is in charge of Turespaña responsible for:

- the management of Turespaña and its staff;
- the formulation of project budgets;
- the implementation of Turespaña's general plans.

The promotional objectives of Turespaña are:

- the establishment of a government foreign tourism promotion policy following the general guidelines laid down by the Tourism Under-Secretariat;
- the coordination and encouragement of promotional actions abroad, financed by public funds, to support the activities and initiatives of the private sector.

The promotional activities of Turespaña consist of:

- the development of activities designed to help marketing, notably information, advertising and public relation campaigns;
- the preparation, production and publication of all types of tourism information;
- the management of tourism organisations and facilities;
- the programming and organising of Spain's participation in travel and tourism trade fairs;
- the formulation of plans and tourism promotion programmes in cooperation with private sector companies;
- the allocation of financial aid to organisations and companies to encourage their promotional activities abroad to open and develop new tourism markets;
- the granting of financial aid to organisations and companies to help set up and develop commercial networks abroad;
- the implementation of all necessary actions to successfully achieve their goals.

The annual promotional budget in 1992 was 8,547 million pesetas, of which 72 per cent was provided by central government. These promotional actions are designed to put into effect marketing plans aimed at strengthening Spain's tourism position.

Essentially, Turespaña's role is to improve the competitiveness of Spanish tourism products. Quality is imperative. For this reason, central government and the seventeen communities have signed a Competitiveness Plan which will be implemented over four years (1992–6).

The competitiveness of the Spanish travel market is very important for the private sector and Turespaña's involvement is more than just support. Already, the private sector collaborates actively with Turespaña (fairs, workshops etc.) by contributing significantly to the organisation. In fact, Turespaña is striving to develop an even more active collaboration with the private sector by supporting initiatives introduced by companies, particularly when they meet the following conditions:

- the global launch of sustainable promotion activities;
- the promotion of specific products;
- the promotion of high-quality environmentally sound products;
- the promotion of brands developed by private sector companies requiring management, training, quality and services.

In this way, the private sector is involved in the plans and activities of Turespaña. In particular, one of the current objectives of the public authorities in Spain is diversification and specialisation of products in order to market distinctive products in generating markets.

International tourism policies in the United States

The United States defined a national tourism policy in 1961 and created the United States Travel Service as the country's official tourism organisation. It was given the responsibility for coordinating and applying tourism policies at national level. In 1981, the United States Travel Service was renamed the US Travel and Tourism Administration (USTTA) with essentially the same responsibilities.

As an official multisectorial organisation in charge of tourism at a federal level, the USTTA presides over an interministerial committee which coordinates policies and projects involving tourism from the federal level to international levels. The USTTA collects, analyses and disseminates statistics on trends and changing tendencies in the travel sector.

The USTTA is responsible for promoting the United States abroad and advising American companies on the best methods of selling their services in foreign markets. It also collaborates with fifty states to develop domestic tourism.

Although the USTTA is responsible for promoting the United States as a general destination, the fifty states must promote tourism to their areas individually. Many of these states have divisions responsible for tourism, usually forming part of the trade or Economic Development Office. Congress allocates them a budget which they manage themselves. Its size can vary between US$4 million and US$14 million depending on the financial resources of the state and on their financial priorities.

The USTTA and the private sector cooperate to varying degrees and for varying lengths of time in tourism promotion activities. Although it is a government organisation, the USTTA calls on private financing for certain projects. The acceptance of these funds is strictly regulated.

The USTTA is located in the US Department of Trade and reports to the Secretary of Trade who is a member of the 'President's Cabinet' (council of ministers). It has regional offices in the major cities of nine countries: Paris, London, Amsterdam, Milan, Sydney, Frankfurt, Tokyo, Mexico City and Toronto. In the United States, it has an office in Miami responsible for Latin American countries. In countries where the USTTA does not have an office, like Spain and Argentina, the US Foreign and Commercial Service is often responsible for the promotion of tourism.

The objectives of the USTTA are to develop tourism to the United States in order to stimulate economic growth, improve international competitiveness and increase foreign currency receipts. The national tourism policy aims to encourage foreign visitors to the United States, encourage tourism product development at competitive prices and promote the use of American airline companies.

The objectives behind its programmes and activities are:

- to inform certain trade quarters of the importance of tourism as an export market and the general advantages of tourism;
- to stimulate demand for travel to the United States;
- to facilitate access to international markets for American tourism;
- to launch, in cooperation with professionals in the tourism industry, campaigns for the growth of exchanges;
- to promote the development of tourism as an option for economic development in rural zones and for ethnic communities;
- to undertake research in international markets for the American tourism industry;
- to coordinate tourism policies and legislative initiatives and eliminate obstacles for the growth of tourism services in the United States.

The basic budget of the USTTA is financed by annual federal credits. It amounted to US$17.5 million in 1993 and was complemented by private sector contributions in the form of partnership of approximately US$20 million.

The USTTA is a relatively small organisation, with limited financial and human resources. Its main difficulty, therefore, is to use these resources as efficiently as possible and raise other funds in an increasingly competitive world environment.

Its budget is apportioned in the following manner:

Operational cost of the head office (general costs, salaries and the cost of centralised services)	10.5%
Salaries of staff abroad	42.3%
Information and promotional activities	23.7%
Marketing and research	16.8%
Advertising in cooperation with the private sector	2.5%
Promotional material (printing costs, films, photographs, brochures, presentations)	3.5%
Miscellaneous costs	0.7%

As a federal organisation, the objective of the USTTA is to preserve and develop a dynamic tourism industry in the United States which can confront worldwide competition and stimulate the development of enterprises and local economies while preserving the historic and cultural heritage and natural resources.

To this end, the USTTA concentrates on the design and development of new products like rural tourism or ethnic tourism. These do not only constitute extra means of economic development but also new experiences for international tourists who already know all the main tourism areas and have experienced all tourism activities. The USTTA also advises enterprises operating in the tourism industry on the best ways of developing products and services for international visitors and how to sell them abroad.

☐ *International tourism policies in France*

International tourism policies in France are controlled by the 'Direction du Tourisme', a section of the 'Ministère de l'Equipement, du Transport et du Tourisme', and by the 'Maison de la France' which is responsible for promoting French tourism products in France and abroad.

In 1987, the French tourism industry was losing international market share. As a result, the public authorities decided to intervene:

- The Maison de la France was created as the organisation responsible for the promotion of French tourism in foreign markets. Its objective is to coordinate and develop activities abroad and to establish and build a coherent image of French tourism supply
- The government introduced policies to enhance the quality of French products, notably by advising and informing tourism professionals on the expectations of foreign visitors

The Maison de la France consists of:

- 70 staff at the head office in Paris;
- an international network of 38 offices ('Services Français du Tourisme à l'Etranger') in 29 countries and employing 200 people.

The unique feature of the Maison de la France is that it is an association bringing together the state, private or other public organisations working in a partnership (travel agencies, hotels, transport companies, Regional Tourism Committees, Departmental Tourism Committees and Tourism Offices). This grouping of economic interests (GEI) associates the government, the Ministry of Tourism and approximately 850 different organisations who are members of the Maison de la France (to which they pay an annual subscription). In this way, the members are represented at the General Assembly and at the Administrative Council.

The objectives of the Maison de la France are:

- to increase tourism receipts;
- to increase and regulate tourism flows effectively;
- to increase the length of stay of tourists;
- to increase receipts per tourist;
- to foster the loyalty of the clientele and to encourage them to visit again.

The mission of the Maison de la France, apart from disseminating information abroad, is the worldwide promotion of its members' products. It provides them with a range of services – some free, others charged for – which, from individual services to collective operations, cover all that the professional needs to get to grips with the market.

Their commercial activities include participation in trade fairs, exhibitions, workshops, publicity campaigns and specific promotional ventures. They also provide access to strategic information on different markets and competitors, training (particularly in marketing), advice, use of database information, help in prospecting for new markets, tactical advice and support and so on.

Because the GEI is based on a partnership system which brings together several promotional budgets, its impact is very strong. In 1994, members contribute 45 per cent of the total budget.

The key to the Maison de la France's success rests in its capacity to sound out the market. By constantly analysing variations in tourism consumption, the slightest trends can be detected. The Maison de la France uses this knowledge to formulate and implement different promotional strategies in each market.

Priority markets are defined by their current size, their potential and their elasticity. Germany, the United Kingdom, the USA and Japan contribute more than 50 per cent of French tourism receipts; in the 1990s the Netherlands, Italy and Spain are the growth markets.

The Maison de la France intervenes by organising targeted promotional actions which it details annually in the 'Partnership Operational Guide'. The actions are jointly developed by the Maison de la France and its partners.

For the sake of effectiveness and coherence, products are classified in four general categories: Business, Lifestyle, Relaxation and Active Leisure. These categories correspond broadly to the types of products required by generating markets. Different strategies are devised for each category which take into account the specificity of the target markets.

The Maison de la France extends the possibility of grouping into promotion clubs based on different themes to its (private and institutional) members. In its general marketing plan, the clubs undertake, in cooperation with the Maison de la France abroad, their own promotional activity programmes: publication of brochures, commercial and promotional campaigns, trade fairs and so on.

There are eleven Maison de la France promotion clubs: Club Français du Tourisme d'Affaire Réceptif; Club Français du Tourisme des Jeunes; Club Français de Nature et Découverte; France Golf International; Club Français du Naturisme; Club Montagne; Club Français Pêche et Tourisme; Club Français Festival; Club Français Gastronomie; Club Châteaux, Musées, Monuments; Club France Mer.

In 1992, the Maison de la France's budget was 380 million francs which was allocated to the following activities:

Information	22%
Advertising	30%
Sales promotion and public relations	34%
Operational costs	8%
Miscellaneous	6%

- *Information* (22 per cent of the total budget) This includes the following aspects:
  - *For the general public* Most of the Service Français du Tourisme, the overseas offices, are open to the general public and distribute brochures and information on all French tourism products. In 1991, the overseas offices gave information to 2 million people (representing 6 million people in all) and distributed 650 tonnes of brochures. A network of interactive computerised information stations is being developed in nine European countries.
  - *For members* Members can consult the Maison de la France for advice. They can consult files, database information and market research studies.
  - *Publications* These include guides and general or specific brochures (approximately 1.9 million issued).
- *Advertising* (30 per cent of the budget) Advertising campaigns (magazines, posters).
- *Sales promotion and public relations* (34 per cent of the budget)
  - This category includes trade fairs and workshops (14), seminars (32), visits to countries (24), towns (105) (certain towns several times) and involves 1,600 exhibitors and 12,000 visitors.
  - Informing the press is an essential element of the Maison de la France's promotion policy. This includes the usual methods of communication (bulletins, press releases and conferences) as well

as familiarisation trips which are extremely influential. These trips make up half the organisation's hospitality activities.
- In 1991, the Maison de la France's 'Welcome' service received 1,305 tourism professionals (radio, television and newspaper journalists) and travel professionals (tour operators, travel agents, incentive travel organisers). Additionally, private partners and local authorities have contributed approximately 8.3 million francs to the hospitality fund. Over a five year period, the Maison de la France has welcomed some 7,900 professionals of which 3,900 were journalists.

While every year the budget is increasing significantly, the government's contribution is actually decreasing. Thus, the consolidated budget was 302 million francs in 1990, 377 million in 1991 and 380 million in 1992. The contribution of the state (through the Ministry of Tourism) and of the private sector (including local administrative units) has changed over the years (see Table 10.1).

Table 10.1 *State and private sector contributions to the Maison de la France, 1990–2*

Year	State contribution (%)	Private sector contribution (%)
1990	63	37
1991	56	44
1992	55	45*

* 25% contributed by local administrative units and 20% by private enterprises.

Since 1990, French tourism promotion has been very successful in foreign markets. It is estimated that for each franc invested in promotion, one hundred francs of tourism receipts are generated, although this is a macroeconomic calculation. More precisely, the Maison de la France undertakes performance evaluations in several markets (two or three times a year). The best effectiveness indicator is still the fact that members are willing to renew their financial contribution each year.

One objective of the public authorities is to encourage partners to undertake several *ad hoc* advertising operations over predefined periods of time.

In France, the role of the state is to coordinate activities in a field where there are many participants and many decisions to be made. A totally private and unanswerable organisation could never have achieved this. The way the GEI is structured has allowed the state to intercede in the promotion of tourism in a sector which is traditionally individualist and which, under different circumstances, would not have withstood such an intervention. Although the partnership system has been difficult to manage, the experience since 1987, when the Maison de la France was created, has proved worthwhile.

The impact of the Maison de la France shows the multiplier effect of public investment when it is associated with private investment.

International tourism policies in the United Kingdom

International tourism policies in the United Kingdom are the responsibility of the British Tourist Authority (BTA). Together, domestic and international tourism contribute around £25 billion annually to the British economy and account for approximately 5 per cent of the country's GNP. In 1992, direct expenditure by international tourists was £8 billion. The British tourism industry employs more people than either the health service or the construction industry, around 1.5 million, which represents 7 per cent of the active population. Over 200,000 businesses are either directly or indirectly involved in the tourism industry.

In 1992, the United Kingdom was the seventh most visited tourism destination in the world after France, the United States, Spain, Italy, Hungary and Austria. It received 18.5 million international tourists. The most important clients ranked by receipts generated are the United States, France, Germany, Ireland, Italy and Canada. However, the Japanese market, currently in seventh place, is growing at the fastest rate.

The organisations involved in the British tourism sector are the British Tourist Authority, which is responsible for promotion abroad, and the English Tourist Board (ETB), which were both created in 1969. In April 1992, they were transferred from the Department of Employment to the newly created Department of National Heritage.

The ETB is concerned with domestic tourism and has no international involvement. Scotland, Wales and Northern Ireland all have their own organisations which promote and develop tourism in their region. They cooperate with the BTA for promotion abroad. These three organisations report directly to the ministry responsible for their respective regions (the Scottish Office, the Welsh Office and the Northern Ireland Office).

Nearly 400 people work for the BTA, half in London and the rest abroad. The Director of International Marketing in London oversees three general managers based abroad in the main generating markets: North America, Europe and the Asia–Pacific region. The London offices are responsible for the other regions in the world and have a department solely concerned with promotion. The BTA manages a total of 29 offices abroad and has agents in seven other countries.

The main activities of the BTA are:

- *international advertising campaigns* designed to promote tourism to the United Kingdom in the press, on television and on the radio. These are always launched in cooperation with commercial partners;
- *joint marketing campaigns* usually for particular types of product such as Manor House Hotels or English Country Gardens. Normally, the BTA launches the campaign and then, after two or three years, the rest of the industry takes over;
- *conference organising* to encourage contacts between foreign travel professionals and their British counterparts;
- *public relations activities* the BTA organises excursions to introduce British tourism products and the work of the department in charge of business travel to foreign journalists;
- *publications* the BTA produces a great quantity of brochures which are essentially destined to be distributed by its offices abroad and through the post by using mailing lists;
- *information* the network of BTA offices and agents abroad disseminate information on tourism in the United Kingdom to interested tourists and to travel professionals. Some offices are located in the same buildings as those of commercial partners so that visitors can make their reservations after having received information;
- *research* the BTA manages a large programme of research, progress reports and performance assessments.

The BTA receives public funds to help private sector enterprises. Its main objectives are to maximise British tourism receipts and to ensure that the destination of the United Kingdom is promoted in the greatest number of markets.

The first objective concerns tourist expenditure rather than the volume of tourists. Hence, the BTA tends to concentrate its efforts on the most lucrative markets.

The second objective concerns endeavours to encourage a better distribution of tourism activities. Two factors are important. First, the advantages brought by tourism activity are more significant for poorer areas of the country. Second, strong concentrations of tourists on certain sites at certain times are both counter-productive and expensive, because tourists may not enjoy the experience and may not repeat their visit.

The BTA has also defined other specific objectives concerning the development of tourist facilities and infrastructure, the dissemination of information to respond to the needs of foreign tourists and advising the public authorities on tourism.

The tourism industry often has the tendency to adopt a short-term view on the value of investments. The BTA has the important responsibility of exploring new markets to ensure long-term profitability.

The 1990–3 BTA budget was provided by government subsidies and private financing by the tourism sector but also by other sources such as the local authorities. In 1992–3, this budget amounted to £49 million of which £30.9 million were public funds. This increased to £32.7 million in 1993–4 and will reach £33.5 million by 1996.

The contribution by the private sector has remained constant since 1990 at approximately a third of the total. However, if just the budget spent on marketing is taken into account, the private sector contribution is two-thirds. Indeed, the BTA insists that the private sector provide 66 per cent of funding for marketing projects. On the other hand, the contribution of the private sector to the cost of running the offices abroad is very small and limited to those enterprises which share buildings with overseas offices.

In the 1992 financial year, more than 40 per cent of the BTA budget was allocated to advertising and marketing and approximately 25 per cent to administrative costs of offices abroad. The publication and printing of brochures and documentation is the third area of high expenditure.

As a comparison, the Scottish, Welsh and Northern Ireland Offices receive a budget of between £11.9 million and £13.7 million a year. National funding for the English Tourist Board is being drastically reduced by central government, much to the concern of the English tourist industry. Its funding is being cut from £15.9 million in 1991–2 to £9 million by 1996. The Heritage Secretary in 1993, Peter Brooke, set out his reasons for the reducing the ETB's funding in the following statement published in *Tourism Enterprise*:

The BTA's role in promoting Britain abroad is an important one. The case is much less strong for central government funding of the promotion of tourism to England. The ETB has done a great deal over the years to raise standards, to improve access to information and to show the industry how its products can be developed and marketed. As the industry matures and the Regional Tourist Boards developed, it appropriate for other bodies to carry on many of the ETB's central activities.

Certain regional offices and local authorities also undertake promotional activities abroad, but there are no precise details on this expenditure. Within the private sector, the airline companies spend the most on promotion, but only a fraction is destined to finance the promotion of the destination United Kingdom.

The performance of the BTA in terms of profitability of public funds is evaluated in three ways:

1. Because of the great number of promotional campaigns jointly under-taken with private sector partners, the turnover in these partners' businesses compared with what had been projected gives an indication of the impact of these campaigns.
2. It is equally possible to measure this impact by the number of written enquiries received in response to advertising, or the number of telephone enquiries.
3. The BTA regularly interviews tourists to estimate the number of visitors who asked for information before their trip to the United Kingdom and to find out if this information had been useful. For instance, a 1990 survey showed that 24 per cent of visitors to the United Kingdom had obtained information from the BTA prior to their visit and 87 per cent of them found the information very useful.

Furthermore, these evaluations also indicate whether the two main objectives have been achieved: an increase in tourism receipts and a better distribution of tourism flows.

Table 10.2   *Comparison of national funding levels in Britain*

	1991–92 £m	1992–93 £m	1993–94 £m	1994–95 £m	1995–96 £m
BTA	29.2	30.9	32.0	32.7	33.5
ETB	15.1	15.3	13.9	10.8	9.0
Development	0.8	3.3	0.3	–	–
Total ETB	15.9	15.6	14.2	10.8	9.0
NITB	5.1	7.6	7.6		
Development	N/A	3.3	4.3	N/A	
Total NITB	5.1	10.9	11.9		
STB	9.1	10.1	10.1		
Development	3.6	3.5	3.6	modest increases	
Total STB	12.7	13.6	13.7	indicated	
WTB	7.6	9.9			
Development	3.6	3.8	+3%	N/A	
Total WTB	11.2	13.7			

Source: Tourism Enterprise.

The information obtained on the effectiveness of the different programmes and the reactions observed from the different markets are ultimately used in tourism planning.

■ Tourism strategies and policies of the European Union

The objective of the tourism policies of the European Union (EU) is to encourage a coordinated development of tourism in the member countries. The Union has identified the priority areas in which joint actions can contribute to solve problems and encourage the growth of tourism in the member countries.

The objectives of the Union's policies focus on four main areas:

- free movement and the protection of tourists;
- work in the tourism industry;
- transport;
- regional development.

☐ *The free movement and the protection of tourists*

The policy aims are:

- to ease custom controls (raising allowances limits for goods bought within the Union);
- to ease police controls at borders;
- to inform European tourists of their social security rights, so that they make full use of them (Europeans have the right to receive medical services in any country of the Union);
- to harmonise car insurance and assistance throughout the Union, so that victims of accidents suffered during a trip within the Union are assisted. These policies aim to provide the same protection in all countries of the EU;
- to protect the interests of tourists against misleading (and even untrue) advertising and when promised services are not provided; and to increase security in areas visited by tourists.

☐ *Working in the European tourism industry*

The EU aims to improve the work structure for professionals in the tourism industry, in order to establish the most favourable conditions for the best development of tourism activity.

To this end, initiatives are launched in the following areas:

- *The right to establish and operate tourism services*   The European Union has created *a common market of tourism services* which allows the citizens of the Union to set up businesses and operate services in member states. However, national regulations concerning access to tourism professions often impede the freedom of establishment and operation of tourism services. The objective of EU policy is to propose measures for the elimination of the barriers, particularly in the transport and travel agency professions.
- *Professional training and the mutual recognition of qualifications and employment*   In terms of professional training, the member states should recognise each others specialised courses in hotel and catering activities. The European policy aims to encourage more high-level specialised training courses in tourism organisation and management.

   Furthermore, the tourism sector can receive financial aid from the Social Fund in order to improve the possibilities of employment and geographical and professional mobility.
- *Spreading holiday periods*   The Union wants to reduce the concentration of school and professional holidays in certain months of the year because this hampers regional development and the growth of tourism services, and means that prices are set high for peak periods where the spread is insufficient or non-existent.
- *Tourism fiscality*   The VAT (value added tax) rate applied to tourism services (notably the hotel trade and restaurants) differs from country to country in the Union, a situation which needs harmonising.

   However, before introducing a gradual levelling of VAT across the countries, the objective of the EU's policy is to examine whether the fiscal disparities existing in the tourism sector divert tourism flows from some countries to the benefit of others.

☐ *Transport and tourism*

Economic integration has had a positive effect on communications within the European Union, particularly for *road transport*, and the policy has been to liberalise the access to the road transport market. To achieve this, several measures have already been taken: the introduction of common regulations for international passenger transport by coach and the regulation of scheduled and specialised coach services between EU countries.

The policy for passenger *rail travel* is to improve the service (speed, frequency) and to create European commercial products (for instance, the EURALC ticket for the overseas clientele, the BIGE ticket with a 40 per cent discount).

The policy for *air transport* aims to introduce changes to the air tariff structure for scheduled services, so that fares for leisure and interregional travel can be reduced. It will also encourage the liberalisation of the 'skies' within the Union with the introduction of the cabotage right from April 1997. To this end, two policies are pursued simultaneously.

The first policy encourages increased transparency by requiring that clear and detailed information on applied tariffs and on the initiative margin of each airline company be made available. The objective is to bring down air fares substantially, which is very favourable to the development of international tourism.

The second aims to improve regional coverage and to increase competition, which will also have a positive effect on tourism traffic.

☐ *Regional development and tourism*

The European Union wants to promote tourism to underdeveloped regions with tourism potential. For this, two instruments of regional economic policy are used:

- *The European Fund for Regional Development (EFRD)*, which contributes to the financing of tourism projects when presented as part of a regional development plan.
- *The European Agricultural Guidance and Guarantee Fund (EAGGF)*, which encourages the development of tourism activity complementing agricultural activity.

The different initiatives demonstrate that the European Union is taking an active role in the development of tourism without, however, intervening in national policies which are adapted to the particular situation of individual member countries. For this reason, Union policy tends to concentrate on priority areas like the promotion of social, cultural and rural tourism, the extension of the tourism season, heritage and architectural conservation.

The industrialised countries are pursuing the most advanced policies of tourism development. For many developed countries where unemployment is high, tourism is one of the largest job-creating sectors, particularly in zones of low economic activity. For this reason, efforts have been concentrated on land development policies, the protection of the environment, the renovation of existing tourism products and the development of new tourism resources.

However, developing supply to satisfy a greater demand constitutes just one aspect of international tourism. Tourism-marketing and promotion policies to encourage more visits are increasingly important to ensure the financial profitability of the investments. Budgets allocated to promotion have become very large as rich countries regularly increase them in their constant battle to gain competitive advantage. Some developing countries have insufficient financial means to pursue promotion policies and little-known countries cannot be marketed properly. Consequently, they do not receive enough income from tourism to develop new infrastructure and superstructure and the gap between rich and poor countries widens further. To redress this, an important development in international tourism has been introduced: joint tourism policies by groups of developing countries.

Reference

1. OECD. *OECD Tourism and International Tourism Policies in OECD Countries*. Paris, 1991–92.

Further reading

Airey, D. 'European Government Approaches to Tourism', *Tourism Management*, 4(4), pp. 234–44, 1983.

EC. Commission Report to the Council of the European Parlament and to the Economic and Social Committee on Community Actions affecting Tourism, *The Council's Decision*, 92/421/EEC, Brussels, April 1994.

Foin, T. C. 'Quantitative Studies of Visitor Impacts on Environments of Yosemite National Park, California, and their Implications for Park Management Policy', *Journal of Environmental Management*, 5(1), pp. 1–22, 1981.

Lavery, P. and Van Doren, C. *Travel and Tourism: A North American/European Perspective*. Huntingdon: Elm Publications, 1990.

Middleton, V. T. C *Marketing in Travel and Tourism*. Oxford: Heinemann, 1988.

Mill, R. C. *Tourism, The International Business*. Englewood Cliffs, NJ: Prentice-Hall, 1990.

Pearce, D. *Tourism Organisations*. Harlow: Longman, 1992.

■ *Chapter 11* ■

International Tourism in Developing Countries

The features of international tourism in developing countries
The impact of international tourism in developing countries: the economic
    impact of international tourism; the socio-cultural impacts; the
    environmental impacts
Tourism development policies in developing countries: tourism promotion
    and the matching of demand; new tourism products and the modernisation
    of the supply; adaptation of air transport to the development of tourism;
    facilitation and installation rights; training

According to Antonio Enriquez Savignac, Secretary-General of the WTO
(1995), tourism undeniably acts as a driving force for world development.
Its growth has overtaken that of international trade which in turn
progresses faster than the creation of wealth, particularly for developing
countries.

Tourism contributes to the transfer of wealth from North to South and
from the industrialised to the developing countries. The latter account for
a quarter of world arrivals and receipts but could potentially perform
much better. For them, international tourism is unquestionably paramount
as a creator of jobs and the most readily exploitable source of foreign
earnings to finance investments or reduce foreign debt.

■ The features of international tourism in developing countries

Tourism is already a strong component of the economy in major
developing countries (such as Egypt, India, Morocco and Mexico). It has
enabled several countries in the Caribbean and Indian Ocean to achieve
take-off and is helping the newly industrialised countries of the East Asia
and Pacific area to do likewise.

Table 11.1   *The developing countries, 1991*

Ratio of developing countries' tourism receipts	32%
Share of total world arrivals	23%
Share of total world receipts	23%
Ratio of developing countries' tourism receipts to their total exports	9%
Ratio of developing countries' tourism receipts to their total trade in services	32%

Source: WTO.

Despite many differences, developing countries have certain common characteristics with regards to international tourism polices:

- Developing countries are mainly tourism receptor destinations
- International tourism is considered to be a means of acquiring foreign currency
- Tourism flows involving developing countries are principally North–South which broadly corresponds to the main commercial flows:
  - North America → Latin America and the Caribbean
  - Europe → Africa, the Caribbean and the Indian Ocean
  - North America, Europe and Japan → Asia and the Pacific
- Although intraregional tourism between developing countries in some regions is currently growing at a faster rate than intercontinental tourism, tourism flows are still very weak as developing countries themselves generate few tourists (and sometimes none at all).
- International tourism is a technologically advanced activity in which many developing countries are lagging behind. They have problems of transferring compatible technology, adapting to new technology, financing, training staff and integrating technology in the national economy.

  Tourism investments may not be profitable during the initial period, which is needed to adapt resources for commercial exploitation, meaning that private enterprises are reluctant to invest. The responsibility, therefore, usually falls on the state, despite its low financial resources. This often results in the state accruing large debts. It frequently makes franchise agreements with international hotel chains in order to benefit from the advantages of building such hotels. This allows the country to be represented in an international chain, and to use the chain's brand name, technology and marketing network. Management contracts are also agreed to introduce foreign know-how and expertise. The developing country pays for these services whether the occupancy rate of the hotel is high or not, thus running the risk of deficit in the management costs.

- The socio-cultural systems of developing countries receiving tourists often differ greatly from those of industrialised tourist-generating countries. When tourism flows from generating countries reach a certain size, these differences may be the cause of problems (culture differences, objections to behaviour, cultural degradation, rejection, etc.).
- The importance of tourism varies between different developing countries. Some countries (generally the new industrial countries) are very important international tourism destinations (Mexico, Caribbean islands, certain South-East Asian and North African countries) whereas international tourism in other developing countries is very limited.

International tourism presents many advantages, but also certain disadvantages which must be analysed for each country and compared with other economic sectors. This analysis indicates the relative importance of tourism in the economic activities of the country and assesses whether tourism contributes enough to the economic and social development of the country. As a result, measures are taken to reduce the inconveniences caused by international tourism and to increase the advantages.

Empirical studies provide general information necessary to carry out comparisons and formulate hypotheses which allow strategists to select the most appropriate tourism policies for each country. Regional and national analyses are essential as international tourism policies differ between regions (for instance Africa and the Caribbean) or countries (Tunisia and Kenya).

The least developed countries often have great tourism potential and a comparative advantage in low-cost employment, particularly in the hotel and catering trade. However, the tourism sector also requires very high investments and certain jobs can only be performed by highly skilled workers.

The impact of tourism in low-income countries can be analysed from statistics compiled by the WTO, which show tourism flows, tourism receipts and hotel capacity in relation to the level of economic development. This analysis confirms the large gap between developing countries and industrialised countries in the level of international tourism particularly relative to GNP per inhabitant. Indeed, tourism flows towards low-income countries accounted for 18.4 million arrivals in 1991, just 3.9 per cent of the world total. Their share of international tourism receipts was only 2.2 per cent of total world receipts and amounted to US$5,872 million. Furthermore, tourism flows towards low-income countries are largely concentrated towards two countries, China and India, which together accounted for 76.8 per cent of arrivals and 71.4 per cent of receipts. Consequently, in many low-income countries, the international tourism sector is virtually non-existent despite the fact that there may be a great tourism potential. Nearly 50 per cent of low-income countries receive less than 50,000 tourists annually. In terms of receipts, the difference is even greater with 11 countries out of 34 surveyed by the WTO receiving less than US$10 million a year from international tourism.

Middle-income developing countries account for a much larger proportion of world tourism flows, both in terms of receipts and in terms of arrivals. In 1991, they received 130 million international tourists, 28.5 per cent of the world total and US$54,163 million from international tourism, 20.7 per cent of total world tourism receipts. The difference between countries at the lower end of the middle-income bracket and those at the higher end is not important in terms of international arrivals. However, in terms of receipts, the difference is considerable. Countries at the lower end of the middle-income bracket secured 35.5 per cent of this group's receipts, while countries at the higher end received 64.5 per cent.

■ The impact of international tourism in developing countries

The impact of international tourism expansion policies on the development of Third World countries has often been hailed as an 'economic miracle' needing minimal investment and providing vast sums in foreign currency. However, international tourism can create economic, social and ecological problems for developing countries. They do not have the same capacity for assimilating foreign tourists as industrialised countries, which, in most cases, have a long tourism tradition and much experience in welcoming foreign tourists, and can offer them economic and socio-cultural systems similar to those they are used to (North America, Western Europe).

The main impact of international tourism on developing countries is economic, socio-cultural and ecological. Measures must be taken to encourage the positive effects and reduce the negative effects. These measures must be incorporated into tourism plans and more generally into the country's international tourism policy.

Table 11.2 *International tourist arrivals (excluding same-day visitors) (000)*

	1981	1982	1983	1984	1985	1986	1987	1988	1989	1990	1991
Low-income economies	7,615	7,916	7,811	9,275	11,646	13,951	15,809	17,643	14,932	16,336	18,404
China and India	5,046	5,212	5,096	6,335	8,392	10,451	12,244	13,952	11,097	12,191	14,142
Other low-income countries	2,569	2,704	2,715	2,940	3,254	3,500	3,565	3,691	3,835	4,145	4,262
Middle-income economies	78,443	70,813	74,374	84,012	88,206	90,758	98,717	107,980	118,583	136,596	130,315
Lower-middle-income	33,152	31,380	33,482	35,848	36,647	38,254	41,673	47,771	52,670	60,774	60,326
Upper-middle-income	45,291	39,433	40,892	48,164	51,559	52,504	57,044	60,209	65,913	75,822	69,989
Industrial market economies	170,838	177,872	178,791	194,198	198,914	203,532	215,449	227,111	247,781	258,281	262,376

Source: WTO and World Bank.

☐ *The economic impact of international tourism*

International tourism has an economic impact on the national income, employment, prices, the state budget and the balance of payments.

☐ The impact on the national income

Expenditure by foreign tourists constitutes a contribution, often very large, to the national income of a developing country. Employees and suppliers in the different tourism sectors receive salaries or payments. There are also indirect effects on the national income resulting from work on infrastructure, communications, transport, accommodation and procurement.

However, in many developing countries, an increase in consumption by foreign tourists does not always mean quantitative or qualitative increases in national production. Importing food products, durable goods and equipment often becomes necessary, resulting in revenue increases for foreign suppliers. Furthermore, foreign tourism enterprises repatriate a proportion (sometimes a large one) of the profits earned in the developing country (particularly in the hotel trade); foreign technicians and experts are paid salaries; and repayments and interest on loans must also be met.

Faced with the problems of integrating international tourism into their economic activities, the main objective of developing countries is to find the right balance between tourism policies and the needs of their national economy. To this end, the following factors must be taken into consideration:

- *The short-, medium- and long-term effects*   For instance, in the short term, it is necessary to spend foreign currency in order to generate it in the long term.
- *The different choices*   Are there alternative methods of economic development? Could international tourism be successfully replaced (because the costs involved are smaller) by agricultural or industrial development?
- *The impact of sectorial and regional production policies*   These policies gradually integrate international tourism into the economy of the country, notably food production, handicraft manufacturing and services (transport and accommodation, etc.).

For instance, a 150-room hotel (300 beds) can be designed as a tower block and built and run with imported materials and technology. It can also be built with local materials and with local know-how (professional training of local workers on the building site), with imported equipment kept to a minimum (generators, air-conditioning, kitchens, lifts). The local architectural style of the second option is often better appreciated by foreign tourists who are tired of identical architectural structures in hotels with similar comfort and service standards found all over the world.

Developing countries must attempt to supply tourism complexes with national or local food products in order to reduce imports and integrate tourism into their economy. However, the products they supply must reach the required standards of hygiene so as not to jeopardise the success of their tourism industry.

The impact of international tourism on national income can be very different from country to country. This depends on whether the country has integrated tourism into its economy or not. If tourism has not been properly integrated, foreign tourists are accommodated and catered for by foreign hotel companies which import virtually all equipment and consumer goods and repatriate profits and the salaries of their foreign staff. International tourism is a 'transformation' industry and it is important to determine precisely its final direct and indirect impacts (employment, taxation etc.) on the national economy. Negative economic impacts (inflation), socio-cultural impacts (degradation of the cultural and ethnic heritage) and ecological impacts must also be assessed.

Each developing country should base its choice and level of tourism investment on detailed analysis of its particular situation.

☐ The impact on employment

The governments of developing countries place great importance on the effects of international tourism on employment because, very often, these countries suffer from very high unemployment rates. It is therefore vital to create new economic activity. Tourism, as a labour-intensive service industry, is ideal because it employs a large semi-skilled and unskilled workforce.

In countries highly dependent on tourism, up to 50 per cent of the workforce is involved in economic activities directly and indirectly linked to tourism for part of the year. These are principally countries with small insular economies which, before developing their tourism industry, were reliant on just one economic activity (like agriculture) or on one product (like sugar in the Caribbean).

Nevertheless, in most developing countries, international tourism is very limited, and the employment it creates is less than 5 per cent of total employment. Furthermore, the potential of international tourism as an

employment creator must be compared to the number of jobs that could be created if other economic sectors were to be developed. The results of such comparisons are difficult to interpret because the capacity of tourism activities to create jobs depends on the professional sector. For instance, within the accommodation sector, a deluxe hotel has a quite different investment/employment ratio from a one-star hotel, particularly if different levels of technology are used.

Consequently, developing countries must concentrate on examining the potential for creating the maximum amount of employment, using technology which corresponds to the development level in each country. Labour costs and equipment replacement costs must also be taken into account so that the tourism product remains competitive.

☐ The impact on prices

The influence of the tourism industry on the general price level of goods and services in a country depends on how much it contributes to the national income. However, in developing countries which have a high concentration of tourism demand to visit for particular geographic areas or for specific products, its impact is generally influential. This is because their markets tend to be very narrow and imbalances become apparent very quickly.

The movement of land prices

Rises in land prices are either linked to the development of new infrastructure or attributed to speculation resulting from increases in demand for a good of which there is a limited quantity. An increase in the price of land in tourism areas causes a general increase in the price of land around the country, which not only affects tourists but also agricultural, industrial and social users (social accommodation, schools, hospitals etc.). The profitability of many enterprises and even the whole agrarian policy of the country can also be affected. Consequently, the aim of tourism policies is to define areas of tourism development by imposing certain conditions which regulate the transfer of property, thus dissuading speculation. Land reserves can be created for subsequent development.

Product shortages

Shortages of certain products usually consumed by the local population (fish, meat, fruit) can be caused by tourism, because they are also in great demand by foreign visitors. The result is inflation which can spread to the whole economy. This inflationary risk is higher in developing countries because supply is generally inelastic and it is often not possible to import extra products because of a lack of foreign currency. Without imports to satisfy demand, the price of available goods goes up with repercussions on the whole economy, notably the triggering of salary increases.

Inflation can be tackled either by reducing national and foreign tourism demand or by increasing imports financed by currency brought in by foreign consumers. Nevertheless, adjustments have to be made which require short-, medium- or long-term measures, depending on the solution adopted (imports, reductions in demand or increases in national production).

The risk of inflation caused by the success of the tourism industry indicates the necessity of effective planning for the management of the growth of the tourism sector, while also taking into account the general situation of the economy. Economic liberalism, where all import restrictions are eliminated, may naturally adjust supply to demand at a low enough level to stifle the risk of inflation. However, this could bring certain sectorial and social imbalances.

A more general problem is the seasonal increase in prices during peak tourist periods. Appropriate measures are adopted by all countries and not just developing countries.

☐ The impact on the national budget

Expenditure on tourism infrastructure constitutes the largest burden on the state budget. This includes ports, airports, roads, telecommunications, water distribution networks, electricity, gas, water disposal and treatment systems; and health services and equipment. The cost is particularly high in developing countries because of the shortage of natural resources. However, to remain competitive, they must provide high-standard services and equipment comparable to those in industrialised countries, facilities that are not normally available to the country's population. Developing new equipment and services has the added advantage of benefiting the local population and contributing to the improvement of its standard of living.

The major problem for developing countries is the time delay between the government expenditure on developing the infrastructure and the increased receipts raised by the tourism sector. The time delay causes particularly difficult problems for developing countries which have to rely on public or private financing from foreign sources. This has become increasingly costly because of rising interest on funds borrowed and the rising US dollar (the international currency usually adopted).

To lessen their reliance on foreign finance, developing countries are sometimes tempted to adopt short-term measures to increase receipts from international tourism, like the following:

- taxation and levies on goods and services specifically imported for the tourism sector and its suppliers;
- special taxes imposed on international tourists, such as airport taxes or taxes on length of stay in the country;
- differential between prices charged to foreign tourists and the local population.

These policies may increase foreign currency reserves in the short term but, in the long term, are generally detrimental. They have a negative impact on the country's competitiveness and on its tourism image abroad. The extra receipts that they generate may have to be used to finance additional tourism promotional efforts to compensate.

On the other hand, the country can generate extra revenue from tourism through its fiscal system without damaging its tourism industry. This is achieved by direct and indirect taxes on income from tourism. However, these fiscal receipts can only be levied by the state once the infrastructure has been developed and once the commercialisation of the country's tourism products is under way. In these conditions, the impact of international tourism on the state budget of developing countries depends on the economic and financial situation in each country. The main difficulty is in forecasting accurately the necessary expenditure to develop the infrastructure and the capacity of the country to raise international loans.

☐ The impact on the balance of payments

Often the principal objective of international tourism policies of developing countries is increasing foreign currency reserves to finance economic development. To estimate accurately if this objective is being achieved, it is important to identify the contribution of the international tourism industry to the balance of payments of the country.

This is generally impossible to estimate. As a rule, the tourism industry's contribution to the balance of payments is calculated as the difference between expenditure by foreign tourists in the country and expenditure by residents of the country abroad.

This calculation is very complicated for developing countries because they are often obliged to import many consumer goods (including food) and equipment for tourism superstructures and infrastructures. There are five main categories of foreign currency expenditure attributable to international tourism:

- the import of equipment, goods and services to develop tourism infrastructures;
- the import of goods and services used by foreign visitors. These are both finished products and products where one or more elements are imported and combined with elements found nationally to produce a final tourism product;
- interest and repayment of borrowed foreign capital;
- rental payments, salaries paid to foreign staff and the repatriation of profits by foreign companies;
- the cost of promotion and publicity abroad absorbed by the country's national tourism administrations and by tourism professionals in the country.

The impact of international tourism on the balance of payments depends on the production capacity of the country, which is a function of its geographical, economic, technical and social characteristics and its level of development. Nevertheless, international tourism can be the driving force in the economic growth of many developing countries and, if managed properly, can have a positive impact on their balance of payments.

☐ *The socio-cultural impacts*

Developing countries are particularly sensitive to the socio-cultural effects of international tourism. The arrival of foreign tourists from industrialised countries may cause friction because of differences in culture and lifestyle. This may lead to cultural degradation in the receptor country as well as resentment and ultimately rejection of foreign tourists by local residents. This friction is particularly apparent during periods of strong tourism flows at certain times of the year (peak periods) and in certain areas (areas of high tourist concentration) and can manifest itself in many subtle and varied ways.

Unless policies of complete isolation, economic self-sufficiency and structural underdevelopment are pursued, the friction between visiting and resident cultures is inevitable in a situation of rapid expansion. However, the problems should not be blamed solely on tourism. Television, the importation of consumer goods, equipment and technology, fashion, contact with immigrant workers returning to their original country, and technical and scientific training all have strong influences on the culture of developing countries.

One of the aims of international tourism policies is to control the effects of international tourism in order to avoid or reduce potential cultural clashes. To this end, two methods are used.

- The first method is to concentrate most tourism installations away from densely populated areas, so as to avoid confrontation between the two lifestyles (for instance, on sparsely inhabited beach-fronts or islands such as the Maldives). Unfortunately, this solution may create zones of economic activity cut off from the economic and social environment of the country. Furthermore, the equipment, installed for tourism purposes, is only used by foreign tourists and does not benefit the local population. However, experience has shown that this may be the only appropriate solution for the promotion of large-scale international tourism in countries with small populations (for instance, the islands in the Caribbean).

- The second method consists of limiting international tourism flows to attract a mainly high-income foreign clientele. The high receipts generated compensate for the small number of tourists visiting the country. This very selective tourism policy requires an exceptional, and therefore rare, environment and high-quality equipment and services which are seldom compatible with the means of most developing countries, the competition they are up against or their socio-economic development objectives. Despite these conditions, certain countries have actively pursued this policy with considerable success (for instance, Mauritius).

Policies which aim at integrating foreign tourists into the social and political life of the country may appear to be very beneficial to destination countries (social and cultural exchanges etc.) but are, in reality, very difficult (sometimes virtually impossible) to pursue in most countries. Large-scale integration is often opposed by both the local population and foreign visitors. The presence of a large number of tourists produces a 'demonstration effect'. This effect, usually involuntary on the part of the tourists, causes resentment because of their apparently superior material wealth. The social and cultural upheaval this creates results in cultural degradation or the rejection of foreign tourism.

To avoid these risks, international tourism policies in developing countries aim at channelling tourism flows:

- towards growth areas where the concentration of tourists is inevitable but can be controlled;
- on to organised tours and stays integrated into the social environment of the country, but with a limited number of tourists. This is done by fixing higher prices or limiting the accommodation supply.

These objectives also protect the health of foreign tourists whose immune defences and lifestyles may be different from those of the local population.

☐ *The environmental impacts*

International tourism in developing countries is both:

- a factor which develops the natural heritage of the country;
- and a factor which damages and even destroys this environment.

Consequently, the objective of international tourism must be to encourage the positive effects and to limit the negative effects.

- *The positive effects of tourism on the environment* Tourism contributes to the preservation and conservation of the national heritage. For instance, national and regional parks are created to protect the local flora and fauna. International tourism often awakens a conscious reevaluation of the natural heritage of developing countries and the possibilities of exploiting it.

  From this point of view, the effects of international tourism are very positive. Furthermore, compared with other manufacturing industries, tourism produces relatively little pollution. Quite often it initiates the maintenance of sites and landscapes hitherto abandoned.

  However, in many developing countries, tourism is developed without following any real policies of protection and maintenance of the environment. This is because they lack finance and are insufficiently aware of the damage that can be caused. In fact, the receipts provided by tourism are often spent on other areas of the economy deemed more important and are rarely replaced in the tourism budget. As a result, the negative effects of tourism on the environment often override the positive effects.

- *The negative effects of tourism on the environment* These are the damage to various ecological elements which constitute the tourism heritage of these countries: the destruction of the fauna (e.g. wild life in Africa), the destruction of sites (excessive concentration of high-rise hotels along beach-fronts), the destruction of historical monuments (unprotected monuments are vulnerable to vandalism and theft), pollution of rivers, seas, lakes and underground lakes by the discharge of impure water and untreated sewage.

Policies designed to protect the environment are vital to reduce the negative effects of tourism. They are profitable in the long term because they ensure the continuity of tourism activity in the future. However, in the short term, many developing countries ignore environmental protection in favour of commercial or financial considerations, largely because of their inexperience in tourism planning.

Developing countries need to follow very specific tourism policies to control all the economic and social impacts caused by an increase in international tourism flows.

Thus, the concept of carrying capacity is very important for the sustainable development of developing countries. Mathieson and Wall (1982) define the carrying capacity of an area as 'the maximum number of tourists that can be catered for while making full use of the recreational facilities and without damaging the environment. Limitations to capacity may be physical (crowding, visual deterioration) or social/cultural (unacceptable change of local lifestyles.'[1]

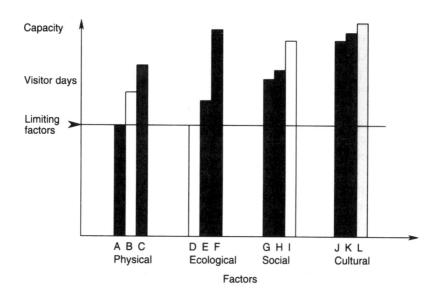

Source: Trevor Atherton, WTO Round Table on Planning for Sustainable Tourism Development, 10th Assembly of WTO, Bali, Indonesia, October 1993.

Figure 11.1   *Carrying capacity of a destination*

Figure 11.1 highlights the issues associated with carrying capacity. According to Trevor Atherton (1993),

> In theory there is an infinite number of factors. To measure sustainable development, however, only those which are potentially limiting factors are relevant.
>
> The most important thing to note is that limits are not absolute. It is possible to increase the capacity of many limiting factors by planning and management techniques and by using technology. For example, if the limiting factor is A: *availability of space on the beach*, you can increase the carrying capacity by zoning, restoring or building more artificial beach. However, there are likely to be some factors which may be absolute limits. For example, if another factor is D: *the beach is a rookery for endangered green turtles*, it may be prudent not to interfere with it all.
>
> There is also a limit upon how much planning, management and technology can be justified. It costs money. Economists can calculate whether the returns from the increased tourism will outweigh the cost involved in increasing the capacity of the limiting factors.
>
> So conceptually it is possible to integrate the methodology of all disciplines involved (including economics) and to define the limit of sustainable tourism development in terms of tourism carrying capacity.[2]

Tourism policies must aim at preventing the risks of economic dependency that could be caused by the unchecked growth of international tourism. The bodies responsible for tourism in developing countries must develop their bargaining powers, and collaborate with international organisations, to negotiate with the main agents of international tourism. This is very important, since they cannot run the risk of diverting tourism flows away from their country once the necessary infrastructure and superstructure (airports, hotels etc.) have been developed. They must negotiate with tourism professionals in industrialised countries so that the developing countries are included in their plans and not passed over for other more profitable destinations.

But how can developing countries influence and contribute to developing a new North–South relationship (in other words, a new international tourism order). They intervene directly in generating markets, either individually, if they have the financial resources, or collectively with other organisations. Well-conceived, well-run and competitive operations allow developing countries much more independence and permit them to expect a guaranteed numbers of tourists.

When countries have no multinational companies or offices, they can achieve comparable results by grouping their national tourist offices and their airline companies. However, this can only really be successful if the operations they carry out are of international quality and, therefore, competitive. The different governments coordinate their tourism policies and the financial resources they are prepared to commit. These arrangements involve regional development organisations or specialised tourism and financial organisations (the African Development Bank, the Asian Bank, the Inter-American Bank, etc.), air transport organisations and especially the Regional Commissions of the World Tourism Organisation.

▌Tourism development policies in developing countries

The main objective of development policies in the tourism sector is to ensure sustained growth by matching supply as closely as possible to international demand. To this end, specific actions are implemented concerning both regional cooperation and cooperation between countries with very different levels of development. They are designed to encourage tourism development and tourism exchanges. These include:

- Tourism promotion and the matching of demand
- New tourism products and the modernisation of supply
- Adaptation of air transport to the development of tourism
- Facilitation and installation rights
- Basic and professional training

Each of these actions can contribute to solving problems associated with the growth of the tourism sector in developing countries. However, to be operational, these actions must be analysed stringently before being implemented and substantial international cooperation must be agreed.

Tourism promotion and the matching of demand

This generally involves regional cooperation. Indeed, promoting and disseminating tourism information in the large generating markets (the USA, the European Union, Japan) require considerable financial resources, usually far too high for most developing countries. Thus, developing countries are compelled to pool their resources to launch promotional campaigns and market the tourism products of all the countries in the region. However, joint promotion can result in the different countries involved losing their identity. In fact, surveys and market studies show that potential tourists in generating markets are hardly motivated if they do not have a clear and precise perception of a tourism destination. Consequently, there is a risk of the tourism image of the country becoming 'diluted'. It is important that tourism promotion activities based on regional cooperation highlight the individuality of each tourism destination. It is particularly useful to adopt several levels of regional cooperation at the same time.

☐ Extended regional cooperation

The main aim of this form of cooperation is to ensure the promotion of entire regions. One of the primary examples of this type of cooperation is PATA (Pacific Asian Travel Association) which includes most of the destinations of East and South-East Asia and the Pacific. PATA is organised into groupings by country and by wider market which allows both an overall promotion of the zone and the targeting of specific country–market actions.

Today, countries in the Indian Ocean are striving to put in place an extended regional cooperation along lines similar to PATA. The objective of the Indian Ocean Tourism Association is not only to represent the islands of the Indian Ocean (Mauritius, Madagascar, the Seychelles, the Comoros, Réunion Island) but also countries bordering the region such as Australia, Malaysia, Singapore, India, Pakistan and the Far Eastern countries. Within this kind of cooperation, tourism firms in these countries can coordinate promotional activities, not only in their traditional markets, but also worldwide. However, if this extended regional cooperation could be developed for other areas such as the South Atlantic and the Mediterranean, it must be complemented with specific regional cooperation measures.

☐ Restricted regional cooperation

The objective of restricted regional cooperation is to promote a small group of countries located in the same geographic zone and exhibiting similar characteristics. The advantage of this kind of cooperation is that these countries can be jointly represented at large events and tourism fairs. The Tourism Council of the South Pacific groups Fiji, Kiribati, Papua New Guinea, the Solomon Islands, Tonga, Tuvalu, Vanuatu and Western Samoa together. The primary objective of the Indian Ocean Commission associating Madagascar, Mauritius, the Comoros, Réunion and the Seychelles is tourism promotion abroad under the banner of 'The Islands of the Indian Ocean'. However, there are problems identified with joint promotion programmes, notably competition between countries offering similar tourism products and often insufficient funds submitted to the joint promotion budget.

☐ North–South regional cooperation

This kind of cooperation involves countries with different levels of development. The objective of regional cooperation between countries within the same tourism zone is to launch promotional campaigns in generating markets which are independent of those launched by each state of the region, but which complement them. A notable example of this type of agreement is the interregional and intra-regional cooperation between the EU (the European Union) and the countries of the ACP (Africa, Caribbean and Pacific). Countries signatory to the Lomé Convention have access to the European Development Fund (EDF) for financial aid to sell tourism products of their zone (for instance, the Caribbean, West and East Africa and the Indian Ocean) on the European market. In this way, new mixed tourism products can be created which bring together several destinations on the same tour.

These three levels of cooperation help to adapt tourism products of developing countries to international demand and also ensure a sustainable development of the tourism sector in these regions.

☐ *New tourism products and the modernisation of the supply*

Regional cooperation is often difficult when it comes to supplying tourism products. The assumption is that enterprises in different countries are capable of creating and commercialising common products. For this to occur, all obstacles to international tourism exchanges must be abolished, particularly when they concern the movement of people. To this end, UNCTAD has created a databank of rules concerning the temporary movement of people linked to the exchange of services. This regional cooperation can involve groups of countries located in the same region, or countries with different levels of development situated in different regions.

Intra-regional cooperation principally concerns conditions for the creation of new tourism products involving several countries. Two or three destinations can be commercialised in international markets and marketed as one tourism package. While each country has its individual character, cooperation can be developed on a complementary basis (for instance, projects involving Singapore, Malaysia and Indonesia, projects involving islands in the Indian Ocean and East Africa and projects between Mexico and Central American countries).

However, there are financial, technical and political problems associated with creating mixed products. From a financial point of view, they are generally high-priced products, because more than one means of transport (air and road) or type of accommodation have to be used. These products tend to attract a low-volume, high-spending clientele. From the technical (as well as financial) point of view, foreign enterprises which want to create tourism products encounter certain restrictions, notably in the repatriation of profits.

Accordingly, interregional cooperation programmes tend to concentrate on the transfer of technology to help developing countries adapt their supply to the requirements of demand so that they can offer competitive tourism products both in terms of price and quality. To achieve this, specific programmes have been initiated such as the Interreg, Regis and Leader programmes created by the EU. At an international level, these programmes have been implemented by the WTO.

Adaptation of air transport to the development of tourism

For many developing countries, air transport is a major obstacle for the development of their tourism industry. For instance, in African countries, the recognition of this problem has recently led to much attention being focused on analysing causes in order to find a solution. Three main causes have been identified:

- inequitable and exorbitant fees charged to airline companies, hoteliers, travel and tour operators for access to the system;
- monopolistic controls imposed by a cartel of owners which make the development of new computer systems in developing countries difficult;
- restrictions which are imposed when access is being sought through systems which are not part of the major network.

Faced with these problems, the tourism authorities in African countries feel that there is discrimination against the airlines and all others in the travel and tourism industry in countries not served by GDS networks.

Box 11.1   *The problem of communication in developing countries: the case of West Africa*

At a presentation delivered at the jointly sponsored ECOWAS/WTO seminar on the organisation of air transport and development of tourism in the ECOWAS sub-region, Dr Edmund Premph (Chairman of M & J Travel and WAPTOURS) highlighted the lack of technology in communications between countries in the region by relating the following case:

Case of a typical WAPTOURS West African itinerary. Australia–Côte d'Ivoire–Mali–Togo–Ghana[3]

The original communication for this tour came from M & J Tours Associates in South Africa who wanted five Australian tourists visiting West Africa for the first time to be given VIP service and a hassle-free inaugural trip.

The operators involved with this tour were as follows:

(a)   Air Afrique, Air Ivoire and British Airways.
(b)   The ground operator in Côte d'Ivoire was Haury Tours; in Mali, ATS; in Ghana, M & J Travel and Tours; in Togo, Pronto Voyage.
(c)   Hotels involved were the Intercontinental Golf Hotel in Abidjan; Hotel President in Yamoussokro; Hotel de l'Amitié in Mali; Hotel Sarakawa in Togo and in Ghana, the Labadi Beach Hotel.

The problems

M & J Travel and Tours was the coordinator for the entire tour. The problems encountered were essentially those of communication.

First of all, in Côte d'Ivoire, before the tourists arrived from South Africa, there had been problems regarding the booking and confirmation of the two hotels. It was a hard battle getting immediate confirmation of the hotel reservation and thus the clients arrived before we actually got information by telephone, even though it appeared that the hotel had received our earlier messages and had also tried desperately to make contact.

The same problem applied to our ground operator associates who could not tell us that our clients had left for Mali because they could not get through by telex, fax, telephone or by any terminals (because of different systems).

Meanwhile, our South African colleagues were constantly on the telephone to our office because we were the co-ordinators of the project, seeking information as to the whereabouts of the clients. We could only answer by reference to the itinerary, without being exactly sure where the clients were and whether all the reservations and excursions had gone on well.

Two days after they were supposed to have arrived in Mali, we finally managed to get through to our colleague by telephone, whereupon we were assured that our clients were safe and enjoying their holiday. That was to be the last time we heard from them until a desperate message came informing us that they were on their way to the Ghana border by road.

At every stage, what saved the day was the sheer professionalism and complete confidence in the individual abilities of the tour operator and the occasional success of telephone calls.

It is clear from what I have said that the existence of a common regional or even sub-regional distribution system would have enabled us to deliver our services with less stress and inconvenience to all parties concerned. This problem could cost all the companies involved future potential lucrative business, for it turned out that these clients were very important and likely to generate much trade.

As it is, inconvenience was caused all round which took the form of wasted time, extra communication costs (which diminished our profit) and the depreciation of our professionalism, which was saved only by the actual pleasures and attractions of the sub-region which the clients enjoyed.

Source: ECOWAS/WTO, Cotonou, February 1994.

Indeed, one of the key conditions for the development of tourism is for countries to actively pursue a policy of reducing air tariffs. Unfortunately, airports in developing countries are often too basic to receive tourists and there are either too many or too few airline companies using them. The cost of operating certain African airlines is 40 per cent higher than the world average. To resolve such a situation, policies must be designed to encourage competition and increase productivity, because they are crucial in order to strengthen the foundations of tourism development. These policies can only be effectively introduced by regional cooperation and joint ventures to create new tourism and air transport hubs. These are not the same as the hubs operated by airline companies in the United States which are exclusively based on their air transport strategy. The objective of developing these tourism and air transport hubs is to create real synergy by channelling international tourists towards several countries in the region. The economy of scale produced by using jumbo jets gives the tourism destinations concerned a considerable competitive advantage. Examples of this type of hub already exist in the Caribbean with airports in Barbados and Martinique which receive European tourists whose destination are other islands in the area.

□ *Facilitation and installation rights*

Regulations and practices which impinge on the activities of tourism enterprises in developing countries are often linked to general measures which relate to property rights, equity participation, capital transfer limitations controlling exchanges, rules concerning foreign personnel employment and import or fiscal restrictions.[4]

Furthermore, there are a number of restrictions applied to tourism enterprises which generally slow down the development of tourism. For instance, certain measures which limit the financial participation to the registered capital of a company restrict the establishment of branches abroad, notably in the travel agency sector.

Other measures affecting the activities of tourism enterprises include employment professional rights restrictions. In some countries, national qualifications are required to practice certain professions (tour guide, for instance) which are very difficult for foreigners to obtain. Switzerland restricts the access to most tourism careers by regulating professions. To work in the hotel catering industry, a proficiency certificate is required. Each canton has its own criteria and no equivalence system exists at the federal level. As such, the only way foreigners can pursue a career in tourism or in the hotel trade is by associating professionally with Swiss nationals.

Many developing countries impose restrictions on imports and on the use of essential factors of production such as foreign promotional material, capital equipment and most especially the consumer goods needed by the hotel trade to maintain international quality standards. In a number of countries, these restrictions hinder the hotel franchise system. Equally, fiscal or financial restrictions relating to the employment of foreign management and training staff have a negative impact on the tourism sector. There may also be problems accessing and using global reservation systems, because there may be a shortage of specialised staff.

☐ *Training*

Training can be considered as the most important feature of tourism cooperation. In order to adapt the tourism supply of developing countries to the requirements of the international market successfully and to improve quality, effective professional training programmes should be established, particularly:

- hotel catering schools, for basic training of professionals in the hotel and catering sectors;
- high-level tourism management and marketing courses, designed to train administrative and commercial managers in both the tourism and the hotel industries;

- on-going professional courses, to train staff working in all sectors of tourism in new developments in the industry (for instance training travel agency personnel in the use of new computerised reservation systems).

Tourism development policies in developing countries are also concerned with the following areas:

- The promotion of tourism investment
- Joint financing of basic tourism infrastructure
- Measures aimed at guaranteeing the security of international visitors
- The protection of the consumer in terms of prices and tourism services
- Environment protection policies and the integration of equipment for the leisure industry

Tourism development strategies must pursue all of these policies to reduce the structural vulnerability of the tourism sector in developing countries.

International tourism development policies are increasingly important for developing countries. They not only introduce another sector to the economies of countries without an established tourism industry (like China in the early 1980s), they also fulfil certain macroeconomic objectives. Tourism as an export sector plays a major role in the balance of payments. This is why most developing countries are focusing their efforts on attracting tourists from other countries to increase their foreign currency reserves. However, the local population of these countries may not always be willing to accept tourism. At times, even outside peak periods when tourism flows are weak, a compatibility problem caused by the presence of tourists in the social and cultural environment of the receptor country may exist.

For this reason, tourism policies in developing countries must include both economic and social objectives. Only then will global policies of tourism development result in establishing a tourism sector sufficiently important to achieve the desired macroeconomic objectives.

Thus, accurate forecasts of world tourism must take into account policies pursued in both industrialised and developing countries as well as worldwide economic trends and influences.

References

1. Mathieson, A. and Wall, G., *Tourism: Economic, Physical and Social Impacts*, Harlow: Longman, 1982.

2. WTO Round Table on Planning for Sustainable Tourism Development, 10th General Assembly of WTO, Bali, Indonesia, October 1993.

3. Dr Edmund O. T. Premph (WAPTOURS), 'Practical Problems Encountered at the Level of African Travel Agents on the Improvement of Access to the International Information and Distribution Network', WTO–ECOWAS Seminar, Cotonou 22–3 February 1994.

4. Confer. Document, GATT, MTN.GNS/W/61.

Further reading

Ahmed, S. A. *Perceptions of Socio-Economic and Cultural Impact of Tourism in Sri Lanka – A Research Study*. Working Paper 84–18, Faculty of Administration, University of Ottawa, Ottawa, 1984.

Archer, E. 'Estimating the Relationship between Tourism and Economic Growth in Barbados', *Journal of Travel Research*, 22(4), pp. 8–12, 1984.

Britton, S. G. 'The Political Economy of Tourism in the Third World', *Annals of Tourism Research*, 9(3), 331–58, 1982.

Cazes, G. 'Le Tourisme Alternatif: Reflexion sur un Concept Ambigu', Paper presented at Colloque du CNRS sur le Tourisme, Paris, 15–18 June 1986.

De Kadt, E. *Tourism – Passport to Development?*, Oxford: Oxford University Press, 1979.

Francisco, R. 'The Political Impact of Tourism Dependence in Latin America', *Annals of Tourism Research*, 10(3), pp. 363–76, 1983.

Harrison, D. *Tourism and the Less Developed Countries*. London: Belhaven, 1992.

Inskeep, E. *Tourism Planning*. New York: Van Nostrand Reinhold, 1990.

Jenkins, C. L. 'The Effect of Scale in Tourism Projects in Developing Countries', *Annals of Tourism Research*, 9(2), pp. 229–49, 1982.

Lea, J. *Tourism Development in the Third World*. London: Routledge, 1988.

Pearce, D. *Tourism Development*. Harlow: Longman, 1992.

Williams, A. M. and Shaw, G. *Tourism and Economic Development*. London: Belhaven, 1988.

■ *Chapter 12* ■

Trends and Forecasts of International Tourism

WTO forecasts for international tourism
WTO forecasts for European, American and East Asian–Pacific tourism:
  forecast for the European region; forecast for the American region;
  forecasts for the Asia–Pacific region
The predicted trends in tourism development policy: more competitive
  quality–price ratio and better productivity; diversification of tourism
  products; stronger economic effects of tourism

After a period of sustained worldwide growth (even throughout the economic crisis), international tourism has entered an unsettled period. Since 1986, the growth rate has been around 3 per cent annually despite the negative impacts caused by the economic crisis in industrialised countries and more especially by the effects of the Gulf War. After the war, the buoyancy of international tourism was fragile and the economic mechanisms (particularly monetary) took a while to register an impact. Furthermore, there were only sparse indications of recovery and resumed economic growth in the United States, Europe and Japan which are, of course, the main generating countries.

As a result, the development of the international tourism market relied increasingly on qualitative factors.

■ WTO forecasts for international tourism

WTO forecasts indicate that over the 1990–2010 period the growth rate of world tourism arrivals should increase at about half the rate of that achieved in the 1950–90 period. This represents an average annual growth rate of between 3.5 per cent and 3.8 per cent. However, this modest growth of tourism demand could be revised if economic recovery leads to strong economic growth, particularly in Europe which is the world's main tourism market.

Figure 12.1, on the following page, shows that international tourist arrivals worldwide will reach 661 million in the year 2000 and 937 million by 2010. Between 1990 and 2010, the number of international tourists in the world will have doubled. This strong increase in volume implies that hospitality and accommodation capacities will need to be adapted. Consequently, international tourism will remain in the foreseeable future an economic sector of high job creation and will continue to contribute much value added.

Table 12.1   *World tourism growth trends and forecasts*

	Tourist arrivals (average annual growth rate, %)
1950–1970	9.9
1970–1980	5.7
1980–1990	4.7
1990–2000	3.8
2000–2010	3.5

Source: WTO.

WTO forecasts for regional trends show that the changes in the distribution of tourism flows between regions already identified will continue for the foreseeable future. The share of European and American regions will decrease until 2010 whereas the share of East Asia and the Pacific region will increase strongly. It is interesting to note that Europe's forecasted share is set to drop by 17.3 percent and East Asia's forecasted share is set to rise by exactly the same percentage (17.3 per cent).

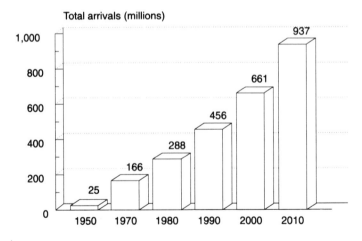

Source: WTO.

Figure 12.1   *International tourist arrivals worldwide: trends and prospects, 1950–2010*

Table 12.2 *Trends in regional market share, 1970–2010 (as % of world international tourist arrivals)*

Region	1970	2010	Change (percentage points)
Europe	68.1	50.8	−17.3
Americas	25.3	22.1	−3.2
East Asia/Pacific	3.0	20.3	17.3
Africa	1.2	3.8	2.6
Middle East	1.2	1.9	0.7
South Asia	0.6	1.1	0.5

Source: WTO.

The estimated annual growth rate over the 1990–2000 period is 2.7 per cent for Europe and 6.8 per cent for East Asia and the Pacific (see Figure 12.2). In the other regions of the world, the forecasted trends show weak growth in Africa and even weaker in South Asia.

The WTO forecasts that the share of tourism will remain stable until 2010 at a quarter for interregional tourism and three-quarters for intra-regional tourism.[1] Of the tourism-generating countries, Japan will

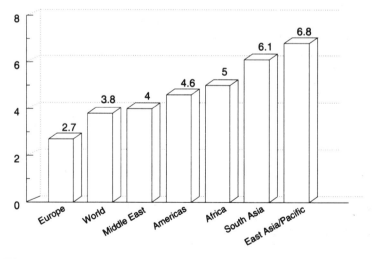

Source: WTO.

Figure 12.2 *Growth of international tourist arrivals worldwide by region of origin (average annual growth rate, %), 1990–2000*

experience the strongest growth with an annual rate of 7 per cent until the year 2010. On the other hand, there will be a weaker growth rate in tourist arrivals from the United States and the United Kingdom.

Table 12.3   *Forecast of tourist arrivals worldwide from five major generating markets, 1990–2010*

Major generating markets	Millions of arrivals			% average annual change	
	1990	2000	2010	1990–2000	2000–2010
France	19.47	26.96	35.37	3.31	2.75
Germany	57.19	82.84	109.17	3.77	2.80
Japan	17.32	34.65	67.75	7.18	6.93
United Kingdom	34.24	44.54	57.57	2.66	2.30
United States	55.51	70.57	87.83	2.43	2.21
Total of 5 major markets	183.73	259.56	357.69	3.52	3.26

Source: WTO.

The differences in forecasted growth are mainly due to trends in economic growth and exchange rates in each country. Thus, it is forecast that the economic growth rate in Japan will remain relatively high and the yen will appreciate against the major currencies. Moreover, Japan will continue to pursue its successful policy of encouraging its residents to travel abroad. This policy, initiated in the late 1980s with the 'Ten Million Programme', has doubled in less than a decade the number of Japanese tourists who travel overseas. Thus, expenditure by Japanese tourists in countries that are Japan's commercial partners will partly solve the problems of bilateral imbalances in the balance of payments.

▍ WTO forecasts for European, American and East Asian–Pacific tourism

The WTO has forecast future trends in the three main tourism regions: Europe, America and East Asia and the Pacific.

□ *Forecasts for the European region*

These are particularly pessimistic with a growth rate over the 1990–2000 period of 2.7 per cent and over the 2000–10 of just 2.5 per cent. This indicates that the European countries' share of world tourism will decline further. According to these forecasts, tourist arrivals in Europe will reach 372 million by the year 2000 and 476 million by the year 2010.

Table 12.4   *Tourism growth trends and forecasts in Europe*

	Tourist arrivals (average annual growth rate, %)
1950–1970	10.9
1970–1980	5.3
1980–1990	4.1
1990–2000	2.7
2000–2010	2.5

Source: WTO.

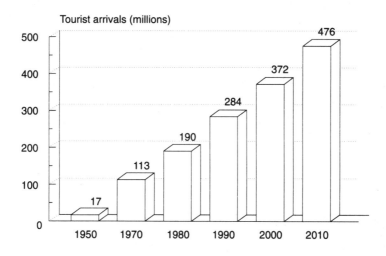

Source: WTO.

Figure 12.3   *International tourist arrivals in Europe: trends and prospects, 1950–2010*

This relative decline in growth rate may be caused by Europe's heavy reliance on certain forms of tourism, like mass tourism. This is particularly evident in the coastal zones of the Mediterranean which are prone to vulnerability and to economic dependency.

- *Vulnerability* Tourism in areas such as Southern Europe and parts of the United States is mainly seasonal and based on the 'sun, sea, sand' formula. Since the 1970s, this type of tourism has survived by charging low prices for services that are all too often mediocre.

    A lack of tourism products and intense competition between the principal receptor countries (Spain, France, Greece, Tunisia and Morocco on the one side and the United States, Mexico and the Caribbean on the other) have resulted in anarchic developments of high-density accommodation structures which have created many problems (noise, pollution, excessive traffic).

    After the fall in demand in 1989 and 1990 (a drop of 4 per cent in tourist arrivals), the desirability of this type of development has been challenged. Spain, for instance, which suffered a great loss of competitiveness (a drop in the quality–price ratio) caused by inflation, a lack of new products and the rise of the peseta in the exchange market, is now pursuing alternative development strategies.

- *Economic dependence* Countries offering products predominantly based on the 'sun, sea, sand' formula aimed at the lower end of the market have not succeeded in stimulating sufficient economic effects in receptor areas.

    Certain industrial countries have developed a 'tourism complex', in the sense of an industrial complex. Indeed, international tourism contributes to the development of capital goods and services industries: agri-industry, transport and the hotel trade.

    But opposite effects have been observed in many developing countries. They have become, to a varying extent, economically dependent on generating regions.

Faced with such a situation, the future of international tourism to Europe is a decelerating economic growth rate between 1995 and 2010.

☐ Forecasts for the American region

The tourism growth trends and forecasts in the American region indicate a particularly strong growth over the 1995–2000 period with a rate of 5.1 per cent, higher than the world average (4.4 per cent). The forecasts until the year 2010 show a slight fall in the rate but still equal to (possibly stronger than) the world average.

Table 12.5 *Tourism growth trends and forecasts in the Americas*

Tourist arrivals (average annual growth rate, %)	
1950–1970	9.9
1970–1980	3.8
1980–1990	4.3
1990–2000	4.6
2000–2010	3.5

Source: WTO.

Forecasts for the American zone are largely dependent on the buoyancy of international tourism which in 1993 accounted for 44 per cent of tourist arrivals and 64 per cent of tourism receipts.

International tourist arrivals in the American region should reach 147 million by the year 2000 and 207 million by the year 2010.

The predicted sub-regional distribution of tourist arrivals shows that the North American region will maintain its predominance and that arrivals to the Caribbean will grow at a faster rate than arrivals to Latin America. Despite a lower population, the Caribbean already receives more tourists than all the Latin American countries combined.

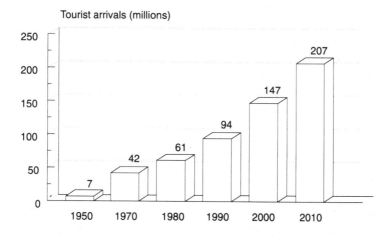

Source: WTO.

Figure 12.4 *International tourist arrivals in the Americas: trends and prospects, 1950–2010*

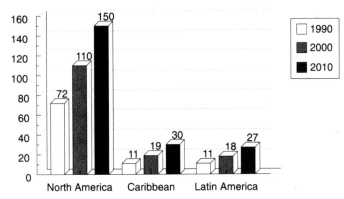

Source: WTO.

Figure 12.5   *Americas – forecasts of inbound tourism by sub-region, 1990–2010 (tourist arrivals, millions)*

☐ Forecasts for the Asia–Pacific region

This region has the strongest forecast growth rate. It is nearly double the world average at 6.8 per cent over the 1990–2000 period and 6.5 per cent over the 2000–10 period. The forecast is all the more remarkable as it follows a period of already strong growth of international tourism in these countries, some of which have become leading countries in tourism development thanks to their competitiveness and the quality of their tourism products. Thus, tourist arrivals should increase from 52 million in 1990 to 190 million by 2010. This growth can be mainly attributed to a very strong increase in intra-regional tourism from 49 per cent in 1980 to 79 per cent in 2010.

Table 12.6   *Tourism growth trends and forecasts in East Asia and the Pacific*

	Tourist arrivals (average annual growth rate, %)
1950–1970	18.1%
1970–1980	14.7%
1980–1990	9.6%
1990–1995	6.1%
1995–2000	7.5%
1990–2000	6.8%
2000–2010	6.5%

Source: WTO.

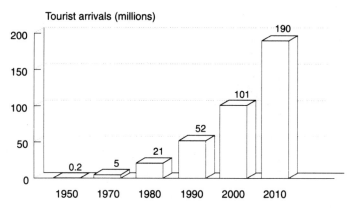

Source: WTO.

Figure 12.6 *International tourist arrivals in East Asia and the Pacific: trends and prospects, 1950–2010*

■ The predicted trends in tourism development policy

The predictions for the future development of the tourism sector and for international tourism demand highlight three main areas:

● more competitive quality-price ratio and better productivity;
● diversification of tourism products;
● induced effects.

⬜ More competitive quality–price ratio and better productivity

To develop an ideal 'tourism complex', the associated industrial and agricultural products must show significant comparative advantages in terms of competitiveness and the quality–price ratio. Most countries possess important factor endowments based on natural tourism resources. However, the economic development of these natural resources does not always generate enough comparative advantages. In fact, traditional tourism countries are increasingly suffering competition from 'new tourism countries', especially the new industrial countries of Asia: Singapore, Hong Kong, Thailand, Indonesia and South Korea. There is a real danger in the future that international tourism in Europe will be limited to intra-regional tourism between countries located near each other.

After the year 2000, European countries may represent the 'past' of international tourism and South-East Asian, Pacific and the Caribbean countries could represent the new developing markets and therefore the 'future' of international tourism. Faced with such an alarming prospect, European countries must adopt different tourism development strategies. To increase (or even just to keep) their share of international tourism, they must pursue two objectives: *better quality* and *increased productivity*.

☐ Better-quality tourism products

The tourism industry is both a labour-intensive and a heavy industry. Yet, it is evident that all too often there has been insufficient investment in the tourism sector, particularly in the coastal regions of France, Spain, Italy, the Greek islands, the Balearics and the Canary Islands. As a result, accommodation supply (hotels, apartment hotels, lodgings, etc.) ages prematurely and is not renovated or converted. To remain competitive, hoteliers have to reduce the quality of their products (catering, leisure facilities, etc.). The financial margins then become too small to allow new investment.

To remedy this situation, public authorities (central and local government) must implement specific policies to improve the quality of hospitality and accommodation infrastructures and superstructures. The objectives of these policies must be:

- to encourage investment in quality from the point of view of both the construction of urban projects and their cultural content;
- to develop professional training programmes in all areas of the tourism industry;
- to establish financial packages appropriate to tourism development.

☐ Better productivity in tourism enterprises

Better-quality tourism products and infrastructure should not be introduced to the detriment of maintaining international competitiveness. Therefore, tourism enterprises must increase productivity.

Productivity gains are possible with the introduction of new technologies. For instance, new technology revolutionised the hotel sector, particularly in the two-and three-star categories. Hotel chains are principally developed through a franchise system which allows individual initiatives but the advantages of belonging to a group. Gains in productivity are achieved by designing hotels for greater efficiency and by introducing new technology in the reception area, in the catering facilities and in the processing of payments. This has reduced the workforce considerably. For instance, the staff needed to run a 40-room hotel can be reduced from twenty to ten or less (even five in one-star hotels).

Productivity gains allow the hotel industry in high-labour-cost countries to compete internationally. France, in particular, has achieved impressive efficiency savings which has enhanced its tourism results. It overtook both Italy and Spain in the early 1990s in terms of international tourism receipts.

☐ *Diversification of tourism products*

The future of the tourism industry in industrialised countries largely depends on the adoption of product diversification policies. Indeed, if it is undeniable that seaside tourism still accounts for the greatest number of tourism visits, in many areas the capacity threshold has been reached and these zones have become saturated. Hence, industrialised countries must concentrate on developing other zones for tourism. To achieve this, new tourism products, new routes and new areas must be developed.

In many countries new concepts are being created to attract tourists to the more remote parts although these may not be traditional green tourism products. These are sophisticated products designed to attract a high-spending clientele.

- *Fitness and health* This type of tourism product is responding to a growing demand from the urban population who want to use their holidays for fitness and health purposes to recuperate from city life. These tourism products are different to traditional thermalism products because they do not have real therapeutic goals. In fact, fitness and health tourism products are usually developed in established tourism resorts, particularly in seaside resorts which want to diversify their supply and lengthen their tourism season. Among these health products thalassotherapy is especially important, notably in France on the Atlantic coast, with centres at Carnac, Biarritz and Roscoff.
- *Theme parks, leisure parks and aqua-parks* The emergence of leisure parks as a tourism product symbolises a new type of domestic and international tourism. They reflect the development of tourism demand which is tending towards shorter stays spread throughout the year. The main leisure parks were introduced in the USA by Disney. There are Disney leisure parks in Florida, California, Japan and, since 1992, in

France (Disneyland Paris). Each of the four Disney parks receives approximately 10 million visitors annually. This number of visitors (both national and international) is equivalent to 10 per cent of the international flow of tourists. Other leisure parks are now being developed, principally aimed at the domestic market in the United Kingdom (Center Parcs, Alton Towers), France (Astérix, Futuroscope), Germany and Belgium. Parks based around particular themes such as aqua-parks and all-weather parks protected by shields have also become very popular. However, the high visitor numbers at these parks are not necessarily a guarantee of financial success because of the size of the investment they require and their high operating costs. Despite 9 million visits annually, Disneyland Paris has been obliged to reduce its staff and restructure its debt to limit its financial losses.

- *The protection and restoration of the environment*   This new type of tourism product focuses on exploring the environment, notably flora and fauna in safeguarded areas. Many experiments are currently under way such as the UNESCO programme of biospheres, where people spend time in a controlled environment. However, the development of this type of product is hampered in two ways. First, it appeals to a small market which means that it tends to be an expensive product, possible even a luxury product. As a result, firms that only specialise in ecotourism are rarely profitable. For example, ecotourism products in the northern region of Uruguay which is endowed with a rich and varied bird population have failed to be successfully marketed in Europe and North America. Second, problems arise when ecotourism products become too successful. High numbers of tourists may damage the ecosystems which attracted them in the first place. Nevertheless, ecotourism products are becoming more important, particularly those that have succeeded in changing the tourism image of a destination. In 1991, the Canary Islands organised jointly with the WTO an international conference on tourism and the environment. The conference concluded that ecological tourism should not be just limited to certain specific experiments but should become a basic factor of tourism development.

☐ *Stronger economic effects of tourism*

The impact of tourism on the economic development of the main tourism countries does not generally result directly from tourism strategies. Consequently, the direct and indirect impacts of tourism on other sectors of economic activity (mainly agriculture) are not great enough. Foreign currency receipts in Greece, for instance, have stagnated. In 1981, Greece received 5.5 million tourists and earned nearly US$2 billion from tourism. In 1989, the number of visitors to the country was more than 8 million but the receipts were only US$2.4 billion. In 1989, a further 20 per cent drop in the volume of receipts was recorded. The average sum people spent during their stay fell from US$308 per person in 1988 to just US$250 in 1989.[2]

This situation can be improved by introducing new tourism products and developing new markets which are likely to increase the secondary economic effects of tourism. To pursue this policy successfully, considerable financial means and the raising of international funds are needed. In Europe, the European Union's Integrated Mediterranean Programme (IMP) finances up to 50 per cent of hotel renovations.

International tourism growth forecasts both confirm and amplify the trends that have recorded up until the mid 1990s. International tourism should continue its expansion at a sustained rate despite the risks of economic recession affecting the generating countries' purchasing power. Indeed, tourism demand has its own determinants based on the demand for holidays and leisure which allow it to progress even in periods of economic downturn. Furthermore, tourism is one of the economic sectors that derives most benefit from economic recovery (for instance, the sale of tourism products in the United Kingdom increased by more than 15 per cent from 1993 to 1994, during a period of slow economic recovery).

There will, however, be considerable changes in the distribution of tourism flows and these will condition the future trends of international tourism. Despite already substantial performances, the growth of tourism flows towards Asia have only just started. The relative rate of decline of Europe's market share will accelerate for the foreseeable future and East and South Asia will experience a very strong growth rate. Thus, the main areas of world tourism growth will move from the Mediterranean region to the Pacific region, as will the growth of the air transport sector.

For many countries, the development of an international tourism industry as an alternative route to economic growth has replaced traditional methods (agricultural production followed by industrialisation). Economic growth strategies based on either internal growth or the expansion of the export sector do not correspond any more to today's economic realities.

The service sector has become an vital part of the economy. As the largest creator of jobs, it generates greater production and increases the export sector. Tourism has become a key service sector within the economies of both industrialised and developing countries.

However, it is undeniable that international inequalities in the tourism sector are larger than in trade. There is an urgent need to ensure that all countries have access to the market. To achieve this, new approaches to encourage the development of tourism must be based on international cooperation, not only between different states but also between states and firms. Indeed, international cooperation and agreements between the key components of tourism (hotel, transport and tourism firms) will guarantee the future development of the industry.

However, it is important that these are backed up by environmental, public health and market liberalisation policies, the success of which will ensure that the tourism sector will extend and expand in a greater number of countries for the benefit of global economic growth.

Tourism policies must seek to address the following key issues:

- increasing the economic impact of tourism without risking the destruction of the environment and the social and human balances in receptor countries;
- ensuring a better distribution of tourism flows and receipts throughout the world;
- and, most importantly, ensuring a sustainable tourism that satisfies the needs of human development and not just material desires.

These objectives will be reached when global economic growth is maintained at a sustainable and constant rate. Then, tourism will be the most important economic activity in the majority of the world's countries. It will be less exposed to fluctuations in international economic, political and social conditions and will become an increasingly important factor for both economic and human development in the twenty-first century.

References

1. WTO definition: 'Residents of countries of a given region travelling to countries of the given region are intra-regional tourists. Residents of countries of a given region travelling outside the given region are inter-regional tourists.' *Tourism to the Year 2000 and Beyond: Regional Forecasting Studies*. Madrid, 1994.

2. National Bank of Greece and the EOT, the national tourist office.

Further reading

Choy, D. J. L. 'Forecasting tourism revisited', *Tourism Management*, 5(3), pp. 171–6, 1984.

Index